Apple Training Series

Mac OS X Advanced System Administration v10.5

Edward R. Marczak

D1504856

Apple
Certified

Apple Training Series: Mac OS X Advanced System Administration v10.5
Edward R. Marczak

Published by Peachpit Press. For information on Peachpit Press books, contact:
Peachpit Press
1249 Eighth Street
Berkeley, CA 94710
510/524-2178
510/524-2221 (fax)

Find us on the Web at: www.peachpit.com
To report errors, please send a note to errata@peachpit.com
Peachpit Press is a division of Pearson Education

Project Editor: Rebecca Freed
Development Editor: Judy Walthers von Alten
Production Editor: Danielle Foster
Copyeditor: John Banks
Tech Editors: Joel Rennich, Shane Ross
Proofreader: Rachel Fudge
Compositor: Danielle Foster
Indexer: Valerie Perry
Cover design: Mimi Heft

ISBN 13: 978-0-321-56314-9
ISBN 10: 0-321-56314-X

9 8 7 6 5 4 3 2 1

Printed and bound in the United States of America

Acknowledgments

First, "I" did not write this book. There are too many contingencies that allowed its creation. Overall, I merely stood on the shoulders of the giants that precede me.

There should also be two other names on the cover: Matthias Fricke and Patrick Gallagher from the Advanced System Administration "team," without whom this book would be about half the volume, and no training course would exist. Thanks also to Ben Greisler for stepping very late into the process to calm nerves.

At the top of my specific list, I need to thank my immediate family, my daughters Emily and Lily, and particularly my wife Dorothy, who took on (even more of) the household burden while I wrote. Also, thank you for having enough sense to force me to *stop* writing and periodically look at the world.

Thanks to my parents for inspiring a young mind and providing it with the tools to learn. Thanks also to the teachers that inspired and prepared me along the way, particularly Ken Graham, Marsha Cohen, Dr. Barry Dutchen, and Dr. Robert Marose.

Thank you to Neil Ticktin for providing me with opportunity and generally having faith in me.

Thanks to Schoun Regan for being Schoun Regan.

Thanks to the crack team at Peachpit. Judy Walthers von Alten, you have made this an immeasurably better product.

Shane Ross, you kept me sane. I hope I did not have the opposite effect on you.

Thanks to everyone at Google, particularly Clay Caviness, Joseph Dries, and Nigel Kersten, who put up with my random ramblings and status reports on my progress.

Contents at a Glance

Contents

Getting Started

Welcome to the official reference guide for the Apple Mac OS X Advanced System Administration v10.5 certification course. This book serves as a self-paced guide and is designed to help you build the basic skills you need to effectively administer Mac OS X and Mac OS X Server systems. Apple Training Series: Mac OS X Advanced System Administration details the tools that Apple provides to configure system services. The primary goal of this book is to advance entry and mid-level system administrators in their technical sophistication. To become truly proficient, you need to learn the theory behind the graphical tools, how to affect many systems at once, and how to troubleshoot system problems—locally or remotely. You'll also learn that advanced administrators plan. For example, not only will you learn how to use command-line utilities and the critical support files for major services, but you will also learn how to document your work and troubleshoot based on investigation and your documentation.

This book assumes that you have a good foundation in Mac OS X and Mac OS X Server, such as the level of knowledge gained in *Apple Training Series: Mac OS X Server Essentials* and *Apple Training Series: Mac OS X Support Essentials* from Peachpit Press.

The Methodology

Apple Training Series books emphasize learning by doing. The lessons contained within this book are designed so that you can explore and learn the tools necessary to manage Mac OS X. Each chapter is grouped according to an overall theme, starting with planning and installation, moving through daily tasks, and ending with ways to optimize and troubleshoot existing systems.

Course Structure

Because Mac OS X and Mac OS X Server are broad, user configurable, and contain several open source initiatives, it is impossible to include all the possibilities and permutations here. System administrators who use Mac OS X on a daily basis and users of other UNIX-based operating systems who are migrating to Mac OS X have the most to gain from this book; still others who are upgrading from previous versions of Mac OS X Server will also find this book a valuable resource.

> **WARNING ▶** The information in this book points users to internals of the operating system and critical data structures. The exercises in this book are designed to be nondestructive. However, some involve restoring data and should only be run on a test system because data restores will overwrite data. Other examples need to be run with root (superuser) privileges, and if performed incorrectly could result in data loss or corruption to some basic services, possibly even erasing a disk or volume of a computer connected to the network. Thus, it is recommended that you run through the exercises on systems in a test environment that is not critical to your work or connected to a production network. This is also true of the Mac OS X computer you will use in these exercises. Please back up all your data if you choose to use a production machine for either the Mac OS X Server or the Mac OS X computers. Apple Computer and Peachpit Press are not responsible for any data loss or any damage to any equipment that occurs as a direct or indirect result of following the procedures described in this book.

This book is divided into four sections:

▶ Lessons 1 through 4 cover planning and initial system implementation.

▶ Lessons 5 and 6 cover networking aspects of Mac OS X administration.

▶ Lessons 7 through 10 cover overall administrative tasks that a system administrator will face when working with Mac OS X.

▶ Lessons 11 and 12 detail optimizing and troubleshooting an existing installation.

▶ The appendix lists further methods of documenting Mac OS X systems.

System Requirements

This book assumes a basic level of familiarity with the Macintosh operating environment. All references to Mac OS X refer to Mac OS X v10.5, which is the primary operating system assumed throughout the book.

Administrator access is required for many commands in this book. Any command-line examples preceded by a dollar sign ($) can be run by any user. Commands preceded by a hash mark (#) require root-level access.

Certification

Apple Training Series: Mac OS X Advanced System Administration provides a thorough preparation for the Apple Mac OS X Advanced System Administration v10.5 certification exam offered by Apple. Before you take the test, you should review the lessons and ideas in this book, and spend time setting up, configuring, and troubleshooting Mac OS X and Mac OS X Server systems.

You should also download and review the *Skills Assessment Guide*, which lists the exam objectives, the score required to pass the exam, and how to register for it. To download the *Skills Assessment Guide*, go to http://train.apple.com/certification.

Earning Apple technical certification shows employers that you have achieved a high level of technical proficiency with Apple products. You'll also join a growing community of skilled professionals. In fact, Apple Mac OS X certification programs are among the fastest-growing certifications in the industry.

Passing any of the Mac OS X certification exams for Mac OS X v10.3 or higher also qualifies you to join the new Mac OS X Certification Alliance, a free program that recognizes and supports the thousands of Mac OS X experts worldwide.

For more information, visit http://train.apple.com.

About the Apple Training Series

Apple Training Series: Mac OS X Advanced System Administration is part of the official training series for Apple products, which was developed by experts in the field and certified by Apple. The lessons are designed to let you learn at your own pace.

For those who prefer to learn in an instructor-led setting, Apple Authorized Training Centers, located around the globe, offer training courses. These courses, which typically use the Apple Training Series books as their curriculum, are taught by Apple-certified trainers, and balance concepts and lectures with excellent and intense hands-on labs and exercises. Apple Authorized Training Centers have been carefully selected and have met the highest standards of Apple in all areas, including facilities, instructors, course delivery, and infrastructure. The goal of the program is to offer Apple customers, from beginners to the most seasoned professionals, the highest-quality training experience.

To find an Authorized Training Center near you, go to http://train.apple.com.

Part 1 Implementation

1

Time   This chapter takes approximately 45 minutes to complete.

Goals   Understand the need for planning prior to installation

Understand power and cooling estimates

Learn items to include in initial system documentation

Chapter 1

Planning Systems

You've been tasked with setting up a new server: A system for the Finance Department, or perhaps an entire data center. How do you know what to actually purchase? Technologists tend to get excited about unboxing new equipment, but they face important decisions before ordering and racking new gear.

Planning is a little-documented discipline, but it is perhaps the most critical task in the process of implementing a system or service. An underpowered system causes only frustration. An overpowered system that adds too much heat to a data center causes just as many issues, in addition to needlessly using up budget. Adding even a single server to a new or existing setup prompts many questions, some unrelated to the server itself, such as "how many client nodes will access the services on this server?" Also, the types of services that a server will run tend to be optimized in different ways and need to be planned for accordingly.

The topics in this chapter help you plan even *before* a purchase is made. Some of the topics remain theoretical here; later chapters will present some of the data-gathering and tools needed for analysis.

Planning Before Purchasing

Determining the resources needed for a business initiative involves many factors, which should guide the implementer to the right resources to purchase. A well-known maxim says that when you fail to plan, you plan to fail. Planning is what makes an advanced administrator, well, advanced!

A system administrator must be conscious of the system. A *system* is greater than the sum of its parts—but remember that many parts are in play, all working together. For example, a server doesn't exist in a vacuum: It connects to a network switch, perhaps to a Fibre Channel network for storage, with a limited set of resources available (disk space, RAM, and so on), and also connects to local and perhaps remote resources over a network or networks. The server also exists physically (yes, virtualized servers still run on hardware *somewhere*). This physical server needs adequate cooling and power, and possibly physical security. Similarly, a network switch must have adequate bandwidth to serve the devices that pass data through it, respond to security policies that may be imposed, and so on.

If you're reading this, most likely you've set up a server or some network component before. Was it a success? If so, why? Planning? Or luck? Were you given a budget that allowed each piece of equipment to be overspecified? If it wasn't successful, why not? What did you learn that you can apply now? Planning means that thought has been given to a setup, its potential utilization, its impact on an existing system (to the extent possible), and any obstacles. Certainly, things crop up that couldn't have been accounted for, and each plan should also plan for change. Unforeseen issues shouldn't stop you from putting together the best plan possible based on past experience.

Checklists and worksheets are great aids and starting points in the planning process. You should fine-tune a worksheet over time as you gain experience. Worksheets help you avoid forgetting important steps in your implementation process and therefore prevent nasty surprises. This chapter will help you come up with some of the basics of a form to use.

Determining Utilization

Ultimately, a server exists to provide services to users. Discussions with users about requirements and expectations should inform purchase decisions. The goal is to inspect various forms of *utilization*. Casually, utilization means how effectively a resource is being used. More formally, it is the ratio of usage to capacity. Perhaps existing infrastructure is *underutilized* and can handle additional load. In a new installation, the questions are how much utilization demand will be placed on the equipment and how much utilization *headroom* is needed for spikes in usage and future growth. Headroom is the margin between usage and capacity.

When planning you need to take into account many forms of utilization: power, cooling, CPU, memory, network bandwidth, disk space (storage), disk bandwidth, service (the processes running on a system), and more. The details of the electronic tools to measure these factors will be presented later in the book; for now, you can certainly map out utilization from a high-level planning perspective.

Another smart idea is to implement a utilization *policy*. Your company may already have one for existing resources. Policy may spell out that when a server CPU is 70 percent utilized, additional resources should be added, such as an additional server. The same could be done for storage utilization.

Determining Heat Dissipation and Load, Power, and Cooling

One of the easier statistics to gather is *heat load*. *Dissipation* is a physics term that describes the loss of energy, typically by conversion to heat. Heat is produced as energy is consumed. Used a MacBook Pro lately? On your lap? Imagine the heat that multiple Xserve units can generate. The heat generated places a heat load on the room in which equipment is placed. Heat load is measured either in British Thermal Units (BTU) or kilowatts (kW). These are numbers you simply collect from a vendor's documentation. Once you have heat load numbers for all the equipment that will be in a room, you add them up for a total. Interestingly, other factors besides equipment affect a room's heat load and may be more difficult to measure. Are there windows in the room that allow sunlight? Human bodies generate heat: Will there be an approximately constant number of people working in the room? The lighting in a room adds heat as well, so that choice also affects the total heat load.

In smaller setups, most of this planning is ignored with no ill effects (everyone has seen the 10-person company with an Xserve stuffed into a coat closet or someone's office). However, tales abound of larger setups that have problems when the cooling system can't keep up.

Power and cooling *supply* must meet or exceed *demand*. The trick is to neither oversupply, thereby causing waste, nor undersupply and thus cause failure. All electrical equipment generates heat; so take all equipment into account.

Most IT equipment is simple: electrical load (power consumed) measured in watts equals heat out, measured in watts. For other equipment you can use formulas to determine heat:

▶ Uninterruptible power supply (UPS) with battery: 0.04 × power system rating (the power system rating is measured in watts and can be determined from the product's documentation)

▶ Power distribution unit (PDU): (0.01 × power system rating) + (0.02 × IT load)

▶ Lighting: 2 × floor area (in square feet)

▶ People: 100 × room personnel (maximum)

Once you've gathered all data, add it up to find the total. For any IT equipment with a BTU rating, convert it to watts with this formula:

Watts = BTU × 0.293

(Many vendors still give the heat rating in BTU. For example, see http://docs.info.apple.com/article.html?artnum=307330 for Apple's information on an early 2008 Xeon Xserve at various points of configuration. Heat output is given in BTU.)

You will see the cooling output capacity of most air-conditioning units referred to in *tons*. You can convert watts into tons using this formula:

Tons = watts × 0.000283

Once you determine all this information, you can find a suitable unit. Other factors in this decision include planning for future growth, giving headroom to current equipment, and planning for redundant cooling.

Sizing power capacity is similar to cooling: Find out the power load for each unit and add it up for a total. You can determine the power load from a manufacturer's literature. The entire room must have the correct capacity. In addition, each UPS must be sized to accommodate the total load of the equipment plugged into it at peak usage. Most UPS units are specified in volt-amperes (VA). Conversion between watts and VA is not entirely straightforward. A good rule of thumb is to size at 60 percent, or, expressed as a formula, available watts equals VA × 0.6. A 3,000 VA UPS can safely handle 1,800 watts. Remember to subtract total watts used from the total available to determine your available headroom.

When planning your first large-scale setup, rather than tackle these calculations alone, use the expertise of data center and cooling engineers and consultants. Talk to them about your needs and get involved in the process.

Given the formulas just discussed, the following example shows how to calculate heat dissipation. Imagine a scenario with this equipment and specifications:

- ► Two Xserve units (both have two 3.0 GHz quad-core Intel Xeon processors); three 1 TB 7200-rpm SATA Apple Drive Modules; 32 GB RAM (in eight 4 GB 800 MHz DDR2 ECC fully buffered DIMMs); Xserve RAID Card; ATI Radeon X1300 graphics with 64 MB RAM; no PCI cards.

- ► One APC 3000 VA UPS.

- ► All equipment can be plugged directly into the UPS; no PDU is needed.

- ► Two permanent operations personnel staff the room.

- ► The equipment will be installed in a 200-square-foot space.

Using Apple's Knowledge Base, you'll find that an Xserve with the preceding configuration will produce a maximum of 1,296 BTU/h (http://docs.info.apple.com/article. html?artnum=307330). Using the preceding formula, this converts to 380 watts each (rounded up). The 3,000 VA UPS is approximately 1,800 watts, which is multiplied by 0.04 (see the preceding formula) to yield a rating of 72 watts. The personnel approximate 200 watts, and lighting dissipates 400 watts. The total heat load is the sum of the values you've determined:

$$(380 \times 2) + 72 + 200 + 400 = 1{,}432 \text{ watts}$$

Using the formula provided earlier for tonnage, the 1,432 watts can be cooled by 0.41 tons of air conditioning capacity. Essentially, this small setup requires a half ton of cooling, not taking into account future expansion.

Planning CPU, Memory, and Service Utilization

The tools to determine *actual* use of CPU, memory, and services are covered later in this book (see Chapter 8, "Monitoring Systems"). Just as with cooling, to plan for these factors you must account for peak usage and future growth, as well as reliability. For example, a server may have a great uptime record, but if users are constantly complaining about slow service, that server isn't really doing its job.

Another factor to consider is the amount of redundancy and load balancing required in a setup. While it may be very possible to run many services on one server, will that provide the best experience to users of that service? Does that provide the greatest security?

Part of the system load equation is simple: Every running service that is added to a machine takes CPU cycles. However, things get fuzzy from there. Each service can (and will) add a different load to the system. Much of this kind of knowledge comes purely from past experience. You will be translating the desires of management and users into actual running processes on a server: For example, when management says, "We need a web server that only employees can log in to," you'll start thinking, "OK, this server will run Apache, with an Open Directory Master configuration." Company policy may dictate that your configuration includes extra services, such as a built-in firewall, or it may simply require spreading certain services over separate hardware.

The bottom line is this: The more work that you ask a single machine to do, the more memory and CPU it will require to keep up with your demands.

Planning Network Utilization

Planning for network utilization, while possibly more straightforward than planning for CPU and memory, shares one decision-making factor with them: Since so many services rely on network connectivity, the more services you run on a single machine, the greater its network bandwidth requirements will be. Also keep in mind that some services require servers to talk to each other, even though no user is involved in the electronic conversation. For example, Open Directory Master and its replica will generate network traffic as they communicate.

Typically, modern network capacity is measured in gigabits per second (Gbit/s). However, a full gigabit each second is largely theoretical, with real-world values approaching the hundreds of megabits per second. This is typically 600 to 700 megabits per second (Mbit/s), or only 60 to 70 percent of capacity. As increasing traffic forces network interfaces to process loads approaching 1 Gbit/s, packet loss and errors increase. This again requires the planner to include ample headroom in the equation.

All modern Macintosh server platforms (Xserve and Mac Pro) include two 1 Gbit Ethernet interfaces that can be *trunked* together to achieve a 2 Gbit pipe. (Trunking is also known as *bonding*, or allowing more than one interface to behave as one.) The Ethernet switch must also support the ability to trunk, following the IEEE 802.3ad standard known as Link Aggregation Control Protocol (LACP). Plan accordingly.

Being able to base your network utilization plans on an existing real-world situation is ideal. If that's not possible, planning will involve using good sense to make some estimates. A video or graphics department will typically use more bandwidth than an office administrative group, for example.

Imagine this scenario in a little more detail: A new branch office for a company is to open. Because the employees and job functions will simply move out of headquarters to the new building, historical data can inform planning. Say that each of the 10 people in the art department has a Mac Pro running with a single gigabit connection to a gigabit switch, and each user averages 20 Mbit/s. Further, each of the two-person administrative staff has a wireless laptop that uses 3 Mbit/s. You can estimate the impact of the staff and its usage with the following formula:

$$(10 \times 20 \text{ Mbit/s}) + (2 \times 3 \text{ Mbit/s}) = 206 \text{ Mbit/s}$$

To calculate utilization:

$$206 \text{ Mbit} \div 1 \text{ Gbit} = 21\% \text{ utilization}$$

This type of utilization is well within reasonable limits. As utilization increases, an administrator may consider trunking the Ethernet ports to increase capacity.

Determining Storage

Planning for storage may be the most straightforward of all these factors, but it does have its wrinkles. Like the other factors presented here, until there is actual use, planning is simply theoretical.

Since storage will be of a fixed size—at least for some period of time—you can easily calculate theoretical planned usage. From there, you can determine an appropriately sized storage solution, taking into account headroom for present needs and expansion space for future growth.

Some simple calculations for storage planning include storage per user home (number of users × max GB/user), storage per project (number of work-in-progress projects × max GB/project), scratch space, and mail storage (number of mail users × max GB/mailbox).

Lastly, when planning storage, don't forget about operating system requirements! While the OS itself takes up a certain amount of space, that consumption should remain relatively static. Placing active files on storage shared with the system disk is typically problematic. Log files, dynamic web shares, user homes, and more can entirely fill a disk in short time. In most default installations these files remain on the system disk. Letting the system run out of disk space and not be allowed to write back to the disk can cause many, many problems—particularly for an Open Directory Master. In no case do you want to allow a disk to fill up, but that caution is amplified in the case of a system disk!

Documenting the Initial Requirements

Much like planning itself, documenting a configuration is a task that can be easily ignored. "Easily," perhaps, but certainly not safely.

There is no better time to begin system documentation than when you have a clean slate. However, documentation certainly should not be created once, put on a shelf, and left alone. Documentation is a process, as each system has a life. Gathering and retaining information about a system is easiest at the beginning of this life. If you've ever been called upon to document an already-in-place system, you'll probably remember wishing that you could just start from scratch! Don't forget to update documentation when hardware changes (for example, memory gets added) or *any* programs are installed (especially "invisible" applications such as background daemons, or scripts that run periodically via launchd or cron).

Also, it's important to document how a system backs up its data, as well as what the restore process entails, if that is ever necessary.

Part of being an advanced administrator is being able to teach others in your organization how to step into your role. More than anything, this lets you take vacations!

Your documentation should include at least the following about a server:

▶ A brief description of the system and its intended use

▶ Hardware specifications (including system serial numbers)

▶ Operating system and version

▶ Network information (TCP/IP address or addresses, and MAC address or addresses)

▶ Software installed and version numbers

▶ Fully Qualified Domain Name (FQDN) DNS information

▶ Storage volumes attached

▶ Backup and restore procedures for the system

As a final note, be aware that some industries may require documentation or require a particular format for documentation. Find out from management if this applies in your situation.

Worksheets are a valuable aid in documenting systems. They provide a template that ensures a thoroughness of values and a consistency between systems. While your company may already have created a documentation worksheet or style, many vendors provide worksheets that can be used as a starting point. See the references in this chapter for an Apple worksheet. The appendix contains more specifics on creating documentation.

What You've Learned

This chapter focused on the importance of planning for installation and considerations in doing so. Topics covered include:

- ► Using worksheets and checklists for thoroughness and consistency
- ► System and component utilization and headroom
- ► Planning for power, heat, and cooling considerations
- ► Planning to size systems correctly so they can handle server-side processes
- ► Planning for proper network capacity
- ► Planning for future storage requirements
- ► Documenting the current system and gathering system data to keep documentation in sync with reality

References

- ► Mac OS X Server Installation and Setup Worksheet, http://images.apple.com/server/ macosx/docs/Worksheet_v10.5.pdf
- ► Data Center and Server Room Design Guides, APC, http://www.apc.com/prod_docs/ results.cfm?DocType=White%20Paper&Query_Type=10

Review Quiz

1. What is the formal definition of *utilization*?

2. Name the common units in which heat load is measured.

3. What is the easiest way to determine the heat output of a piece of electronic equipment?

Answers

1. Utilization is formally defined as the ratio of usage to capacity.

2. Heat load is measured in British Thermal Units (BTU) or kilowatts (kW).

3. Heat output from electronic equipment is documented by the manufacturer, both in printed documentation and in spec sheets listed on the web.

2

Time

Goals

This chapter takes approximately 90 minutes to complete.

Understand methods of initial installation

Understand methods of initial configuration

Understand the installation of software via packages

Understand the installation of third-party and open source software to extend the capabilities of the system

Understand the management of computers through a directory service using managed preferences

Chapter 2

Installing and Configuring Systems

After you've completed planning and have confidently made your purchases, boxes will soon arrive and you'll be ready for installation. You'll have to make several decisions about initial installation. It's possible to automatically set up and configure this and other systems, which can save time and offer consistency.

Mac OS X command-line tools allow you to easily install systems remotely using either Apple Remote Desktop (ARD) or the ssh tool, or by scripting the installation. You can apply these tools to install the initial system or a single packaged application. Remote installation allows you to install an entire system on hardware that is physically separate, such as different floors in a building or computers that are miles apart. This allows you, with Mac OS X Server expertise, to be responsible for many systems regardless of their physical location.

For the first time, Mac OS X Server can be installed in one of several predefined roles or configurations. This chapter discusses initial installation, installation of packages, and methods of configuring systems, either after the initial installation or after systems are already in place (postdeployment).

This chapter focuses on installations specific to Mac OS X Server; Mac OS X-based installations are covered in *Apple Training Series: Mac OS X Deployment v10.5.*

Installing Your System

Installation refers to transferring files to a disk, often in a particular location, to enable an application or entire operating system to run. You can install Mac OS X either interactively, by someone at the console making choices with the graphical user interface, or noninteractively, where Mac OS X is installed on a disk or disk image.

Mac OS X Server adds two remote installation methods to Mac OS X: one based on Secure Shell (SSH) and the other based on Apple Remote Desktop (ARD). You can use one of these methods to access a Macintosh remotely when it is booted from Mac OS X Server v10.5 installation media.

Installing Remotely from a Command Line

The first remote installation method available with Mac OS X Server is via the ssh command-line tool, with which you can perform a full installation. Secure Shell can access a shell on the target machine (that is, the machine on which the installation will take place) once it has the following information: the target machine's IP address, which can be obtained using the command sa_srchr; its user ID (in this case, root); and a password that is the first eight characters of the target machine's serial number.

When booted from Mac OS X Server install media, the target server obtains an IP address using Dynamic Host Configuration Protocol (DHCP) or via Bonjour. The target server also runs the Server Assistant Responder, sa_rspndr, which broadcasts on the local LAN, allowing other machines to locate and identify the target server. A second Macintosh, on the same LAN segment, can run sa_srchr, which reports the IP address of any machine it finds running sa_rspndr. If you are not on the target LAN, you should be able to use the ssh command on a second, known Macintosh to run sa_srchr. After the IP address is known, you can use the ssh command to access a shell on the target machine, as this example shows:

```
# /System/Library/ServerSetup/sa_srchr 224.0.0.1
localhost#1.33 GHz PowerPC G4#192.168.100.156#00:0a:95:e0:95:04#Mac OS X Server
10.5#RDY4PkgInstall#4.0#512


# ssh root@192.168.100.156
The authenticity of host '192.168.100.156 (192.168.100.156)' can't be established.
RSA key fingerprint is ce:bc:6a:ae:17:bc:cb:81:ff:38:42:2e:6b:21:71:a4.
Are you sure you want to continue connecting (yes/no)? yes
Warning: Permanently added '192.168.100.156' (RSA) to the list of known hosts.
Password:
-sh-3.2#
```

After you log in to the target server, a full range of command-line tools is available. If, prior to installation, you need to format or partition disks, or create Redundant Array of Independent Disks (RAID) devices, you can use the command `diskutil`. The `list` command gives an overview of all volumes on the system at that time:

```
# diskutil list
/dev/disk0
   #:                     TYPE NAME              SIZE        IDENTIFIER
   0:      Apple_partition_scheme               *111.8 Gi   disk0
   1:         Apple_partition_map                31.5 Ki    disk0s1
   2:              Apple_HFS ServerHD            64.0 Gi     disk0s3
   3:              Apple_HFS ServerData          64.0 Gi     disk0s5
/dev/disk1
   #:                     TYPE NAME              SIZE        IDENTIFIER
   0:      Apple_partition_scheme               *7.3 Gi     disk1
   1:         Apple_partition_map                30.0 Ki    disk1s1
   2:          Apple_Driver_ATAPI               401.7 Mi    disk1s2
   3:              Apple_HFS Mac OS X Server Install Disc6.9 Gi     disk1s3
```

Choose a disk to partition, if appropriate, and use the `partitionDisk` command, as follows:

```
# diskutil partitionDisk disk0 GPTFormat HFS+ ServerHD 40% HFS+ MacintoshHD 40% HFS+
Abuse 20%
Started partitioning on disk disk0
Creating partition map
Formatting disk0s2 as Mac OS Extended with name ServerHD
Formatting disk0s3 as Mac OS Extended with name MacintoshHD
Formatting disk0s4 as Mac OS Extended with name Abuse
[ + 0%..10%..20%..30%..40%..50%..60%..70%..80%..90%..100% ]
Finished partitioning on disk disk0
/dev/disk0
   #:                     TYPE NAME              SIZE        IDENTIFIER
   0:        GUID_partition_scheme              *111.8 Gi   disk0
   1:                          EFI              200.0 Mi    disk0s1
   2:              Apple_HFS ServerHD            44.6 Gi     disk0s2
   3:              Apple_HFS MacintoshHD         44.6 Gi     disk0s3
   4:              Apple_HFS Abuse               22.0 Gi     disk0s4
```

When an installation disk is ready—partitioned, formatted, configured as a RAID pair, and so on—you can use the installer command to install the base operating system from packages on the installation media. In this example, the installation packages being used are from the Mac OS X Server installation DVD, located at: /Volumes/Mac\ OS\ X\ Server\ Install\ Disc/System/Installation/Packages:

```
# installer -verbose -package /Volumes/Mac\ OS\ X\ Server\ Install\ Disc/System/
Installation/Packages/OSInstall.mpkg -target /Volumes/ServerHD
installer: Package name is Mac OS X Server
installer: Installing at base path /Volumes/ServerHD
installer: Preparing for installation.....
installer: Preparing the Disk.....
installer:       Preparing Target Volume
#
installer: Preparing Mac OS X Server.....
installer:       Running Installer actions
installer:
installer: Installing BaseSystem.....
installer:
installer:       Configuring Installation
###
installer:       Running Installer Script
installer:       Validating package
#
installer:       Writing files
installer:       Writing files: 0% complete
installer:       Writing files: 1% complete
...(output omitted for space)...
installer: Installing OSInstall.....
installer:
installer:       Configuring Installation
installer:       Running Installer Script
installer:       Running Installer Script
installer: Finishing Installation.....
##
```

```
installer:      Finishing Installation
#
installer:
installer: The software was successfully installed.....
installer: The install was successful.
```

The -verbose flag sends additional information and current status about the installation to stdout. The -package switch specifies the package to install, in this case, a metapackage. Finally, the -target switch specifies the volume on which to install the package.

After the installation is complete, the target machine must be restarted. You can do this using the shutdown command and the -r switch, which will cause a reboot:

```
shutdown -r now
```

The system then ejects the install media and reboots from the newly "blessed" volume. (In Mac OS X terms, a "blessed" volume is one that has a bootable system and is currently marked as the boot volume for the next bootup.)

Installing Remotely Using a Graphical Interface

The second remote installation method available through Mac OS X Server is using the graphical interface of the target machine. Mac OS X Server v10.5 provides the capability to remotely access the console of a target machine graphically during initial installation. This access is through ARD, or Screen Sharing, newly built into Mac OS X v10.5 Leopard. Screen Sharing uses ARD technology. Screen Sharing is limited to viewing and controlling a remote screen, whereas ARD contains other management functions such as reporting. Screen Sharing is available in the Finder's sidebar or directly through the application, at /System/Library/CoreServices/Screen Sharing.app. This method requires the target machine's IP address, which you can obtain by using the command sa_srchr, as described in the preceding section, "Installing Remotely from a Command Line." Unlike connecting through the shell, no ID is needed; the password is still the first eight characters of the target machine's serial number.

Screen sharing allows a connection via the underlying virtual network control (VNC)-based protocols. (Any VNC viewer can be used to connect to the target system.) When you're connected, proceed with the initial installation as if you were sitting at the console.

For details on graphical installation, see *Mac OS X Server Essentials, Second Edition*.

Configuring Your System

After you've completed the initial installation and the server reboots, remote access will once again be available. To continue the installation, connect graphically, as described in the section "Installing Remotely Using a Graphical Interface."

Leopard Server offers several configurations that match the needs of different users and groups:

▶   Standard: A simplified configuration ideal for the first server or only server in a small organization

▶ Workgroup: An easy-to-use setup ideal for a workgroup in an organization with an existing directory server

▶ Advanced: A flexible configuration ideal for advanced, highly customized deployments

For more detailed information on the various configurations, see *Mac OS X Server Essentials, Second Edition.*

Configuring the server establishes the following basic settings:

▶ Defines the language to use for server administration and the computer keyboard layout

▶ Sets the server software serial number

▶ Defines a server administrator user and creates the user's home folder

▶ Defines default Apple Filing Protocol (AFP) and File Transfer Protocol (FTP) share points, such as Shared Items, Users, and Groups

▶ Sets up basic Open Directory information, which, at a minimum, creates a local directory domain

▶ Configures network interfaces (ports), and defines TCP/IP and Ethernet settings for each port you want to activate

▶ Optionally, sets up network time service

▶ Sets the server's host name, computer name, and local host name

You can specify the computer name and local host name, but Server Assistant sets the host name to "automatic" in /etc/hostconfig. This setting makes the server's host name the primary name in each of these instances:

   ▶ The name provided by the DHCP or BootP server for the primary IP address

   ▶ The first name returned by a reverse Domain Name System (DNS) (address-to-name) query for the primary IP address

   NOTE ▶ In the case of a Standard or Workgroup install, the name set by existing DNS servers cannot be changed unless the configuration is changed to Advanced.

▶ The local host name

▶ The name `localhost`

This text assumes an advanced configuration. If you're working with a server that is running in standard or workgroup mode, you can convert it to an advanced configuration. Server Admin and Workgroup Manager tools are reserved for working with an advanced configuration; so running them as part of a standard or workgroup installation will result in the display of a prompt, asking to upgrade to the advanced configuration.

You may consider choosing the advanced configuration if:

1.   You want to configure network home folders and mobile user accounts on the new server.

2.   You want to save the setup data from this server's configuration so you can configure other servers automatically.

When choosing to upgrade to an advanced configuration, be aware of the following operational changes:

1.   Automatic provisioning of user's services will no longer occur.

2.   Firewall settings made with Server Preferences will be disabled.

3.   Server Admin must be used to make any postconversion configuration changes.

Upgrading to an advanced configuration is an easy process, but be aware: It's a one-way process. An advanced configuration cannot be changed later to a standard or workgroup configuration. After you make the advanced conversion, you will *not* be able to use the Server Preferences application to configure your services from this point on. If you choose to convert to an advanced configuration, you will be prompted to confirm your action.

As the dialog box explains, after you've converted your server to an advanced configuration, the server cannot be downgraded to a standard or workgroup mode.

Configuring Your System Offline

You can prepare a server's configuration before the server actually goes online, which can help you plan and save time. The Server Assistant application's offline mode can save a full configuration as a file or directory record that a server can use during initial setup. Running Server Assistant (/Applications/Server) offers the choice to "Save advanced setup information in a file or directory record." This option keeps Server Assistant in offline mode.

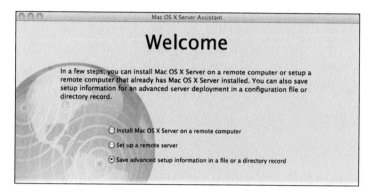

To save information as a file or record, you step through the screens, entering the same information as if you were running an installation. On the Serial Number screen, a tear-off icon appears in the lower right of the window, which indicates that you can save the information on that page by dragging the icon to a Finder window or the Desktop. Just as important, you can drag a properly formatted file into this window to populate the fields. The file has a simple format, all on one line (without carriage returns or line feed characters) and separated by a vertical pipe: Serial #, Registered to, Organization. Here's a sample:

```
XSVR-105-000-N-6GG-XXX-GH6-3CP-OR2-D2G-7|New Server|Radiotope
```

If this information were stored in a file named new_server.sa, you could drag the file into the Server Assistant screen to populate the appropriate fields. (The filename is not important to Server Assistant, although it is important to you.)

As a plain text XML file, this information can be edited by any editor—manual, batch (such as with the sed utility), database-generated, or XML-specific—for any server. You can also use an exported file as a template and add custom settings for any installation.

After all the information is complete, the Confirm Settings screen appears.

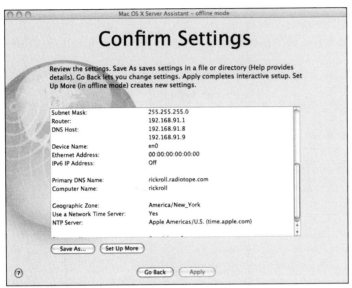

Verify that all the data is correct, and click Save As. In the dialog box that appears, choose Configuration File to use the file as a source for autoconfiguration.

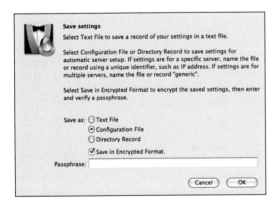

To use this file as a template that can be edited, do not save the file in an encrypted format, even though it stores passwords and machine-sensitive information in plain text. You can protect the configuration file by using any combination of Portable Operating System Interface (POSIX) permissions, access control lists (ACLs), or storage on encrypted media.

To use the configuration file, name it accordingly and place it in a directory named "Auto Server Setup" at the root of any volume mounted in /Volumes. The volume can be on any mountable media, such as a flash drive, iPod in disk mode, CD, or FireWire drive. The server searches in the root directory of mounted volumes for a file with a .plist extension, in this order:

1. The MAC address of the server, less any colons or dashes

2. IP address of the server

3. Host name of the server

4. Serial number of the server

5. Fully Qualified Domain Name (FQDN) of the server

6. Partial IP address of server

7. "generic" (literally—the name will be "generic.plist")

For example, if a flash drive with a volume named "setup" contains a folder named "Auto Server Setup" with a configuration file named 00308a67edcb.plist, the setup application would discover this file and use it to configure the server. Additionally, the configuration file could be named generic.plist. If generic.plist does not contain a valid serial number, that number must be set after the first login, which can be done using Server Admin.app, or over an SSH connection using the serversetup command:

```
serversetup -setServerSerialNumber [serial number]
```

Using these techniques, you can install and configure large numbers of server systems quickly and automatically. Furthermore, these techniques provide a perfect opportunity to keep information tied to a central tracking database.

NOTE ▶ It's common to create an automated deployment with a default password that is not the same as the final admin password. In this way, the password can be configured interactively, or programmatically, without risking its inclusion in a text file.

Performing Third-Party and Additional Installations

After you've completed the initial installation on a Mac OS X system, the installation is not really "complete"—it's really just the beginning. What you have now is a brand-new system that's ready for you to make it do what you need it to do. Normally, you should bring a newly installed server up to date immediately after installation. Typically, even soon after the initial release of an operating system, updates from Apple are waiting to be applied. (In some cases, it may not be desirable to update a newly installed system, for example, if you need to keep a new Open Directory replica of the same version as its master.)

To perform additional installations, Software Update is an applicable graphical tool; however, it's not always the best choice for performing installations across large numbers of machines at once. The shell tool that corresponds to Software Update is softwareupdate, which you can use over a single SSH connection or run en masse over your server systems using Apple Remote Desktop. softwareupdate must be run with root privileges.

You can have the -l (ell) switch instruct softwareupdate to *list* any available updates, as follows:

```
# softwareupdate -l
Software Update Tool
Copyright 2002-2007 Apple

Software Update found the following new or updated software:
* MacOSXServerUpd10.5.2-10.5.2
        Mac OS X Server Update (10.5.2), 389137K [recommended] [restart]
```

The -i switch tells softwareupdate to *install* a given package, and the -a switch is used along with -i to install *all* updates. Both the GUI-based Software Update and the command line softwareupdate utility log information about installations in the /Library/Log/Software\ Update.log file. On a new server, you should typically run these instructions as soon as possible after the initial installation to fetch and install all outstanding updates:

```
# softwareupdate -i -a
```

Apple supplies several different types of updates via the softwareupdate mechanism. Some patches are operating system bug fixes or enhancements. Some are printer or low-level drivers that interact with hardware and make new features available. Apple also uses the softwareupdate mechanism to update Apple applications such as Pages, Logic, and Final Cut. Finally, Apple distributes security updates via softwareupdate. You should evaluate and install security updates as soon as possible.

The Software Update framework works by asking Apple's update server, swscan.apple.com, for a list of offered updates, based on the system configuration. Software Update then downloads a localized .dist (distribution) file for each corresponding package. These distribution files contain installer scripts that check to determine if the package can be installed. There's no payload at this point, only scripts that verify whether the offered package is appropriate. If the update package qualifies, it's offered as an update in the list.

Certain updates require a restart. For these cases, Software Update downloads the necessary updates into the /Library/Updates/ directory and creates .SoftwareUpdateAtLogout in /var/db/. These packages are then installed after all users are logged out from a GUI session. After the machine reboots, the .SoftwareUpdateAtLogout file is deleted.

In addition to the download and installation process used by the Software Update framework, the following preferences also guide the application's behavior:

▶   /Library/Preferences/com.apple.SoftwareUpdate.plist stores general software update parameters and lists any updates waiting to be installed at logout.

▶   ~/Library/Preferences/ByHost/com.apple.SoftwareUpdate.(GUID).plist controls per-user display settings, affecting the font size of the GUI-based Software Update.app.

▶   ~/Library/Preferences/com.apple.SoftwareUpdate.plist controls the behavior of software updates per user. This file stores information about the frequency of checking for updates and whether attempts should be made to update.

You can adjust these preferences using the Software Update preference pane in System Preferences, or the softwareupdate command-line tool. For example, to disable automatic checking, per user, you can use the following command:

```
$ softwareupdate -schedule off
```

See the man page for softwareupdate for other options; see "Getting Help" in Chapter 9, "Automating Systems," for instructions on using man pages.

Software Update is ideal for installing Apple-supplied software packages. However, there is much third-party software that can enhance an administrator's and end user's experience. As described in "Installing Remotely from a Command Line" earlier in this chapter, the installer tool can install any Apple package to any valid destination. Often, third-party software is provided in the form of a package, stored on a disk image, and made available via HTTP. Shell tools can automate the entire download, mount, and installation process.

The following example shows how to use a remote shell to download and install MacPorts, a system for compiling, installing, and upgrading open-source software. This is an important exercise: The open standards and UNIX foundation of Mac OS X provide enormous benefits and flexibility to the entire system, with the support for open-source software that augments the capabilities of Mac OS X. Most open-source software can be downloaded, compiled, and installed with very little effort.

A system like MacPorts, however, has two main benefits. For software that needs to be patched to compile under Mac OS X, volunteers maintain and provide patches for you, making the software ready to compile and install. In addition, MacPorts uses a separate installation location, keeping the software that it compiles and installs apart from the main system software.

> **NOTE ▶** MacPorts, while useful, commonly falls into the category of developer tools. Many organizations restrict developer tools from being installed on production servers due to potential security risks or increased resource use.

This separate installation location means that you can have newer experimental versions of software installed on your system without waiting for Apple to patch it officially, and that software installed by MacPorts can use its own versions of libraries without affecting the rest of Mac OS X. For example, you may want the latest version of the Perl scripting language. Mac OS X ships with Perl version 5.8.8, but more recent versions are available. MacPorts makes it possible to have both versions on your system without conflicts. Perhaps most important is that you now have access to the many open-source tools and utilities that help system administrators perform their job more efficiently.

To download MacPorts, first use the ssh command in the target machine. Then download the MacPorts disk image using curl:

```
# curl -O http://svn.macports.org/repository/macports/downloads/MacPorts-1.6.0/
MacPorts-1.6.0-10.5-Leopard.dmg
  % Total    % Received % Xferd  Average Speed   Time    Time     Time  Current
                                 Dload  Upload   Total   Spent    Left  Speed
100  412k  100  412k    0     0   111k      0  0:00:03  0:00:03 --:--:--  359k
```

The -O switch is necessary to write the file to disk. To mount this disk image, the hdiutil command and the mount verb attach the image and mount it in the default /Volumes location:

```
# hdiutil mount MacPorts-1.6.0-10.5-Leopard.dmg
Checksumming Protective Master Boot Record (MBR : 0)
Protective Master Boot Record (MBR :: verified   CRC32 $3A3AE94A
Checksumming GPT Header (Primary GPT Header : 1)
 GPT Header (Primary GPT Header : 1): verified   CRC32 $2D9334D6
Checksumming GPT Partition Data (Primary GPT Table : 2)
GPT Partition Data (Primary GPT Tabl: verified   CRC32 $BA067A2F
Checksumming  (Apple_Free : 3)
                   (Apple_Free : 3): verified   CRC32 $00000000
Checksumming disk image (Apple_HFS : 4)
...................................................................
..........
         disk image (Apple_HFS : 4): verified   CRC32 $A375867E
Checksumming  (Apple_Free : 5)
                   (Apple_Free : 5): verified   CRC32 $00000000
Checksumming GPT Partition Data (Backup GPT Table : 6)
GPT Partition Data (Backup GPT Table: verified   CRC32 $BA067A2F
Checksumming GPT Header (Backup GPT Header : 7)
  GPT Header (Backup GPT Header : 7): verified   CRC32 $0EDC5A35
verified   CRC32 $8FA77E7A
/dev/disk1              GUID_partition_scheme
/dev/disk1s1           Apple_HFS                 /Volumes/MacPorts-1.6.0
```

installer can also report which volumes are eligible targets for any package in question using the volInfo switch. To verify the MacPorts package, specify it with the -package switch, pointing to the newly mounted disk image:

```
# installer -volinfo -package /Volumes/MacPorts-1.6.0/MacPorts-1.6.0.pkg
/Volumes/Data1
/Volumes/Data2
/
```

The -target switch works with any of the reported volumes, which lets you install in alternate locations. If the volinfo verb returns no information, the package is not appropriate for installation on any currently mounted volumes. To install MacPorts on the system volume (as reported valid by -volinfo), issue the following:

```
# installer -verbose -package /Volumes/MacPorts-1.6.0/MacPorts-1.6.0.pkg -target /
```

The -verbose switch is optional. After the download is complete, a fully functional version of MacPorts will reside at /opt/local/bin. See the MacPorts home page at http://www.macports.org for more information on ports and using the ports system.

Finally, be kind: Don't forget to *unmount* the disk image. Unmounting and deleting the disk image conserves system resources and disk space. You need to know the mount point or the disk ID, both of which you can obtain using the mount command. The disk ID also was provided when the disk was attached. In this case, the disk ID is /dev/disk1; you can unmount it using the hdiutil detach verb:

```
# hdiutil detach disk1
"disk1" unmounted.
"disk1" ejected.
```

The man page for hdiutil also provides other useful options, such as info, create, and resize.

Verifying Installations

You should always question the validity of software downloaded from a website. Fortunately, many sites also provide checksums against which to verify the download. Apple provides SHA-1 cryptographic checksums for its downloads. The checksum is verified for you when you use Software Update to install updates. However, you may periodically need to download an update and install it outside of that framework. In that case, or whenever a checksum is provided, you should verify the checksum. For example, the web page that provides the download for Security Update 2008-002 (http://www.apple.com/support/downloads/securityupdate2008002v11leopard.html) displays the SHA-1 digest:

Security Update 2008-002 (Leopard) SHA1 Digest:

SecUpd2008-002.v1.1.dmg=

SHA1= 9e50032326611245bb5382099a60cbcd4d1852c9

After downloading, the SHA-1 digest can be verified using the `openssl` command:

```
$ openssl sha1 SecUpd2008-002.v1.1.dmg
SHA1(SecUpd2008-002.v1.1.dmg)= SHA1= 9e50032326611245bb5382099a60cbcd4d1852c9
```

Compare the checksum received from the `openssl` command with the checksum provided on the download page. If they do not match, you should not install this software. From time to time, downloads become corrupted, causing the checksum not to match. Also, from time to time, websites get hacked, or downloads are replaced with bogus versions that, once installed on your system, may leave it vulnerable to attack.

If you provide software for download, you can use the same procedure shown earlier in this section to determine the SHA-1 digest of your software. Provide it along with the download so that users can verify that they have the genuine article.

Inspecting Packages Before Installation

In addition to verifying downloads using checksums, another important security measure is inspecting packages before you install them.

The software delivery system on Mac OS X revolves around *packages*, a system developed by Apple that can include running scripts to place or install files. Packages have these unique properties:

- ▶ They have the extension .pkg.
- ▶ They are directories, presented by the Finder as a single file (you can examine their contents by Control-clicking the package and choosing Show Package Contents from the context menu, or by examining them in a shell).
- ▶ They contain various files and directories in well-defined locations within the package.
- ▶ The files and directories in a package together provide the information needed by the Installer application to present the packaged software for installation.
- ▶ Double-clicking a package launches the Installer application.

During installation, Installer creates another package file (with extension .pkg) to serve as an installation receipt, and stores it in /Library/Receipts. The presence of a receipt file causes the Installer to treat future installations of this same package as upgrades—even if the installed files are removed.

Apple's sophisticated packaging system can do more than simply take files from point A and install them on point B. Packages can run scripts—typically, an important capability for installers. Scripts often have other tasks in addition to placing files. For example, the Installer program may ask you for an admin-level password. Be aware that if you supply it, you give the package access to the entire system.

While most packages are completely trustworthy, using them can surreptitiously install software. For example, when running the Apple Installer, choosing File > Get Info obtains a list of files that the installer will extract from an archive and install. Plus, a package can easily contain separate archives that a script, hidden from the GUI, will install. These archives will not appear in the list displayed by File > Get Info, and with admin-level credentials, they can install software anywhere on the system. A script can also alter system settings.

You can inspect packages before installation in three ways:

▶ Load the package into a package creation tool, such as the Apple Package Maker utility. This enables you to investigate the file contents and learn the scripts that will run as part of the installation process.

▶ Examine the package contents from a shell. This gives you access to all archives, files, and scripts in the hierarchy. Particularly, look at scripts that may run as part of the installation process.

▶ Query the Bill of Materials (BOM) file using the lsbom utility. The lsbom command operates on a .bom file, typically "Archive.bom." For example:

```
$ lsbom Archive.bom
```

You can specify a full path, and examine BOM files from installed packages in /Library/ Receipts. The -d switch to lsbom limits output to directories in the installer. This is ideal when you need only a high-level view of the contents. For example:

```
$ lsbom -d /Library/Receipts/iWeb.pkg/Contents/Archive.bom
```

Without the -d switch, this example lists 19,046 files rather than 52,921; the switch makes the output much more manageable.

For more information about security on Apple-provided packages, see the Apple security updates page at http://support.apple.com/kb/HT1222. Apple also maintains a broader page on security at http://www.apple.com/support/security/. Also, consider signing up for the "security-announce" mailing list found at http://lists.apple.com.

Using Managed Preferences

An incredibly powerful way to configure a system running Mac OS X is using Managed Preferences (MCX). Managed Preferences allow a directory service to push preferences to a client. Preferences can be managed at all levels—the user, group, or machine—and a policy derived from the entire set. *Policy* is a set of preferences defined by an administrator and enforced for particular users of a machine.

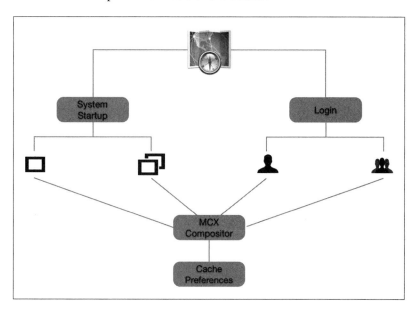

Managed preferences is largely a centralized, directory services topic, as MCX records are stored in a directory; but changes in Mac OS X v10.5 make that centralized distinction a little less clear. (Nowhere is it written that the issuing directory service *has* to be centralized, even if that may be the natural way to deal with machines on a large scale.) Managed preferences also can be applied locally, especially as all user, group, and machine data for local accounts are stored in a local directory service.

Possibly the easiest way to apply managed preferences is built into Workgroup Manager. Contrary to popular belief, Workgroup Manager can work with records in any directory service—including the local directory store running on every Mac OS X machine—not just Open Directory. You can manage preferences with Open Directory or by using the new Managed Preferences (mcx) extensions in the dscl command-line utility.

To manage preferences with Open Directory:

1 Launch Workgroup Manager (WGM) and authenticate to the Lightweight Directory
   Access Protocol (LDAP) directory, either at the WGM login window, or by clicking
   the Lock icon in the upper right corner of the main WGM window.

2 Choose Workgroup Manager > Preferences and select the Show All Records Tab and
   Inspector preference.

   This preference must be turned on for access to some of the LDAP hierarchy. The
   Preferences tab now displays a fifth tab, the Inspector (a bull's-eye target), in addition
   to the Standard User, Group, Computer, and Computer Group tabs:

3 Select the object that you wish to manage—a user, group, or computer—and click the
   Preferences button in the toolbar.

   This action displays a pane with preferences that can be managed.

4 Choose a category to display more detail and set preferences. For example, the mobil-
   ity preference has three tabs, most with subtabs of options that can be managed.

5 Choose the desired frequency for managing parameters. Management for most
   parameters can occur with a frequency of Never, Once, Often, or Always. (WGM
   does not use Often.)

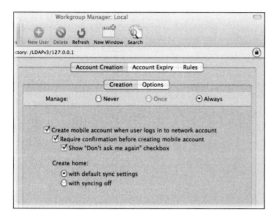

The Once option sets the preference initially, but then allows the user to change it. The Always option enforces the preference, disallowing any changes. In the middle is the Often option (not shown in the figure, because WGM does not use the Often option), which reapplies the preference whenever preferences are refreshed (which is at least at every login).

6   Save the options. The main pane displays an arrow button next to any category that is managed.

You can also create, view, and manipulate these settings using the new .mcx extensions in the dscl command-line utility. For example, to read all MCX-enabled preferences for the user "marczak", use dscl with the mcxread command:

```
# dscl localhost -mcxread /Search/Users/marczak
App domain: com.apple.dock
Key: AppItems-Raw
State: always
Value: (
        {
        "mcx_typehint" = 1;
        "tile-data" =           {
```

```
        "file-data" =              {
            "_CFURLString" = "/Applications/Safari.app";
            "_CFURLStringType" = 0;
        };
        "file-label" = Safari;
    };
    "tile-type" = "file-tile";
},
...

(voluminous output snipped for space)
```

Just as interesting is the ability to push policy (managed preferences) onto local accounts. This capability lets an administrator make settings once that can be enforced for any user on that local system, including any new accounts that are set up. There is no real difference between setting up managed preferences in a central directory versus the local directory. To access the local directory of a Mac OS X machine using Workgroup Manager, simply choose Server > View Directories. This will display the local node, allowing access to local user, group, machine, and machine group records. You can set preferences on any of these records.

| Overview   Details |

Apple has provided a preference manifest that allows management of many aspects of the system. A preference manifest is a list of preferences provided by an application that lets the managed preference system know which preferences can be set for that particular application. To import a preference manifest, click the Preference button on the toolbar, and then click the Details button.

Most likely the list is empty, but you can quickly fill it with useful preferences. To select an application containing the preference manifest, click the Add (+) button beneath the list. One useful example is contained in the ManagedClient.app bundle supplied by Apple. Using the file dialog box, navigate to /System/Library/CoreServices and add the ManagedClient.app file.

After you've added the ManagedClient.app file, preferences will populate the list. To apply a preference, choose the object to which you want to apply the preference, select the preference in the Detail pane, and then click the Edit button (pencil icon). Click the disclosure triangle next to the management style that you want to enforce: Once, Often, or Always.

Highlight the row to select it, and click the New Key button at the top of the window. Click the new key that you added to display a pop-up menu of values to manage.

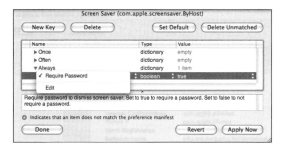

Sometimes what you want to manage is not predefined in the list. You can easily add arbitrary values to the list (as long as they can function appropriately). Arbitrary values don't damage anything, but values in the directory have to be correct to do something. For example, Mac OS X v10.5.2 introduced a menu bar item (menulet) for Time Machine. To disable it, edit the Menu Extras preference, and choose Edit from the pop-up menu. Type `TimeMachine.menu` and set it to False. Workgroup Manager will show a warning that the entry does not match the preference manifest. The entry can then be safely ignored.

Troubleshooting

The material covered in this chapter was broad and fairly deep. Each topic presented has specific ways of troubleshooting. These measures will be addressed here by subject.

Initial Installation

When you perform an initial installation, whether remotely over `ssh`, at the console locally, or using Screen Sharing, little can go wrong. Because the system is booted from installation media, the disks are entirely under the installer's control. Problems in this realm typically stem from bad media—optical or magnetic. If the install DVD is in question, let the graphical installer verify it during installation, or simply use another DVD.

Ideally, run disk checks prior to any installation. If you find disk errors before installing a system, take the opportunity to swap out any bad disks before beginning the installation. Disk errors only get worse over time.

If errors occur during an initial system installation, check the destination for errors. You can access the GUI-based Disk Utility while booted from the Leopard DVD by choosing Utility > Disk Utility. If you're performing a remote installation over ssh, the console-based diskutil also is available. Verify a volume's integrity with the verifyvolume verb:

```
diskutil verifyvolume disk2s3
```

If you find errors, use diskutil repairvolume to try to correct them:

```
diskutil repairvolume disk2s3
```

You can specify the device passed to diskutil as either a device node entry, such as /dev/disk2; a volume mount point, such as /Volumes/ServerHD; a disk identifier, such as disk2; or a disk's UUID (Universally Unique IDentifier).

If you encounter problems connecting to a remote machine to perform the installation, ensure that the target machine has finished booting from the install DVD. To obtain a remote target's IP address, you must use sa_srchr on the same subnet as the target. If you cannot use the same subnet as the target, have someone (or something) on the remote network tell you what the IP address is.

Subsequent Installations

Often, problems with installations on already-running systems come down to permissions. Ensure that the user ID performing the installation has sufficient permissions on the target. If you're sure that the user ID in question has permissions (for example, running under root), the problem may fall into the same category as the type of disk errors outlined in the previous section; see "Initial Installation" for methods of verifying a disk's integrity.

A subtle variation of a permissions problem is when installer packages are poorly constructed. Remember: With admin-level rights, an installer can do anything on your system, including cause problems. Developers have sometimes packaged applications with incorrect permissions. If these files are installed into system-supplied directories, such as /bin or /etc on which the system relies, an installer can inadvertently change the permissions on these directories. You can find this problem and correct it with the Disk Utility.app verify and repair disk features. These options also exist in the command-line diskutil utility.

Managed Preferences

Managed preferences traditionally have been difficult to troubleshoot. This was especially true in larger installations that push policy from all domains (user, computer, group, and computer group) where each source potentially adds to the mix. Apple took this into consideration and provides a new-to-Mac OS X v10.5 tool, `mcxquery`, which can composite all policy items for an object and display the results.

```
# mcxquery -user marczak
com.apple.homeSync
      loginSyncDialogTimeoutSeconds  marczak (User)  always  60
com.apple.screensaver.ByHost
      askForPassword                 marczak (User)  always  1
```

The `mcxquery` tool can access any domain and composite it with another domain. For example, if there is a conflict between a group—such as the "students" group—and a user-level preference, the user-level preference takes precedence. The students group sets the "Launch Animation UI Disabled" flag (shown as `launch-anim-immutable` in the following example) in `com.apple.dock` to true (or `1`), but the user policy allows it by setting the preference to false (or `0`). The `mcxquery` command combines the results and shows only the final policy:

```
# mcxquery -user m2 -group students
com.apple.dock
      launchanim-immutable           m2 (User), students (Group)  always  0
com.apple.homeSync
      loginSyncDialogTimeoutSeconds  m2 (User)                    always  60
com.apple.screensaver.ByHost
      askForPassword                 m2 (User)                    always  1
com.apple.systempreferences
      EnabledPreferencePanes         students (Group)             always  ( "com.apple.
preference.dock", "com.apple.preference.desktopscreeneffect", "com.apple.preference.
displays", "com.apple.preference.expose", "com.apple.preference.general" )
```

Other managed preference issues stem from the directory that is supplying the managed preference records. Is the client correctly bound to the directory? Is the directory reliable?

Is the user ID in the correct groups in the directory service? The `id` command is helpful in determining this information:

```
$ id
uid=88721(marczak) gid=4500(mac_admins) groups=4500(mac_admins),98(_
lpadmin),1003(share_masters),1001(reports),20(staff)
```

See the `man` page for `id` for more options.

MCX records are cached for use. This reduces network traffic so that a client does not need to contact the directory service each time it needs to refer to policy. It also allows managing of mobile devices, such as laptops, that may be entirely offline or unable to contact the central directory service. Because the cache and the directory service itself are two separate things, they can become out-of-sync.

Clients with a cache try to refresh on every directory service transition (such as login, wake, network interface change, and so on). This attempt is successful only when the client can contact an appropriate server.

Another useful way to verify the source of preferences and how they are being applied is to examine the directory cache for each managed object and the cache file named complete. plist. A complete.plist file exists at each point in the /Library/Managed\ Preferences file system hierarchy where preferences are composited, at a user, group, or computer level. This plist file represents the set of all managed preferences. Interestingly, each entry has a key that lists its source—much like using `mcxquery`.

If it seems that cached results are causing problems or not picking up new values, you can take some corrective actions. One way to flush the cache is to use the `dscacheutil` command with the `-flush` verb:

```
# dscacheutil -flush
```

A network transition is another action that causes the cache to try to refresh. You can simulate this action by killing the `DirectoryService` daemon (on the client, with root-level access):

```
# killall DirectoryService
```

If that does not solve the problem, first find a directory for each managed object within the /Library/Managed\ Preferences directory. You can examine and remove these plists (any removed will be re-created on the next refresh). If necessary, you can even remove the entire contents of the /Library/Managed Preferences directory.

As you explore the system, you'll find many useful command-line tools. Sometimes, you'll find tools that are really useful but completely undocumented by Apple, so you must be cautious.

The ManagedClient.app file also contains a useful application binary of the same name. You can use the application to refresh cached MCX records. Provide the -f switch to recomposite the preferences, plus the -u switch with the user ID to act on, in single quotes:

```
/System/Library/CoreServices/ManagedClient.app/Contents/MacOS/ManagedClient -f
'-u 15798'
```

Finally, if no other troubleshooting solution is successful, the MCX compositor has a debug mode, which you can enable with these two commands:

```
sudo defaults write /Library/Preferences/com.apple.MCXDebug debugOutput -2
sudo chmod 666 /Library/Preferences/com.apple.MCXDebug.plistcompositor
```

A log is then created, and can be followed at:

```
/Library/Logs/ManagedClient/ManagedClient.log
```

While not officially documented by Apple, this log contains a wealth of information.

What You've Learned

In this chapter you learned about a wide range of topics, from initial system installation through updating and configuring systems. Specifically, you should now know the following:

▶ It's possible, and relatively easy, to install Mac OS X Server on remote hardware.

▶ Use sa_srchr to find the IP address of the machine booted from the server install media. The utility must be run from the same subnet as the target.

▶ Use the installer command to install, verify, and determine the validity of packages.

▶ Converting a standard or workgroup server installation to the advanced configuration is a one-way operation. Once converted to an advanced configuration, a server cannot go back to a standard or workgroup configuration.

▶ You can create a configuration file offline, before using any target hardware, to automate configuration choices.

▶ Open-source software is a great fit with Mac OS X. Many programs that ease the burdens of system administrators and users alike can be easily downloaded, compiled, and installed. Configuration systems such as MacPorts also greatly aid in this process.

▶ `softwareupdate` is a useful command-line tool that fetches packages from Apple, verifies their contents, and installs them on the target system.

▶ Use `openssl` to verify SHA-1 checksums on downloaded files and verify their authenticity.

▶ After you supply admin-level credentials to an installer, you give it free access to do anything with your system. Investigate packages before you trust them.

▶ Managed preferences, also known as MCX, are a powerful way to configure preferences and push policy to Mac OS X devices. MCX records reside in a directory, either centralized to many machines, or local.

Review Quiz

1. What are the two methods of remote installation for Mac OS X Server?

2. What are the two processes that broadcast and receive notifications for a machine booted from Mac OS X Server installation media, ready for installation?

3. Name the command-line utility that allows manipulation of disk devices, such as partitioning and repair.

4. Name the command-line utility that allows you to install Apple packages from the command line.

5. Name the three configurations in which Mac OS X Server can be installed and run.

6. After a server configured in a standard or workgroup mode is converted to advanced mode, can Server Preferences.app still be used to manage the server?

7. What is the command-line utility that allows an administrator to retrieve operating system and other updates from Apple, verify, and install them?

8. Where does Apple list the SHA-1 cryptographic hash that allows you to verify the authenticity of files that you download from the Apple website?

9. Which utility do you use to verify the SHA-1 hash?

10. What is the purpose of a package receipt?

11. Which command-line utility is used to query bill-of-material (BOM) files?

12. Name the four domains to which managed preferences can be applied.

13. Where are managed preferences initially stored?

14. What is a preference manifest?

Answers

1. Graphical, using Apple Remote Desktop or Screen Sharing, and text-based via `ssh`.

2. `sa_rspndr` runs on the server awaiting installation and `sa_srchr` runs on the local client machine.

3. `diskutil` allows manipulation of disk devices, such as partitioning and repair.

4. `installer` allows you to install Apple packages from the command line.

5. Standard, workgroup, and advanced are the three configurations in which Mac OS X Server can be installed and run.

6. No. Once converted to advanced mode, Server Preferences.app cannot manage the server. Advanced mode requires Server Manager.app and Workgroup Manager.app.

7. `softwareupdate` allows an administrator to retrieve operating system and other updates from Apple, verify, and install them.

8. The SHA-1 hash is listed on the same webpage, along with the download itself.

9. `openssl` lets you verify the SHA-1 hash.

10. A package receipt serves two purposes: to track the files installed with a package, and to inform the installer whether a particular package has previously been installed.

11. `lsbom` is used to query bill-of-material (BOM) files.

12. User, group, computer, and computer group are the four domains to which managed preferences can be applied.

13. A directory service, such as Open Directory, stores managed preferences.

14. A preference manifest is a list of preferences provided by an application that lets the managed preference system know which preferences can be set for that particular application. To use a preference manifest in Workgroup Manager, it must first be imported.

3

Time

This lesson takes approximately 60 minutes to complete.

Goals

Prepare for the upgrade of Mac OS X Server

Back up and export critical server settings

Export user and group records

Import settings on an existing server

Import user and group data

Chapter 3

Upgrading and Migrating Systems

It is rare to have the opportunity to plan and install 100 percent of a network. Usually, existing systems need upgrades or older hardware has to be retired, forcing a migration to new hardware. This chapter covers strategies for upgrading and migrating Mac OS X-based servers.

Upgrading Your System

As with any major changes to a system, upgrades must be planned. Most upgrade scenarios are fairly straightforward. That is why administrators choose to upgrade rather than reinstall a system—the promise of less work.

It is important to distinguish between a software update and a software upgrade.

In general, an *update* refers to an update within one version of the operating system. The numbering scheme in Mac OS X might add some confusion, because version 10 is always used. It might be easier to think in terms of the "code name," such as Jaguar, Panther, Tiger, and Leopard (10.2, 10.3, 10.4, and 10.5, respectively). So if you change in Tiger, say from version 10.4.10 to 10.4.11, then you're said to be *updating*. If you change to a newer version of the operating system, say from Tiger (Mac OS X v10.4) to Leopard (Mac OS X v10.5), then you're said to be *upgrading*.

Each generation of Mac OS X Server includes major structural changes, which can cause issues. Currently, Mac OS X Server v10.3.9 and versions 10.4.10 or later can be directly upgraded to v10.5. The minimum hardware requirements for Leopard must still be met.

Planning an Upgrade

In planning a version upgrade, one of the major issues is to determine if current production software—whether system software, third-party software, or an in-house custom solution—will be compatible with the new version. Always have a backup ready before upgrading. You should run a test upgrade and have a postupgrade plan in case you must stop the upgrade and regroup.

A backup provides a way to roll back in the event of problems. Problems can be hardware-related (such as a bad disk) or they can be less obvious.

Ideally, an administrator can preflight an entire upgrade. With appropriate hardware—spare or soon-to-be-production hardware—the administrator can clone a production image to a test system and perform an upgrade.

You should also prepare a postupgrade test plan, which will give you a threshold for knowing when to abort the rollout and restore the previous system from backup.

When upgrading the Mac OS X Server, you need to understand the impact on services that upgrading a server will cause. You should follow all of the installation guidelines for the version of Mac OS X Server, ensure that hardware requirements are met, and plan and have a functioning network infrastructure—particularly the Domain Name System (DNS).

(DNS converts names to IP addresses and IP addresses to names. DNS is covered in detail in Chapter 5, "Working with DNS and NTP.")

Many settings on an Open Directory master rely on the server seeing the correct DNS records, because many Lightweight Directory Access Protocol (LDAP) records embed the fully qualified domain name (FQDN) of the server. You should verify forward and reverse DNS before and after an upgrade using the changeip and checkhostname commands:

```
# changeip -checkhostname

Primary address      = 192.168.100.18

Current HostName     = dawn.radiotope.com
DNS HostName         = dawn.radiotope.com

The names match. There is nothing to change.
```

If changeip reports any problems, correct them before upgrading.

Upgrading from Tiger, Panther, and Jaguar

Upgrading to Leopard is supported from Mac OS X v10.4.11 Tiger, v10.3.9 Panther, and v10.2.8 Jaguar. (In all cases, Macintosh Manager is not supported in Mac OS X Server v10.5.)

When you upgrade from Mac OS X Server v10.4.10 or later, virtually all existing data and settings remain available for use; however, note the following:

▶ NetBoot images created using Mac OS X Server versions 10.3 and 10.4 are reusable. NetBoot images created using earlier versions cannot be used.

▶ When upgrading to Mac OS X Server v10.5, the launch daemons (/System/Library/LaunchDaemons) are replaced by the Mac OS X Server v10.5 version of these daemons.

▶ Upgrading to v10.5 removes the QTSS Publisher application but leaves the files used by the application.

▶ Hypertext Preprocessor (PHP) 4 reached the end of its life on December 31, 2007, and critical security fixes won't be made after August 8, 2008, as announced at http://www.php.net. If you upgrade to Mac OS X Server v10.5 and retain PHP 4.4.x and Apache 1.3, plan to switch to PHP 5.x and Apache 2.2 before August 8, 2008 to maintain a secure PHP.

When you upgrade from Mac OS X Server v10.3.9, virtually all existing data and settings remain available for use. However, note the following:

▶ NetBoot images created using Mac OS X v10.3 can be reused.

▶ In Mac OS X v10.5, Watchdog was replaced by `launchd`. To enable automatic hardware restart, use the Energy Saver pane of System Preferences. To migrate settings for services that you added to /etc/watchdog.conf, create a `launchd` plist file and install it into /System/Library/LaunchDaemons/. For more on `launchd`, see "Using launchd" in Chapter 9, "Automating Systems."

▶ In Mac OS X v10.5, `hwmond` has been replaced by `launchd`.

▶ Upgrading to Mac OS X v10.5 removes the QTSS Publisher application but leaves the files used by the application.

Upgrading from version 10.2.8 is complex enough to be beyond the scope of this book. Typically, computers running Mac OS X v10.2.8 will require hard disk reformatting or replacement with a newer computer.

Exporting Settings and Data

You may want to export system settings for various reasons, including backing up, documenting, or migrating a system from an earlier version of Mac OS X to Leopard, often when moving the system to newer hardware. Typically, you won't need to migrate a Mac OS X v10.5 system to another v10.5 system, because you can clone the source system to the target system. In cloning from a PowerPC-based system to Intel, however, there are some issues with certain services. This section covers several techniques for dealing with those issues.

When upgrading from Mac OS X Server v10.4.11, the following services can be migrated:

▶ Web configuration data

▶ Web content

▶ MySQL data

▶ Mail database

▶ WebMail data

- ► FTP configuration files
- ► LDAP server settings
- ► NetBoot images
- ► WebObjects applications and frameworks
- ► Tomcat data
- ► JBoss applications
- ► Apple Filing Protocol (AFP) settings
- ► Server Message Block (SMB) settings
- ► IP firewall configuration
- ► DNS settings
- ► DHCP settings
- ► NAT settings
- ► Print settings
- ► VPN settings
- ► User data, including home directories
- ► QuickTime Streaming Server files and folders
- ► QTSS Publisher files and folders
- ► User and group accounts
- ► iChat server settings

You can export settings with the `serveradmin` command, running with admin-level privileges. Run `serveradmin` with the `settings all` directive, and redirect the output to a file:

```
serveradmin settings all > server_settings.txt
```

On Mac OS X v10.4 systems, this all-in-one approach has been known to fail. However, each service can export its settings individually:

```
serveradmin settings afp > afp.sabackup
serveradmin settings appserver > appserver.sabackup
serveradmin settings dhcp > dhcp.sabackup
```

```
serveradmin settings dirserv > dirserv.sabackup

serveradmin settings dns > dns.sabackup

serveradmin settings filebrowser > filebrowser.sabackup

serveradmin settings ftp > ftp.sabackup

serveradmin settings info > info.sabackup

serveradmin settings ipfilter > ipfilter.sabackup

serveradmin settings jabber > jabber.sabackup

...

serveradmin settings vpn > vpn.sabackup

serveradmin settings web > web.sabackup

serveradmin settings webobjects > webobjects.sabackup

serveradmin settings xgrid > xgrid.sabackup

serveradmin settings xserve > xserve.sabackup
```

NOTE ▶ Using .sabackup as the extension for exported settings is only one convention, and not necessary.

You can display a full list of services with serveradmin list directive. You can also export service settings using the Mac OS X v10.5 Server Admin application. Select the server from which to export settings and choose Server > Export > Service Settings. A dialog box appears, prompting you for a name and location for saving the information. The Export Service Settings command saves settings as a plain-text XML file.

Moving end-user data is fairly easy: Mount a remote volume and copy, or connect a removable storage device and transfer (with the resulting sneakernet move, or physical data transfer). However, this migration is complicated by one aspect: permissions.

Permissions are enforced by mapping the file's owner and group back to a directory. If the target system is not using the same directory, or a copy of it, as the source, those mappings will fail to align. You should verify the state of a target system's directory service before moving end-user data in bulk.

In the case of migrating an Open Directory master between hardware products, you can choose to do the following:

▶ Clone and upgrade. This applies to v10.4 systems moving to v10.5.

▶ Use Workgroup Manager to export users and groups.

▶ Use dsexport to export users and groups.

▶ Back up Open Directory data in its entirety using Server Admin.app or serveradmin.

Each option has advantages and disadvantages.

Cloning and Upgrading

Any server running Mac OS X v10.4.10 or later can be cloned to new hardware and then upgraded. This method provides an easy path to upgrade the operating system and hardware at the same time.

If you choose to clone and upgrade, first run Disk Utility, or its command-line equivalent diskutil, to check for disk errors. You can also use Disk Utility, while booted from another volume, including the installer media, to create the clone. Prior to upgrading, also export print service settings using serveradmin, as described in the preceding section, "Exporting Settings and Data." If you plan to clone and upgrade to an Intel target from a PowerPC, back up Open Directory (see "Backing Up Open Directory" in this section).

Once on the new system, do not boot from the clone, but rather from v10.5 installation media. Perform a standard upgrade, which upgrades settings and minimizes the amount of manual work that you need to do—but not entirely. You will still need to manually upgrade some services in the transition to v10.5 from v10.4, including print and web services and Open Directory.

After the upgrade, you must manually re-create all print queues using System Preferences > Print & Fax. Only then can you restore print settings (again, using serveradmin; see "Importing Settings and Data" later in this chapter for more details).

Under v10.5, the web server running by default is Apache v2.2; however, after an upgrade, Apache v1.3 remains running. (Both versions of software are installed; however, settings and data must be migrated.) Moving from v1.3 to v2.2 is a manual process, not handled by the Apple upgrade.

Issues with migrating to Open Directory arise only when moving from a PowerPC to an Intel target. After a PowerPC-to-Intel clone-and-upgrade migration, an Open Directory master might fail to function due to issues of endian differences. A CPU is either "big-endian" or "little-endian." Big-endian chips order the most significant byte of a number first, while little-endian orders the least significant byte first. This can cause issues when moving data between a big-endian PowerPC chip and a little-endian Intel chip. However, you can still use the clone-and-upgrade migration method, if you backed up Open Directory before upgrading. After cloning and upgrading Open Directory, you can demote the server to standalone services, re-promote the server, and restore Open Directory.

See the Apple server documentation at http://www.apple.com/server/documentation for extensive notes on upgrades.

Using Workgroup Manager

Using Workgroup Manager to clone and upgrade may be useful for some smaller deployments, but it is not appropriate for larger-scale upgrades.

When migrating to a new version of the operating system, it is often advantageous to perform a fresh installation and migrate settings manually as needed. With a large number of users and groups, it's more efficient to automate this process as much as possible. You can use Workgroup Manager to export both users and groups.

 Open Workgroup Manager, located in /Applications/Server by default, and authenticate with directory administrator credentials when asked. Click the Accounts button in the toolbar, and make sure that the Users tab is chosen.

Click a user and then press Command-A to select all users. Note that the command selects only all *visible* users. If the LDAP server only returned a portion of users (due to filters or a limit), you will need to perform multiple exports (or, perhaps, increase the server limit). To perform the export, choose Server > Export.

Export groups by selecting the Groups tab and repeating the process described in the previous paragraph.

One note of caution: Passwords are not exported as part of this process. Depending on the size and sensitivity of your user base, this may or may not be an issue. To export users, groups, *and* passwords, see the section "Backing Up Open Directory."

Using dsexport

Unique to Mac OS X v10.5, `dsexport` is a command-line utility that exports records from directory services. This utility is useful only for backups or for v10.5-to-v10.5 migrations. The `dsexport` utility exists on Mac OS X machines as well as Mac OS X Server, and can be used to export records from the local node (/Local/Default). The process for exporting user or group records is straightforward:

```
dsexport [filename] [node] [record type]
```

For example, to export users from the Open Directory master (while running this command *on* the master) to a file named user_list.exp:

```
dsexport user_list.exp /LDAPv3/127.0.0.1 dsRecTypeStandard:Users
```

To export groups, the record type would use `dsRecTypeStandard:Groups`.

New to v10.5 is the loss of `NetInfo`, replaced by `dslocal`.

Backing Up Open Directory

Open Directory is a combination of several different technologies that work in concert. Backing up or capturing each subsystem can be complicated, but Apple has built into Server Admin the ability to back up all relevant parts of Open Directory.

To back up Open Directory, launch Server Admin, authenticate, and choose an Open Directory master. (Backup will not work on a replica, because you would be just resynchronizing from a master.) Choose the Open Directory Service, and then click the Archive button in the toolbar. Choose a location for the backup and click the Archive button in the window. The backup writes files to a single encrypted disk image at the location you specify.

The disk image contains, in addition to other Open Directory information, a dump of the LDAP database; data from PasswordServer; settings from local directory nodes; and settings for DirectoryService (plists), Kerberos, and Samba. All these files are stored in a volume named ldap_bk. Bear in mind that the contents of this file are extremely sensitive, containing everything that an attacker would need to successfully access a server, and, potentially, every machine that is bound to this server. *Always* take the proper cautions and care in handling this file and its information.

This backup reduces the task of taking a snapshot of the Open Directory environment to a few mouse-clicks. However, while a snapshot is good for a single backup, as in the case of a migration, it is a poor technique for regular backups that should always be automated and require as little human involvement as possible. The Server Admin's command-line equivalent, serveradmin, can be fed a list of commands and effectively scripted. Following is a script to do just that:

```bash
#!/usr/bin/env bash
(umask 077 ; touch sacommands.txt)
BACK_DIR=/var/backups/odbackup-`date "+%Y%m%d"`
echo "dirserv:backupArchiveParams:archivePassword = somepass" >> sacommands.txt
echo "dirserv:backupArchiveParams:archivePath = $BACK_DIR" >> sacommands.txt
echo "dirserv:command = backupArchive" >> sacommands.txt
/usr/sbin/serveradmin command < sacommands.txt
rm sacommands.txt
```

You should mark this script as executable, protected appropriately (rights for root *only*), and set it up as a recurring job via `cron` or `launchd`. Additionally, you should periodically prune the backup location to ensure that it does not take up excessive disk space.

When writing scripts that make multiple simultaneous changes using `serveradmin`'s `command`, `settings`, or `writeSettings` options, keep the following in mind:

▶ `writeSettings` will include `<svc>:needsRecycleOrRestart` in its output with a value of *yes*

▶ You must end your `serveradmin` input with the Control-D characters.

See Chapter 9, "Automating Systems," for more details.

Importing Settings and Data

Settings exported with Server Admin or the command-line `serveradmin` program can be imported using either tool. To import settings using Server Admin.app, launch the program and authenticate to the server with admin-level rights. Then, choose Server > Import > Service Settings.

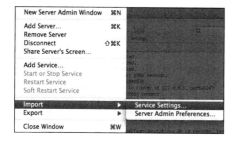

In the standard file open dialog box that appears, select the file that you exported earlier.

To import settings using the command-line `serveradmin` program, redirect the exported settings file contents into `serveradmin`:

```
serveradmin settings < backup.sabackup
```

You follow the same procedure to import an individual service's exported settings: Simply redirect the file into `serveradmin`.

Just as in exporting data, you can follow several methods to import user and group data, which correspond to the method of export:

▶   Use Workgroup Manager.

▶   Use dsimport.

▶   Restore Open Directory.

Each method, described in the following sections, has advantages and disadvantages.

Using Workgroup Manager

If you have already exported users and groups using Workgroup Manager, you can use Workgroup Manager to import these records. If you have exported *both* users and groups, you should import groups first, and then users. The method is similar for both, however.

To import users and groups, launch Workgroup Manager and authenticate with directory admin privileges. Once authenticated, choose Server > Import. The file open dialog box has several options.

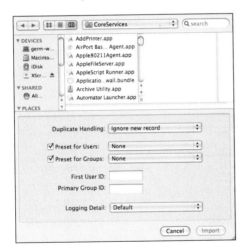

The Duplicate Handling drop-down list has several self-explanatory options, as shown here; "Ignore new record" is the default.

If user or group presets are defined, you can select and apply them to each imported record. The First User ID field enables you to set the base ID, to which all other imported records in this session will relate. The Primary Group ID field enables you to add all imported user records to a group as their primary group. The Logging Detail drop-down list can change the level of detail of the log that will be written to ~/Library/Logs/ImportExport. The log file is named DSImportExport.(timestamp).log. You can check this log for more information if import errors occur.

Using dsimport

You can import records into Open Directory with the important utility `dsimport`. The source of these records may come from `dsexport`, as described in the previous section, "Using dsexport." The source may also be a file generated by another system in your network, such as an education application or a company acquisition, where thousands of new users may need to be added at once. If a registrar or HR system is capable of handing off this data to you electronically, you can use `dsimport` to bring the records into Open Directory.

The `dsimport` options are closely related to `dsexport`:

```
dsimport (-g|-s|-p) filepath DSNodePath (O|M|A|I|N) -u user -p password [options]
```

To import the file exported in "Using dsexport," use the command:

```
dsimport -g user_list.exp /LDAPv3/127.0.0.1 O -u diradmin
```

The `-g` switch denotes the type of file being imported. In this case, it is a delimited file, as exported by Workgroup Manager. The node path must be supplied as applicable. If you are running this directly on the Open Directory master that is receiving the records, /LDAPv3/127.0.0.1 is appropriate. The choice of `O`, `M`, `A`, `I`, or `N` controls how duplicate records are handled, as follows:

▶ `O` overwrites any existing records that have the same record name. All previous attribute values will be deleted.

▶ `M` merges the imported records into an existing record. This merge prefers the new values; old values are kept only if no new value is present. This option does not create a record if one does not already exist.

▶ A appends values to fields within existing records. This option does not create a record if one does not already exist.

▶ I ignores a record with the same name if it already exists.

▶ N tells dsimport that no duplicate checking should be done.

Finally, the -u switch specifies a user with admin-level credentials. In addition, a -p switch allows specifying this user's password, but leaving it out will prompt for a password. Using the -p switch will expose the user's password in process listings—if possible, you should avoid using the -p switch.

Since dsimport rides on top of DirectoryService, any errors reported are generated from that subsystem. The DirectoryService man page contains a list of error codes. Additionally, the dserr command can also help look up errors.

```
dserr 14171
-14171: eDSAuthPasswordTooLong
```

You can specify error codes with or without the negative (-) sign.

All uses of this utility are written to a log file in ~/Library/Logs/ImportExport. The log file is named DSImportExport.<timestamp>.log, and is a good source for troubleshooting import errors when the error code is not descriptive enough.

Restoring Open Directory

Server Admin can restore the encrypted disk image backup it created. A server must be acting as an Open Directory master to restore previously backed up settings. The same pane in Server Admin that creates a backup is used to restore the backup. There is no need to mount the disk image before restoring.

To restore a backup, launch Server Admin, authenticate, and choose Open Directory in the left pane. Click the Archive button in the toolbar. For the Restore From option, simply choose the entire disk image, and click the Restore button.

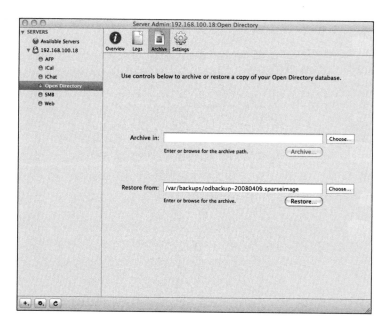

Using this feature restores all directory services, Kerberos settings (crucial to Open Directory), Samba, and user and group records, to the point when the backup was last taken.

Migration Overview

To knit the export and import process together, following is a summary of the steps needed to migrate a server running Mac OS X Server v10.4 to a new server running a clean install of Mac OS X Server v10.5.

To export the data from the source (v10.4) server:

1   Export Open Directory information (users, group, computers, and computer groups).

2   Record current share points and privileges.

3   Back up/export service settings.

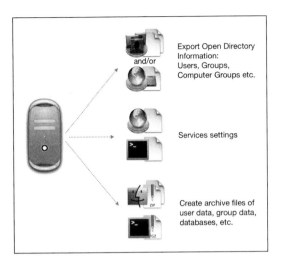

4   Copy the exported Open Directory information to the target (Mac OS X v10.5) server.

5   Set up the home directory infrastructure.

6   Import Open Directory data.

7   Transfer user data and other data files.

8   Re-create share points and privileges.

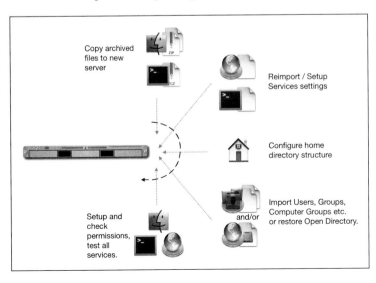

Troubleshooting

Troubleshooting the topics in this chapter is fairly straightforward. Diagnosis or repair may be difficult, but, fortunately, errors are rare.

Errors during upgrading are similar to errors while installing: Typically, they are caused by defective source media or bad target media. Because the system is booted from the installation media, problems are rare. Disk errors can manifest themselves in peculiar ways, however, and lead the troubleshooter astray. Before installation, always check the target media for consistency. If errors are detected, simply swap the source media for known good media, or verify the media during a graphical installation.

Importing and exporting data relies heavily on DirectoryServices. If error codes are returned during an import or export, record the error number. You can look up specific error codes with the dserr utility or in the DirectoryServices man page.

Also, DirectoryServices is particularly sensitive to DNS results. At a minimum, you should verify the DNS lookups using the changeip command and the checkhostname flag. The result should be only "The names match. There is nothing to change," as the following shows:

```
# changeip -checkhostname

Primary address     = 192.168.100.18

Current HostName    = dawn.radiotope.com
DNS HostName        = dawn.radiotope.com

The names match. There is nothing to change.
```

If the server or other machine is not hosting DNS, verify that the DNS server listed returns good results. Mac OS X can act very strangely with DNS that does not conform to the published specifications. A particular problem is when a DNS server (such as OpenDNS) uses an all-encompassing wildcard that returns a positive result for a nonexistent record. Also, a misbehaving DNS server that answers but never returns will manifest itself as a problem with DirectoryService. The simple remedy is to verify DNS, and verify again.

If there is a mismatch in addresses reported, use the `changeip` script to correct the problem. For example, to update a server with an IP address of 192.168.0.12 and a name of old.example.com, to have an IP address of 192.168.0.10 and a name of new.example.com, use the following command with root-level privileges:

```
# changeip /LDAPv3/127.0.0.1 192.168.0.12 192.168.0.10 oldhost.example.com
newhost.example.com
```

`changeip` is a Perl script and relies on several other scripts to accomplish its task. `changeip` calls the following scripts:

▶ `changeip_ds` updates user, machine, computer, mount, LDAP, and Password Server config records and changes these files:

> /Library/Preferences/DirectoryService/DSLDAPv3PlugInConfig.plist
>
> /etc/openldap/slapd_macosxserver.conf
>
> /etc/hostconfig (if there is a static host name)
>
> /etc/smb.conf

▶ `changeip_afctl` changes the adaptive firewall configurations.

▶ `changeip_web` updates the Apache 2 configuration.

▶ `changeip_pcast` updates the pcast server configuration.

▶ `changeip_jabber` updates the Jabber configuration using `serveradmin`.

▶ `changeip_mail` updates the Mailman, Postfix, and Internet Message Access Protocol (IMAP) configurations using `serveradmin`.

When a network address change is detected, no matter how the change happened, `changeip` is invoked, so this process should not be necessary. However, it is critical to run `changeip` when changing the name of a host. When the name returned from DNS is out of sync with the names encoded in the directory, many services and functions will fail to work properly. The server setup program uses this information to configure other server components (such as Open Directory, Kerberos, and Password Server). As such, the IP address and the DNS settings of the primary interface and these other components must always match.

What You've Learned

This chapter discussed strategies for migrating data between two servers, particularly server settings, users, and groups. You've learned how to do the following:

▶ Verify consistency before an upgrade. Use the Disk Utility application or `diskutil` to check media, and use `changeip` to verify DNS settings.

▶ Export and import service settings from a configured server using the Server Admin application and `serveradmin`.

▶ Export users and groups using Workgroup Manager or `dsexport`.

▶ Import users and groups using Workgroup Manager or `dsimport`.

▶ Back up and restore Open Directory in its entirety using Server Admin and `serveradmin`.

▶ When in doubt, check DNS.

Review Quiz

1. Which command-line tool is used to verify both the host name and IP address against DNS?

2. Which prior versions of Mac OS X Server can be upgraded to Mac OS X Server v10.5 Leopard?

3. Which command-line tool is used to export service settings?

4. Which command-line tool is used to export user and group records from the directory service?

5. List the three methods of bringing user or group data into Open Directory.

Answers

1. `changeip` verifies both the host name and IP address against DNS.

2. Mac OS X Server versions 10.4.11, 10.3.9, and 10.2.8 can be upgraded to Mac OS X Server v10.5 (Leopard).

3. `serveradmin` exports service settings.

4. `dsexport` exports user and group records from the directory service.

5. Workgroup Manager, `dsimport`, and restoring an Open Directory Backup are three methods used to bring user or group data into Open Directory.

4

Time   This lesson takes approximately 90 minutes to complete.

Goals   Learn to compute network bandwidth utilization

Learn to assess service and hardware utilization

Learn to assess storage utilization

Understand the Apple installer and package formats

Learn to assess a workflow

Chapter 4

Assessing Systems

Successful systems administration relies on clearly and thoroughly understanding how a system uses its resources—its current hardware and software components—and understanding their interaction with, and dependencies upon, user workflows and running services. This chapter discusses the tools and knowledge required to effectively evaluate several key aspects of an existing infrastructure, including current utilization of bandwidth, services, hardware, and storage. This evaluation enables you to plan and implement changes to an existing infrastructure that minimize interruption to the system's operation and maximize the user's productivity.

Determining Current Utilization

It's important to monitor utilization after a new system has been set up, or if an existing system has been serving users for a while. This information is critical to know for new systems to ensure that they run with the best performance. For existing systems, changes in usage (such as a group of video users that have changed to high-definition files) should cause you to reevaluate the setup to make sure that the system is still adequately meeting needs.

Chapter 1, "Planning Systems," defines utilization as the ratio of usage to capacity. In that chapter, you planned for future capacity; here, your concern is watching a current, running system. Fortunately, Mac OS X includes many utilities that can help you determine system utilization.

Computing Network Bandwidth Utilization

How do you determine utilization—ratio of usage to capacity—for network bandwidth? Chapter 1, "Planning Systems," explains the concept, but you need a way to obtain the values used in the computation. No single command neatly lays this out, but a series of commands enables you to assemble all the information.

The first piece of information comes from the netstat command, which displays network status information, including total bytes received and transmitted by a particular interface. To interrogate a network interface (represented here as en0), use the following command:

```
# netstat -I en0 -b
Name Mtu  Network     Address         Ipkts Ierrs   Ibytes Opkts Oerrs   Obytes Coll
en0  1500 <Link#4>    00:1f:5b:e9:87:1e 2852330   0 2908877372 1726539   0 606872778   0
```

The -I switch specifies the interface, and the -b switch asks netstat to display bytes in and bytes out of that interface. These values are taken from the time that the system boots.

You can also figure out how long the system has been running since boot time, with the uptime command:

```
$ uptime
 8:16 up 16:41, 10 users, load averages: 0.08 0.15 0.20
```

That's great output for a person, but not great for a computer. A running variable stores boot time in seconds since the UNIX epoch (the UNIX epoch is the time 00:00:00 UTC on January 1, 1970), accessible by sysctl:

```
$ sysctl kern.boottime
kern.boottime: { sec = 1177954679, usec = 0 } Mon Apr 30 10:37:59 2007
```

sysctl enables you to get or set kernel variables. To obtain a full list of variables, use the -A switch.

You can also retrieve the current date in terms of seconds with the date command:

```
$ date +%s
1208175680
```

That gives you enough information to compute the average utilization of a given interface. Because you'll want to assess this value from time to time, you can automate this entire routine.

This script is pretty straightforward math, with basic definitions of bits, bytes, and megabytes (automation and scripting will be introduced in Chapter 9, "Automating Systems"). The script uses line numbers for easier reference:

```
01: #!/usr/bin/env bash
02:
03: # Defs
04: iface_name="en0"
05: iface_Mbps=1000
06:
07: # Get boot time, clean up output to something useful
08: boottime=`sysctl kern.boottime | sed 's/,//g' | awk '{print $5}'`
09:
10: # Determine interface activity
11: in_bytes=`netstat -I $iface_name -b | tail -1 | awk '{print $7}'`
12: out_bytes=`netstat -I $iface_name -b | tail -1 | awk '{print $10}'`
13: in_bits=$(($in_bytes * 8))
14: out_bits=$(($out_bytes * 8))
```

```
15: in_mbits=$(($in_bytes / 1000))
16: out_mbits=$(($out_bytes / 1000))
17:
18: # Get the current time
19: currenttime=`date +%s`
20:
21: # Determine total uptime
22: upt=$(($currenttime - $boottime))
23:
24: # Gather bandwith stats in bps
25: in_band_bps=$(($in_bits / $upt))
26: out_band_bps=$(($out_bits / $upt))
27: in_band_mbps=$(echo "scale=5; $in_band_bps / 1000000" | bc)
28: out_band_mbps=$(echo "scale=5; $out_band_bps / 1000000" | bc)
29:
30: iface_in_util=$(echo "scale=5; $in_band_mbps / $iface_Mbps" | bc)
31: iface_out_util=$(echo "scale=5; $out_band_mbps / $iface_Mbps" | bc)
32:
33: printf "$iface_name averge inbound bits/s: $in_band_bps\n"
34: printf "$iface_name averge outbound bits/s: $out_band_bps\n"
35: printf "$iface_name averge inbound mbits/s: $in_band_mbps\n"
36: printf "$iface_name averge outbound mbits/s: $out_band_mbps\n"
37: printf "$iface_name average inbound utilization: $iface_in_util\n"
38: printf "$iface_name average outbound utilization: $iface_out_util\n"
```

The definitions on lines 4 and 5 are hard-coded into this script; update as necessary. Line 8 performs the same sysctl call presented previously, but then cleans up the output to retrieve only the boot time timestamp. Similarly, lines 11 and 12 reduce the output of netstat to only the "bytes in" and "bytes out" of an interface. Also of note in the script is the use of bc to perform floating-point calculations, which the Bash shell cannot do alone (lines 27 through 31). The math here is rudimentary:

▶ Read an interface's activity in bytes (lines 11 and 12).

▶ Convert the results to bits by multiplying by 8—8 bits to a byte, remember? (lines 13 and 14).

- ▶ Convert bytes to megabits (Mbit)—unused in this script, but a good exercise (lines 15 and 16).

- ▶ Gather total seconds of uptime by subtracting boot time in seconds since the UNIX epoch from current date in seconds from the UNIX epoch (line 22).

- ▶ Compute average bandwidth in bits per second by dividing total bits on an interface by seconds of uptime (line 25 and 26).

- ▶ Convert bit/s to Mbit/s by dividing by 1,000,000 (10^6) (lines 27 and 28).

- ▶ Compute utilization by dividing used bandwidth per second by the interface's capacity.

For this script to work properly, you need to set the appropriate definitions (interface name and capacity) at the top of the script. Chapter 9, "Automating Systems," shows ways to refine this script.

To single out current utilization statistics—network throughput and currently connected users—for the Apple Filing Protocol (AFP) and Server Message Block (SMB) file-sharing services on Mac OS X Server, you can use the `serveradmin` command with the `fullstatus` verb. Each service displays its current throughput in bytes per second. For example, to display the statistics for AFP, use the following command with root-level access:

```
# serveradmin fullstatus afp
afp:setStateVersion = 2
afp:servicePortsAreRestricted = "NO"
afp:logging = "NO"
afp:currentConnections = 8
afp:state = "RUNNING"
afp:startedTime = ""
afp:logPaths:accessLog = "/Library/Logs/AppleFileService/AppleFileServiceAccess.log"
afp:logPaths:errorLog = "/Library/Logs/AppleFileService/AppleFileServiceError.log"
afp:readWriteSettingsVersion = 1
afp:failoverState = "NIFailoverNotConfigured"
afp:guestAccess = "YES"
afp:servicePortsRestrictionInfo = _empty_array
afp:currentThroughput = 87
```

The `afp:currentThroughput` key contains the value of current AFP throughput. To single out throughput, pass the output through the `grep` command. For example, to single out the current throughput for the SMB service, use the following command:

```
# serveradmin fullstatus smb | grep Throughput
smb:currentThroughput = 39
```

The current throughput for `smb` is also given in bytes per second.

To list currently connected users and information on each user, `serveradmin` allows commands to be specified. The command for AFP and SMB is `getConnectedUsers`. For example, on a server with one user connected via SMB, the command and output would look like this:

```
# serveradmin command smb:command = getConnectedUsers
smb:state = "RUNNING"
smb:usersArray:_array_index:0:loginElapsedTime = -27950
smb:usersArray:_array_index:0:service = "alicew"
smb:usersArray:_array_index:0:connectAt = "Mon May 19 16:45:58 2008"
smb:usersArray:_array_index:0:name = "alicew"
smb:usersArray:_array_index:0:ipAddress = "192.168.40.45"
smb:usersArray:_array_index:0:sessionID = 11148
```

To gather information on currently connected AFP users, use the corresponding `afp` command: `afp:command = getConnectedUsers`.

Determining Services and Hardware Utilization

It's important for an administrator to understand the resources that individual programs consume on a given piece of hardware, as the two are intrinsically linked. Running services use hardware resources. Is the use of resources effective? Overwhelming? Can certain services be paired with other services? *Service utilization* refers to the impact of a single service, and *hardware utilization* refers to considering the hardware as a whole (for example, looking at memory utilization).

Each running process demands CPU time. Mac OS X contains several tools to monitor CPU load and each running process.

The Server Admin framework is specific to Mac OS X Server and can report on unique information. The GUI-based Server Admin.app can display graphs of CPU utilization over an adjustable range of time. To view these graphs, launch Server Admin.app, authenticate when prompted, select the server in question, and choose the Graphs button in the toolbar.

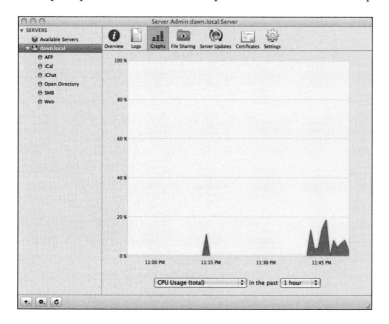

The default view displays CPU usage for the past hour. You can expand the time range to the past seven days using the pop-up menu in the bottom right corner of the window.

Server Admin can also list services being provided by a server. Currently running services are indicated by a green ball next to their name in the servers list at the left of the Server Admin window. Additionally, services configured and running appear on the Overview page of Server Admin, along with high-level graphs of system utilization for CPU percentage, network bandwidth, and disk storage.

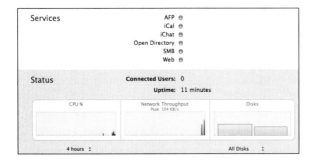

The information provided by the Server Admin framework is valuable, but may not tell a full story. It does not report service status for installed third-party software. Also, the Server Admin tools are specific to Mac OS X Server; there needs to be a way to assess workstation usage as well.

The most straightforward tool is ps, or process status. Typically, executing ps on its own, with no switches, is of little value. By itself, ps simply shows running processes that are owned by the calling ID and attached to a terminal. Of more interest is a list of all processes, owned by any user, with or without a controlling terminal. You can easily achieve such a list with the following command, run with an admin-level account:

```
# ps ax
PID  TT STAT   TIME COMMAND
   1 ?? Ss   0:13.40 /sbin/launchd
  10 ?? Ss   0:00.64 /usr/libexec/kextd
  11 ?? Ss   0:09.48 /usr/sbin/notifyd
... (output removed for space considerations)
25539 ?? Ss   0:00.09 /usr/sbin/racoon -x
25729 ?? Ss   0:00.09 /usr/sbin/cupsd -l
```

The a switch, when combined with the x switch, causes ps to display all processes, from any user, with or without a controlling terminal. However, this does not tell the entire story. Each process in that ps list uses resources—but how much?

You can determine CPU percentage, load, and idle percentage with the top command, which is covered extensively in "top, CPU%, and Load Averages" in Chapter 8,

"Monitoring Systems." You can also find the load average statistic in other places. The uptime command displays load average along with the machine uptime:

```
$ uptime
 8:06 up 2 days, 16:30, 10 users, load averages: 0.55 0.83 0.53
```

Additionally, you can fetch the load average directly from a sysctl variable, vm.loadavg:

```
$ sysctl vm.loadavg
vm.loadavg: { 0.54 0.68 0.51 }
```

You can also find CPU percentage and load averages with the iostat command, covered in the next section, "Determining Storage Utilization."

Each process places load on the CPU by asking it to do work, in the form of making system call requests and placing an instruction to execute in the run queue. To determine which process currently is making the most system call requests, DTrace and Instruments utilities also are very helpful. Both utilities are covered in "Instruments and DTrace" in Chapter 8, "Monitoring Systems."

You can also find virtual memory statistics with the top command, and view them in more detail using vm_stat. Most of the vm_stat columns are the same columns that you can view with the top command: free, active, inac (inactive), wire (wired), pageins, and pageout. If you do not specify an interval, vm_stat prints only a total and exits. If you add a numeric value after vm_stat and run it, it prints statistics repeatedly at the interval specified in seconds (to stop the listing, press Control-C):

```
$ vm_stat 1
Mach Virtual Memory Statistics: (page size of 4096 bytes, cache hits 27%)
  free active inac wire  faults    copy zerofill reactive pageins pageout
174238 408613 301961 162294 193952562 6445537 116503302   44713  309110  60934
174320 408603 301961 162294    186     1    57       0      0      0
174384 408615 301961 162294    184     3    66       0      0      0
174450 408619 301961 162294    977   114   158       0      0      0
174350 408628 301961 162294   1016     0   520       0      0      0
174387 408626 301961 162294    154     0    33       0      0      0
```

Unlike the earlier exercise of writing a script to determine network bandwidth, you can use vm_stat to report on total statistics gathered since bootup. If you run vm_stat with a repeat interval, you should not be surprised by the first set of statistics printed under each banner: a lifetime-accumulated total (since bootup).

The columns have the following significance:

▶ faults—Number of times the memory manager faults a page.

▶ copy—Pages copied due to copy-on-write (COW). COW is a memory-management technique that initially allows multiple applications to point to the same page in memory as long as it is read-only. However, if any of those applications needs to write to that memory location, it cannot without changing COW for every other application pointing to that location. If an application tries to *write* to a shared memory location, it instead gets a *copy*; the original is left intact. The pages copied statistic shows how many times an application tries to write to a shared memory location. It's an interesting statistic for administrators in some ways, but they can do little about it, short of choosing not to run certain applications that cause the behavior.

▶ zerofill—Number of times a page has been zero-fill faulted on demand: A previously unused page marked "zero fill on demand" was touched for the first time. Again, there's not much an administrator can do about this particular value.

▶ reactive—Not what it sounds like; the number of times a page has been reactivated (or, moved from the inactive list to the active list).

See the vm_stat man page for further information.

Determining Storage Utilization

In addition to memory using resources, bandwidth and capacity can also use up storage resources. Systems administrators have several tools they can use to determine input/output activity, disk capacity use, and disk usage for a given part of the disk hierarchy, as well as to pinpoint details about file and disk activity. These tools include iostat, df, system_profiler, du, and Instruments and dtrace, respectively.

iostat displays I/O statistics for terminals and storage devices (disks). Similar to vm_stat, iostat can report on total statistics since bootup, or at a given interval. Running iostat solely with an interval is useful for displaying disk transactions, CPU statistics, and load average; to stop the listing, press Control-C. The -w switch specifies the wait interval between refreshing statistics:

```
$ iostat -w 2
    disk0        disk1     cpu     load average
 KB/t tps MB/s   KB/t tps MB/s us sy id  1m  5m  15m
 21.51 19 0.40  19.48 13 0.25  8 5 87 0.24 0.25 0.24
 4.00  0 0.00   4.00  0 0.00  3 4 94 0.22 0.25 0.24
 4.00  1 0.00   4.00  0 0.00  3 4 94 0.20 0.24 0.24
 12.00  0 0.01  12.00  0 0.01  2 4 94 0.20 0.24 0.24
 4.00  0 0.00   4.00  0 0.00  3 4 93 0.19 0.24 0.24
 12.51 36 0.45  11.50  6 0.07  2 5 93 0.19 0.24 0.24
```

Often, the reason to use iostat is to focus solely on the disk statistics. To drop the CPU and load information—the same information available from the top utility—use the -d switch. To further focus on a specific disk or disks, you can add the device node name or names to the command:

```
$ iostat -dw 2 disk0 disk1
    disk0        disk1
 KB/t tps MB/s   KB/t tps MB/s
 21.51 19 0.40  19.48 13 0.25
 0.00  0 0.00   0.00  0 0.00
 4.00  1 0.00   4.00  0 0.00
 11.30 15 0.17  22.50  1 0.02
 6.42  9 0.06   4.71  3 0.02
```

iostat can also display output in two alternate formats that can complete the I/O story. The -o switch causes iostat to display sectors per second, transfers per second, and milliseconds per seek:

```
$ iostat -od disk0
    disk0
 sps tps msps
 794 18 0.0
```

The -I switch displays total statistics over the time of running iostat, rather than average statistics for each second during that time period:

```
$ iostat -Id disk0
    disk0
  KB/t xfrs  MB
  21.51 6736974 141497.11
```

You can also quickly summarize disk capacity with the df ("disk free") command. Simply type df at a command prompt to display useful information about all mounted volumes:

```
$ df
Filesystem         512-blocks     Used    Avail Capacity Mounted on
/dev/disk4        489955072 118939584 370503488   24%  /
devfs             233       233      0  100%  /dev
fdesc             2         2        0  100%  /dev
<volfs>           1024      1024     0  100%  /.vol
automount -nsl [212]      0       0      0  100%  /Network
automount -fstab [218]    0       0      0  100%  /automount/Servers
automount -static [218]   0       0      0  100%  /automount/static
/dev/disk10       1953584128 1936325520 17258608  99%  /Volumes/Data0
/dev/disk5        361619840 323948976 37670864  90%  /Volumes/Data1
```

This output displays capacities in 512-byte blocks, and lists a percentage-full statistic. You can use two switches to refine this output to make it easier to read:

```
$ df -T hfs -h
Filesystem  Size  Used Avail Capacity Mounted on
/dev/disk4  234G  57G  177G  24%  /
/dev/disk10 932G  923G 8.2G  99%  /Volumes/Data0
/dev/disk5  172G  154G 18G  90%  /Volumes/Data1
```

The -T switch limits the display to file systems of a certain type, in this case, hierarchical file system (HFS) (which also implies HFS Plus, the default file system for Mac OS X Leopard). The -h switch causes df to display capacities in "human-readable" format (output uses byte, kilobyte, megabyte, gigabyte, terabyte, and petabyte suffixes, as necessary, rather than blocks).

system_profiler is a versatile Mac OS X–specific utility. It excels at querying Macintosh hardware. Along with the other command-line utilities presented here, system_profiler can also report on the total capacity and available space on a storage device. For example, to display detailed information on all Serial Advanced Technology Attachment (ATA)–connected disks, use the SPSerialATADataType command:

```
$ system_profiler SPSerialATADataType
Serial-ATA:

    Intel ICH8-M AHCI:

      Vendor: Intel
      Product: ICH8-M AHCI
      Speed: 1.5 Gigabit
      Description: AHCI Version 1.10 Supported

       Hitachi HTS542525K9SA00:

          Capacity: 232.89 GB
...output removed for space considerations...
          Volumes:
            MacintoshHD:
              Capacity: 199.88 GB
              Available: 124.72 GB
              Writable: Yes
              File System: Journaled HFS+
              BSD Name: disk0s2
              Mount Point: /
      Volumes:
            disk0s2:
              Capacity: 199.88 GB
              Available: 124.72 GB
              Writable: Yes
              File System: Journaled HFS+
```

For details on system_profiler, see Chapter 8, "Monitoring Systems."

While df is perfect for quickly determining the overall use of a mounted storage device, you often need more detail. The du ("disk usage") command answers the questions "Where is storage being allocated on a given file system?" and "Where is all the space going?"

Running du with no options will, for the current directory, list each file and directory along with the number of blocks occupied by the given object:

```
# du
0     ./.TemporaryItems/folders.1026
0     ./.TemporaryItems/folders.1027
0     ./.TemporaryItems/folders.1029
(output removed for space considerations)
0     ./xavier/Public
24    ./xavier/Sites/images
0     ./xavier/Sites/Streaming
40    ./xavier/Sites
1411736 ./xavier/untitled folder
10270512    ./xavier
255297560   .
```

The final entry, the dot, represents the total for the current directory. As with df, you can use several switches to tailor the output for easier reading:

```
# du -h -d 1 -c /Users
 0B  ./.TemporaryItems
1.5M  ./andy
333M  ./arthur
202M  ./ashley
(output removed for space considerations)
6.7G  ./mike
1.5M  ./paul
 15G  ./tiffany
1.6M  ./thomas
3.8M  ./william
4.9G  ./xavier
122G  .
122G  total
```

The -h switch generates "human-readable" output, as seen in the df command described previously in this section. The -d switch causes du to output entries only at the given depth, with the current directory being 0, immediate subdirectories being 1, and so on. Use the -c switch to print a final, grand-total line. Also, instead of simply summing up the current directory, you can name the directory path, which in this case is named /Users.

Finally, Instruments.app is an ideal way to examine file activity and impact on a storage system for one or more processes. If df and du do not provide the information that you need, Instruments, with its capability to finely detail file and disk activity, and dtrace offer the necessary power and depth to provide that information. For more information on Instruments and dtrace, see the section "Instruments and DTrace" in Chapter 8, "Monitoring Systems."

Evaluating the Upgrade History

When assessing a system, particularly a server, it is critical to know not only where it is now (the current operating system, load, hardware configuration, and so on), but also how the system got to where it is. Was the current operating system a clean installation? Or was it an upgrade? It is possible to figure this out, even if there is no prior system administrator around to ask. Without this knowledge, it is often difficult to correlate behavior that you see with baseline, known behavior.

Among other tasks, the Apple installer performs two actions when installing a package that can help you figure out the history of installed packages and system upgrades. First, the installer writes *entries* to the installer.log file, located in /var/log, along with several other log files. Second, the installer writes *receipts* to /Library/Receipts.

In the installer.log file, the installer program writes a running list of packages that it installs on the system. Other entries in installer.log are written by Software Update as it finds new software to install, and software update service, if the machine in question is running Mac OS X Server along with the software update daemon, swupd. An example of an initial system install from installer.log is as follows:

```
OSInstaller[197]: =========================================
OSInstaller[197]: Choices selected for installation:
OSInstaller[197]:   Install: "Mac OS X Server"
OSInstaller[197]:   Install: "Essential System Software"
OSInstaller[197]:       BaseSystem.pkg : com.apple.pkg.BaseSystem : 10.5.0.1.1.1192168948
```

For your purposes, the installer.log may have limited information. The system's periodic maintenance (in the daily folder at /etc/periodic/daily/600.daily.server) *rolls* logs—that is, compresses the current log file and starts a new one. Rolling entirely removes the oldest log files from a disk so that the log disk does not fill up. This means that if the server was installed or upgraded months ago, it is unlikely that a record of it will still exist in the installer.log files.

Receipts, on the other hand, do not expire and remain as a record of packages that have been installed.

The Apple installer, after installing the files that it contains (the payload of a component package), places a receipt in the /Library/Receipts directory of the installation volume. An *installation receipt* is a token that the installer uses to determine whether a package has already been installed on a system. If the installer, on subsequent installations of packages using the same package filename on the same volume, encounters a receipt, it processes the installation as an upgrade.

When the installer encounters a package in Mac OS X v10.5 format, Leopard handles receipts differently than earlier Macintosh operating systems. With earlier package formats, receipts were dropped by package name into /Library/Receipts. Each receipt resembled the original package minus the actual payload. The only way to remove receipts was manually.

Leopard, in contrast, drops receipts for v10.5-format packages into /Library/Receipts/boms (or Bill of Materials). Leopard also adds a new package database to the system, /Library/Receipts/db, which stores the receipts database. (You should not manipulate this database manually, or you risk corruption of its format.) Leopard also adds a command-line utility, pkgutil, to manipulate and query the database.

You can use pkgutil to collect information about a given package:

```
$ pkgutil --pkg-info com.apple.pkg.BaseSystem
package-id: com.apple.pkg.BaseSystem
version: 10.5.0.1.1.1192168948
volume: /
location: ./
install-time: 1208628236
groups: com.apple.repair-permissions.pkg-group com.apple.FindSystemFiles.pkg-group
```

You can also display a list of files that were installed by a package:

```
$ pkgutil --files com.apple.pkg.BaseSystem | less
.
.vol
Applications
Applications/Utilities
Applications/Utilities/Disk Utility.app
(output trimmed for space considerations)
```

When assessing a system, you can take advantage of the different methods used by Mac OS X v10.5 to format packages and receipts, as well as earlier methods. A system that has been upgraded to v10.5 will have *both* style receipts for the operating system components. Specifically, if there is a receipt for BaseSystem.pkg in /Library/Receipts on a v10.5 system, the system is an upgrade (that is, not a clean install).

One final note on software installation: While the Apple package formats are useful, not all developers ship their products with package-based installers. Simple drag-and-drop installations are popular due to their ease of use. Third-party and custom installers also exist. You can also download application source code and compile and install it manually. None of these methods uses the Apple installer application and therefore they do not necessarily save a log of their actions, nor do they need to write package receipts.

Evaluating Workflows

The entire reason for setting up a computer system is to serve users. As people use a system, they develop a workflow. Workflows are either imposed or they grow organically. In either case, when you assess an existing system, you must examine and document current workflows. The tools discussed in this chapter will help you accomplish the technical aspects of this evaluation, such as determining storage requirements and CPU bottlenecks.

Evaluating a workflow from end-to-end and taking a high-level look involves nontechnical aspects as well. To fully evaluate a workflow, you should follow these steps:

1 Examine

2 Interview

3 Observe

4 Document

5 Optimize

Examining the Workflow

Examine the workflow to determine what resources are being used and how information flows. Note the following:

▶ Teams in place: What common users and groups use this process?

▶ Shares and files: What files are used and where are they stored?

▶ Software: What software—off-the-shelf or in-house—is involved?

▶ Hardware: How does hardware impact this process?

▶ Information flow: How does information flow from one point to another? What routes does it take and where does it stop?

Interviewing Users

Directly speak with people involved in the workflow. You can split users into two groups, consumers and providers.

When interviewing consumers of data, question them to determine the following:

▶ Requirements: What are the real requirements of the workflow? How does a user's job impact requirements?

▶ Expectations: In what form is the data expected?

When interviewing providers, question them to determine the following:

▶ Their understanding: How well do they understand the needs of the consumers?

▶ Limitations: What may impede the flow?

▶ Collaboration: How does the team work together and pass data between members?

Observing the Workflow

Once you have examined the workflow and interviewed users, you should step back and observe. Follow the process through. Does it match what you've been told? Document what is actually happening.

This intermediary documentation helps you to piece together the workflow on your own:

▶ What information is needed?

▶ Where does the information come from and how is it used?

▶ What tools are used in creating the information?

▶ What steps have to be taken to complete the process?

Documenting the Workflow

When it's time to formally document a workflow, note its key aspects:

▶ Application dependencies

▶ Data formats

▶ Access control

▶ Team collaboration

▶ Processing and automation

▶ Storage requirements

▶ Timing

Optimizing the Workflow

Most workflows, when adequately examined, can be improved in some respect. By taking a high-level view of the entire workflow, you can identify bottlenecks and areas for improvement. It's important when choosing to optimize a workflow that you alter only one area at a time. This allows you to measure the results of that single improvement, and it allows easier rollback if the alteration does not have the desired effect. Finally, it minimizes disruption to user productivity.

This is not to say that every workflow needs changing. Sometimes the workflow is just fine, but upgraded hardware, for example, might improve the workflow by speeding up certain processes.

What You've Learned

This chapter outlines tools that can assist you in evaluating or reassessing a system, including technical and nontechnical aspects. This chapter covered the following tools and techniques:

► How to determine hardware utilization, to assess the usage of storage, network, CPU, and memory

► Displaying vital statistics about a network interface using netstat, and from this information, manually computing utilization

► Displaying information about currently running system processes with the ps utility

► Computing load average as an important metric in determining CPU capacity

► Using sysctl as one way to show the current load average

► Displaying detailed statistics about virtual memory usage, including system average statistics since bootup, using vm_stat

► Displaying statistics about current and average input/output, using iostat

► Displaying disk capacity use with df

► Displaying disk usage for a given part of the disk hierarchy, such as /Users, with du

► Determining the history of system upgrades and installed packages using receipts and /var/log/installer.log

► Querying and manipulating the receipts database using the pkgutil command

► Accounting of user workflows when assessing systems

Review Quiz

1. Which command-line utility supplies detailed statistics and information about a network interface?

2. What is the function of the sysctl command?

3. Which Mac OS X Server command reports detailed information about currently connected AFP and SMB users?

4. Name three ways to display the current load average.

5. Which command-line utility can quickly summarize disk capacity?

6. Where does the installer program write its receipts to?

7. Which command-line utility is used to query the receipts database?

8. Does every installation leave a trail in the install.log file?

9. What are the five steps to follow when evaluating a workflow?

Answers

1. `netstat` supplies detailed statistics and information about a network interface.

2. `sysctl` reads and writes kernel operating variables.

3. `serveradmin` reports detailed information about currently connected AFP and SMB users.

4. The following commands reveal the current load average: `uptime`, `top`, `iostat`, and `sysctl vm.loadavg`. Another possibility is Activity Monitor.

5. `df` (disk free) quickly summarizes disk capacity.

6. The installer program writes its receipts to /Library/Receipts/bom.

7. `pkgutil` queries the receipts database.

8. No. Any method of installation not using the Apple installer is not obligated to log installation activity. This includes third-party installers, drag-and-drop installations, and software compiled and directly installed on the machine.

9. Examine, interview, observe, document, and optimize are the five steps to follow to evaluate a workflow.

Part 2   Networking

5

Time   This lesson takes approximately 60 minutes to complete.

Goals   Learn the basics of Mac OS X implementation of DNS

Learn different configurations for DNS servers

Learn how to secure the DNS service

Learn how to configure the DNS service from the command line, without Server Admin.app

Learn how to configure the NTP client and service using both graphical and command-line tools

Chapter 5

Working with DNS and NTP

A fully functioning Domain Name System (DNS) is increasingly becoming the most critical service of a network infrastructure. Almost as important is Network Time Protocol (NTP). When working properly, these services function quietly in the background. Why are they so important and how do they work? This chapter answers those questions by explaining the foundations of each service, how they function on Mac OS X, and how to troubleshoot them when they do not work as expected.

Using DNS: The Big Picture

The main purpose of DNS is to convert easy-to-remember names into the harder-to-remember numbers that computers require. On smaller networks, it is typical, and perfectly acceptable, to rely on the DNS servers supplied by your Internet service provider. However, in larger installations, a site should provide some level of DNS service by hosting the service in-house. Furthermore, it may be necessary to host DNS internally because of the high number of services that rely on a functioning DNS.

Of the 23 services listed in Server Admin, Directory Services, Kerberos, and email require fully functioning DNS, while the rest of the services benefit from having DNS available. For example, the web service will answer requests made by a straight IP address, but the HTTP v1.1 protocol can access and serve different websites from the same IP address, based on the DNS name passed to it.

All these considerations require a system administrator to fully understand DNS and to provide a reliable, secure, and accurate DNS service. The graphical configuration tools for DNS provided in Server Admin have never exposed the full spectrum of options available, forcing anyone with advanced configuration needs to use the command line. In the past, using the command line typically meant that you could not go back to using the graphical user interface tool. However, Leopard removes that limitation by allowing a mix of styles.

About the Domain Name System

Originally, computers performed name-to-address mapping via a simple text file, the hosts file, which contained a list of every machine that needed to be referenced by name. Using the hosts file, a computer could resolve a lookup. Every computer had a copy of the hosts file. If an IP address changed for any machine in that file, the reference would need to be changed in the hosts file and *every* computer's hosts file would need to be updated to reflect the change. Clearly, the number of machines on the Internet today makes this an impossible task.

The Domain Name System overcomes the limitations presented by the hosts file scheme. DNS is a distributed database, allowing local control over portions of the database. At the top of the Domain Name System hierarchy, about 13 root name servers point the way to other DNS servers responsible for a generic top-level domain (gTLD), such as ".com." Root servers are located at high-bandwidth points around the world. These servers in turn point the way to the authoritative server for the query—the server listed with the registrar that can answer queries with authority. This hierarchy is shown in the following illustration.

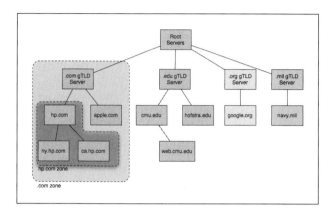

When you register a domain name with a registrar, you must also define the authoritative DNS servers for the domain—the servers that the root servers will ultimately send queries to for your domain. The major registrars tend to provide DNS service for domains registered with them. The mere act of setting up a DNS server does not cause outside entities to suddenly query it—general queries from the Internet will always use the authoritative servers defined by your registrar via the root servers. Turning on the DNS service in Mac OS X Server behind your firewall affects only your local network, as shown in the next illustration of a DNS setup.

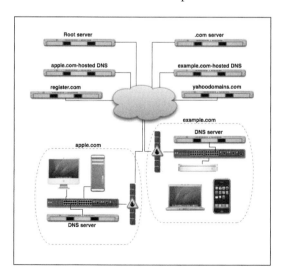

About the DNS Query Path

In the system shown in the figure, all devices at the apple.com site are configured to use the local DNS server. Similarly, all devices on the example.com network are configured to query the local DNS server of that site. In this example, imagine that Apple has registered its domain name with register.com, and the example.com domain has been registered with yahoodomains.com. When a device on the example.com network needs to perform a DNS lookup, it queries its onsite DNS server. If that server can answer the query in some way—from its cache, or because it is authoritative for the domain in question—it will pass the answer back to the client and the lookups are complete. If, however, the local DNS server does *not* have the answer, it must perform a recursive query to fetch the answer needed. A recursive query sends the query up the DNS hierarchy and allows other servers to perform the query on its behalf. The response to the query is ultimately passed back to the originating DNS server, which then passes it on to the client.

Imagine that a device on the example.com network needs to look up partners.apple.com. The device on example.com will not find the IP address of partners.apple.com, neither on its local DNS server nor among the domains listed by its registrar, yahoodomains.com. To find the correct IP address, the local DNS server queries one of the root name servers. The root name server, in effect, says, "Ah—you're looking for information about a server in the .com domain? I know just the server for you to talk to." From there, the root server refers example.com's local DNS server to the generic top-level domain server for the .com zone. This server, in turn, passes back a reference specifically to the DNS server responsible for the apple.com domain. Now, example.com's local DNS server can query the server that is authoritative for the apple.com domain, which can actually answer the question. It retrieves the answer to the query, with a forward or reverse lookup, from the hosted DNS service and passes it to the client that originally made the query. The local DNS server will also now cache this result, allowing it to directly answer this question for any other clients in the future, until the expiration of that record.

About DNS Server Configurations

The previous example discusses several different DNS servers, each running with a particular configuration. This is important to point out, because a particular configuration should be matched to the need at hand. Following are common DNS server configurations:

▶ A caching-only name server, such as a configured server that is not authoritative for any zone, recursively looks up all queries, and caches what it can.

▶ In a split-DNS setup, the local, internal DNS server is configured to be authoritative for the company domain (or domains). Meanwhile, the "master" authoritative DNS server is still hosted, and the local DNS answers all queries from devices inside the network. Devices outside of the network continue to query the hosted DNS service. This provides an interesting opportunity: The internal DNS server does not have to mirror the external DNS database exactly. The administrator may choose to augment the local version with internal-only resources. Because devices on the outside cannot access them, internal-only records do not need to exist in the hosted DNS server database. In essence, this creates one namespace behind the local LAN's edge router, and a separate one for the world at large.

In the case of a company like Apple, with all of its network resources, many internal-only addresses reside behind a security system, intended only for people on the Apple network (or, perhaps, accessing the network via a VPN). An internal DNS server could serve the internal network and the internal-only addresses, as well as act as a DNS cache, saving bandwidth on external lookups.

Finally, if an administrator at Apple decided to enter information about the example.com domain on the local internal DNS server, it would affect only devices on the Apple network. Everyone else in the world would still be referred to the hosted example.com DNS server for authoritative DNS information about the example.com domain.

Configuring DNS Services

Now that you understand DNS from a high-level perspective, you also need to understand some DNS specifics, and details on how Mac OS X implements the DNS system.

Using BIND

The primary interface for configuring DNS services on Mac OS X Server is the graphical Server Admin utility. Similar to many other subsystems on Mac OS X Server, and Mac OS X in general, DNS is handled by a freely available, open source product: the Internet System Consortium's Berkeley Internet Name Domain (BIND). You can configure BIND via Server Admin on Mac OS X Server, or manually on Mac OS X.

BIND is the most widely deployed DNS server on the Internet. Mac OS X includes a full installation of BIND, which includes essential utilities such as the `named` name daemon, which is responsible for handling all queries, and *rndc*, a utility to control the name server. The DNS service can be configured and run entirely from a command-line shell. Also, by basing this service on a standard, Mac OS X easily interoperates with other DNS name servers—both BIND and non-BIND.

The DNS system classifies records into different types:

▶ A: IPv4 address record. Maps a name to an IPv4 address for a forward lookup.

▶ AAAA: IPv6 address record. Maps a name to an IPv6 address for a forward lookup.

▶ CNAME: Canonical name. An alias that points to a separate DNS record.

▶ MX: Mail Exchanger. Supplies the name and priority for a machine that accepts mail for the given domain.

▶ NS: Name server. Defines a name server for the zone.

▶ SRV: Service. Stores information about a service.

▶ HINFO: Hardware info. Stores information about a machine's hardware and/or software.

▶ TXT: Text. Provides descriptive text about a record.

▶ PTR: Pointer record. Maps an IP address to a name, allowing reverse lookups. Basically, a PTR record is the opposite of an A record.

These record types form the database files for each zone created. Database files are created in the /var/named hierarchy on the file system. In Leopard, Apple has chosen to allow a mixed approach: The changes made in Server Admin are written to one set of files, and you can make manual changes to a different set of files. Manual changes update the canonical files, while Server Admin edits some Apple-specific files. Interestingly, this fact shows off Server Admin's ability to interpret these files. Where past OS versions had a much more straightforward graphical user interface–to–config file relationship, new capability is evident in the main configuration file for BIND: /etc/named.conf.

The latest version of BIND, version 9, supports a concept called *views*. Views allow a BIND server to present different zones and zone data to different viewers of the data based on several criteria—all from a single BIND instance. While Mac OS X Server v10.5 is the first version to explicitly use views, the functionality is not exposed in the graphical user interface. In fact, all zones are simply contained in one master view called com.apple. ServerAdmin.DNS.public. To understand this better, look at /etc/named.conf:

```
include "/etc/rndc.key";

controls  {
        inet 127.0.0.1 port 54 allow     {any;    }
        keys    { "rndc-key";      };
    };

options  {
        include "/etc/dns/options.conf.apple";
};

logging {
        include "/etc/dns/loggingOptions.conf.apple";
};
include "/etc/dns/publicView.conf.apple";
```

The comments from this file have been stripped out to show how minimal the code is. Unlike previous OS versions that wrote all configuration options directly into the named. conf file, Leopard puts the "real" directives in external files that are then pulled into the main file via include statements. This same tactic is used for the database files, as discussed below.

Piecing the configuration together in order, the options.conf.apple file contains three statements:

```
directory "/var/named";
forwarders {};
allow-transfer { none; };
```

The `directory` statement sets where `named` should find any zone files referenced in the remainder of the config file. The `forwarders` statement is set to an empty list, and the `allow--transfer` statement is disallowed. If you remember the graphical user interface setup for each zone, "Allows zone transfer" is enabled by default, as shown in the figure below:

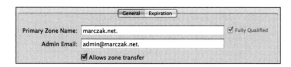

So how is the `allow-transfer` directive set to `none` in the config file? This goes back to the support for BIND views, which will be covered in the discussion below about the publicView.conf.apple file.

The loggingOptions.conf.apple file consists of the following lines:

```
category default {
        apple_syslog;
};
channel apple_syslog {
        file "/Library/Logs/named.log";
        severity info;
        print-time yes;
};
```

These lines ensure that all named logging information is logged to the /Library/Logs/ named.log file.

Finally, named.conf includes /etc/dns/publicView.conf.apple. Its contents vary with the zones configured in Server Admin. Also, a globally unique identifier (GUID) that is unique to each server installation is generated for this file by Server Admin. Here is a sample named.conf file (again, stripped of any comments for space reasons):

```
acl "com.apple.ServerAdmin.DNS.public" {localnets;};

view "com.apple.ServerAdmin.DNS.public" {
//GUID=4E258421-4C6B-4922-A00A-1AA4A5CB923F;

        allow-recursion {"com.apple.ServerAdmin.DNS.public";};

        zone "marczak.net." {
                type master;
                file "db.marczak.net.";
                allow-transfer {any;};
                allow-update {none;};
        };
```

```
        zone "100.168.192.in-addr.arpa." {
                type slave;
                file "bak.100.168.192.in-addr.arpa.";
                masters {192.168.100.12;};
        };

        zone "radiotope.com." {
                type slave;
                file "bak.radiotope.com.";
                masters {192.168.100.12;};
        };

        zone "." {
                type hint;
                file "named.ca";
        };
        zone "localhost" IN {
                type master;
                file "localhost.zone";
                allow-update { none; };
        };

        zone "0.0.127.in-addr.arpa" IN {
                type master;
                file "named.local";
                allow-update { none; };
        };
    };
```

The first line defines an access control list (ACL) named com.apple.ServerAdmin.DNS
.public to be used with a view, and allows the ACL localnets. This corresponds to the
list in the Server Admin DNS Settings pane. While BIND allows very fine-grained use
of ACLs, Server Admin does not press them into service—limiting their use to defining
recursion abilities. The definition of localnets is built into BIND, along with several other
definitions. An ACL of localnet matches all IP addresses and subnets of the server on
which named is invoked. Other built-in values are any, none, and localhost.

The second line defines a view. Views in BIND are an all-or-nothing proposition—once in use, all zones must be defined in a view. This named.conf file takes the simple way: It creates one "master" view and defines all zones inside that.

The next line allows recursive lookups for clients matching the ACL for this view, which is to say, all clients, which matches the setting in Server Admin.

Following are definitions for each zone defined in Server Admin. The `allow-transfer` directives in each primary zone definition match the zone setting in Server Admin.

Several definitions are required without which `named` would not function properly. The first required definition is `zone "."`—the root zone. This allows the name server to contact one of the root name servers on the Internet, as described in the section "Using DNS: The Big Picture." /var/named/named.ca contains the names and IP addresses of all root name servers. It is important that this file be kept up-to-date, because the information about the root servers changes from time to time. Fortunately, this is easy to do using the `dig` utility:

```
dig . ns > /var/named/named.ca
```

Ideally, you should run this simple utility periodically from a `cron` or `launchd` job. The root servers do not change often; scheduling this update to run once a month would be adequate.

```
G5:zones apple$ cat db.pretendco.com.zone.apple
 ;GUID=A5C42059-099F-4209-A359-2B540AA4EA05

$TTL 10800
pretendco.com. IN SOA ns.pretendco.com. admin.pretendco.com. (
  2008052901 ;Serial
  86400   ;Refresh
  3600   ;Retry
  604800  ;Expire
  345600  ;Negative caching TTL
  )

pretendco.com. IN  NS ns.pretendco.com.
ns IN  A 192.168.1.2
_http._tcp IN  PTR http._http._tcp.pretendco.com.
```

```
mail IN  CNAME ns.pretendco.com.
www IN  CNAME ns.pretendco.com.
pretendco.com. IN  MX 0 mail.pretendco.com.
http._http._tcp IN SRV 0 0 80 pretendco.com.
http._http._tcp IN TXT "=/"


G5:zones apple$ cat db.1.168.192.in-addr.arpa.zone.apple
 ;GUID=BE77D3EF-F1BD-40BC-B21A-327C91901A08


$TTL 10800
1.168.192.in-addr.arpa. IN SOA ns.pretendco.com. admin.pretendco.com. (
  2008041400 ;Serial
  86400  ;Refresh
  3600   ;Retry
  604800  ;Expire
  345600   ;Negative caching TTL
 )


1.168.192.in-addr.arpa. IN  NS ns.pretendco.com.
2.1.168.192.in-addr.arpa. IN  PTR ns.pretendco.com.
```

The next and final two zone definitions in the named.conf example file define a forward and reverse zone for localhost, respectively.

Editing and Importing BIND Files

Leopard allows manual editing of DNS configuration files. You can edit the canonical BIND files without having to face any real Apple-specific hurdles. The advantages are clear: People coming from other UNIX-like platforms should immediately feel at home. Any utilities that manipulate DNS configuration or zone files can work unaltered and not cause the loss of Server Admin as a DNS editing utility.

There is a caveat, however: Any zones or machines added into these files are not visible in Server Admin. Importing a zone file is a good example of this issue.

Imagine that a company is migrating from Linux servers to a Mac OS X Server setup. Because DNS is already configured on the Linux servers, the company already has valid and accurate DNS files. These can be used as-is on Mac OS X Server.

To import one or more of these files requires three main steps: Update the /etc/named.conf file; copy the zone file into place; and restart named, as described in the following steps:

1   Update named.conf.

Using root-level access, add the zone definition to /etc/named.conf. Since views are in play, the zone must be wrapped in a view. A sample entry with view and zone definition follows:

```
view "MyView" {
zone "example.com" IN {
        type master;        // Primary zone
        file "db.example.com"; // Name on filesystem
        allow-update { none; };
};
};
```

2   Copy the zone file into place.

Copy the zone file from the original system into the /var/named directory, giving it the same name specified in the zone definition.

3   Restart named.

Again, as root, issue the following two commands:

```
serveradmin stop dns
```

```
serveradmin start dns
```

Alternatively, rndc is available for this task and reduces the work to a single statement:

```
rndc -s 127.0.0.1 -p 54 reconfig
```

Creating Secure and Private DNS Servers

The accuracy and security of a network DNS system cannot be undervalued. Not only do zone files need maintenance to keep data in sync with reality, the system needs to be secured so that results cannot be altered, intentionally or unintentionally. Out-of-date or incorrect zone files may point users or services to incorrect or nonexistent hosts. Similarly, because data in a DNS server contain a "map" of a network, it is important that a DNS server provide protection from attackers. As with any software, bugs in the code have, in the past, allowed attackers to compromise the DNS server. Finally, as with any service, a DNS server uses other resources (such as CPU and bandwidth) and therefore has finite capacity.

This section describes some standard DNS configurations. Protected with a firewall and thereby inaccessible from the public Internet, these configurations are also secure. These standard configurations include a caching-only name server; restricted zone transfers; authoritative-only services (also known as *nonrecursive servers*); and forward servers.

Using Caching-Only Name Servers

One common configuration is a caching-only name server. By placing a DNS server inside a network firewall, DNS lookups can be cached for later use, speeding queries and limiting the number of slower links to the outside world. However, if an enterprise DNS server is not protected, the opposite may occur: Unauthorized queries can unexpectedly load down the system, using greater bandwidth and slowing lookups for internal users. If a caching-only name server is publicly available, or if there is an unexpected number of users within a large organization, performance can suffer and impact other services.

Fortunately, the default configuration forestalls one of the issues out of the box: The problem of allowing unexpected users the use of a DNS server. By default, only localnets are allowed recursion—basically, the use of a DNS server past itself. A caching-only name server is of little use otherwise. The solution to this problem of lock-in is simple: Using Server Admin, set an ACL, using the Settings pane, to restrict recursion to specific machines, subnets, or both. (To see the impact of DNS queries, trace some network traffic and watch how many DNS queries are made—thanks to almost complete reliance on DNS—even on a seemingly idle machine. Multiply this by the number of devices in a large organization, and you can appreciate the impact of DNS queries on a network.)

Restricting Zone Transfers

Another way to keep a primary or secondary DNS server secure is to restrict zone transfers to authorized sources only. By default, the "Allows zone transfer" checkbox is enabled for each zone created, which means that anyone who can issue queries against a server can also request a copy of the entire zone file. This is an especially bad security risk when a server is world-accessible. You should configure named to allow zone transfers only to authorized secondary DNS servers. Locking down zone transfers also prevents denial of service (DoS) by zone transfer to unexpected hosts.

There are two ways to tackle unauthorized transfers: Via the named configuration or by using the firewall. The method you choose depends on your needs and policies.

Going the configuration file route will unfortunately require moving the zone into the /etc/named.conf file (as shown in "Configuring DNS Services"), and losing the ability to manage this zone via Server Admin. Once configured in /etc/named.conf, add the following line to the zone definition:

```
allow-transfer { 192.168.55.22; 192.168.32.18; };
```

The `allow-transfer` statement creates a whitelist of IP addresses that are allowed to transfer the entire zone to themselves. You should add addresses for all the secondary DNS servers that need to transfer the zone.

You can also restrict transfer using a firewall (host-based, like the ones built in to Mac OS X Server) or using router ACLs. For example, you can restrict inbound access from the secondary zone needing to transfer a zone to TCP port 53 on the DNS server, and deny all others. Since standard client queries use User Datagram Protocol (UDP), zone transfers can be limited in this way.

Providing Authoritative-Only Services

Another option for a DNS server is to provide authoritative-only services; this configuration is also known as a *nonrecursive server*. For various reasons, it may be desirable to have a name server that can answer queries about its primary or secondary zones and no others. Such a configuration restricts certain networks from recursion access to the server.

This setup is easy when using Mac OS X Server: Simply set up zones as usual, and then remove all recursion from the DNS Settings pane in Server Admin, including localnets, as shown here:

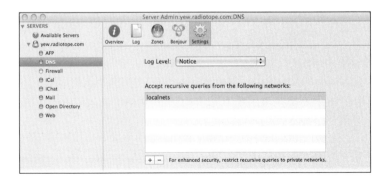

Configuring Forward Servers

A twist on the authoritative-only server is the forward server. When configured in this way, a DNS server forwards any query for which it is not authoritative to a server in its forwarders list. You can enter forwarders in the Server Admin DNS Settings pane.

A forward server typically contains a primary or secondary zone, allowing it to quickly answer queries about the records in its local database, while all others are sent to a separate server. There are several reasons for deflecting queries. A simple reason is security—perhaps a Mac OS X Server is acting as an Open Directory master and DNS server. This server can be locked down from an access perspective, with no external access at all, not even to return DNS queries. To resolve queries about outside entities, the server can forward those requests to another internal DNS server that does have access.

For example, in the following diagram, client computers are configured to use the DNS server at 10.1.17.1, which is configured as a forwarding server. The forwarding DNS server is configured to forward queries to 10.1.0.1 that it cannot answer.

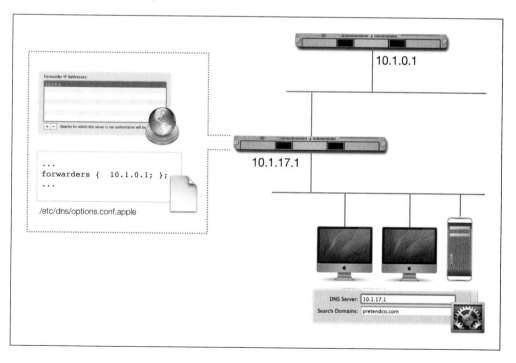

Configuring for Scale

As sites grow to include remote offices accessed via wide area network (WAN) links, DNS infrastructure can become strained. Most of the configurations discussed previously in this chapter can come into play.

Consider using forward servers when you need to build up a site-wide cache. Having all DNS queries go through a single host—or set of hosts on a large network—can save bandwidth by reducing outbound queries.

When several sites share a common infrastructure, keep in mind that secondary servers can also provide zone transfers. So there is no need to mercilessly pound a single DNS server for zone transfers of a particular zone. Secondary DNS servers across a WAN link can provide zone updates to other secondary DNS servers that are closer on the network—do whatever makes sense for a particular topology.

As a final note, remember that a secondary DNS server can be used as a primary server to a network device. In other words, there is no reason to have all clients query a primary name server first. Ensure that the load is spread among all DNS servers as applicable.

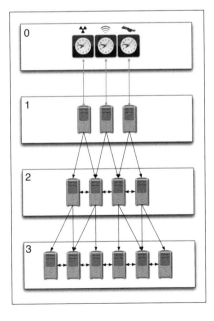

Using Network Time Protocol

Network Time Protocol (NTP) provides a time server that all clients on a network can query to keep their system clocks in sync. It is critical to keep each computer on a network referencing the same time, for several reasons. Several subsystems rely on having correct time, such as Kerberos, which uses synchronized time to prevent replay attacks and synchronize authentication services. A standard time reference also helps preserve the sanity of system administrators—with the integrity of all timestamps ensured (including those for mail headers, database transactions, and file system metadata), correlating log files and events is easier. It would be a waste of time to apply an offset to the timestamps in various files just to match up a login or other event.

NTP is a hierarchical system, disseminating Coordinated Universal Time (UTC), created by several strata of servers. Strata 0 servers, including atomic and GPS clocks, are the highest in the sequence and, therefore, the most accurate. Strata 0 servers feed strata 1 servers, which also have a high level of precision. Strata 1 servers typically include time servers run by governments and institutions of science. Strata 2 servers are any NTP servers that sync their time from a Strata 1 server. Strata 3 servers sync from Strata 2, and so on.

NTP clients can sync to any time server that they are authorized to access. However, two rules apply: The closer the NTP server the better, to reduce latency; and all devices on a given LAN should sync to the same time source. This time source will preferably be an internal resource acting as an NTP server (such as Mac OS X).

Understanding the NTP Service

Mac OS X uses the open source ntpd software suite to provide time services. The ntpd daemon performs the actual work, sending NTP queries on UDP port 123. When enabled, the daemon is active full-time (not on demand), as in the following:

```
# ps ax | grep ntp
   44   ??  Ss    0:24.03 /usr/sbin/ntpd -n -g -p /var/run/ntpd.pid -f /var/db/ntp.drift
```

It is easy to enable the ntpd service using the Server Admin graphical user interface. Select the server, then select the General tab in the Settings pane, as shown here:

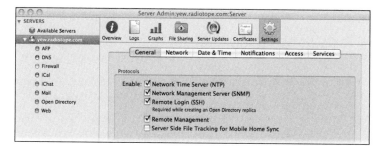

You can configure and control NTP using two command-line utilities: serveradmin and systemsetup. On Mac OS X Server, serveradmin can configure the NTP service with the following commands:

▶ info:ntpServerName = "(server-address)"

▶ info:ntpTimeServe = (yes | no)

▶ `info:previousNTPServerName = "(server-address)"`

▶ `info:ntpTimeSync = (yes | no)`

For example, to set the time source to time.apple.com, you can run the following command:

```
# serveradmin command info:ntpServerName="time.apple.com"
```

The `systemsetup` command configures the NTP client. The following switches are valid when using `systemsetup` to configure NTP:

▶ `getusingnetworktime`

▶ `setusingnetworktime (on | off)`

▶ `getnetworktimeserver`

▶ `setnetworktimeserver (server-address)`

For example, to determine if time sync is currently enabled, you can use the following command:

```
# systemsetup -getusingnetworktime
Network Time: On
```

Like many other services, Leopard brings `ntpd` directly under the control of `launchd`. The plist for this service can be found at /System/Library/LaunchDaemons/org.ntp.ntpd.plist. Interestingly, there is a very Apple-specific thumbprint on this startup: Rather than call `ntpd` directly, the `launchd` plist runs /usr/libexec/ntpd-wrapper. The bulk of the work in the wrapper script is handled by three lines:

```
ipconfig waitall
ntpdate -bvs
exec $sb /usr/sbin/ntpd -n -g -p /var/run/ntpd.pid -f /var/db/ntp.drift
```

The first line pauses execution of this script until a network interface or interfaces are active. This corrects a problem from pre-Leopard systems in which `ntpd` would load before any network was available.

The second line uses the `ntpdate` utility to set the current time before invoking the `ntpd` daemon itself.

The third line also requires a little explanation because the comments have been stripped from the context. The `$sb` variable can contain the path to the `sandbox-exec` loader, which would run the `ntpd` daemon in a *sandbox*. A sandbox is a security utility that imposes rules on a running program. These rules can allow or disallow access to network resources or parts of the file system. By default, `ntpd` does not run in a sandbox—the `$sb` sandbox variable is commented out and left undefined, causing the `exec` statement to ignore `$sb` completely. With the `$sb` variable undefined, `ntpd` does not run in a sandboxed environment.

The final action of the `ntpd` wrapper is to run `ntpd` with these parameters:

- ▶ `-n`—Do not fork. Required for `launchd` compatibility.
- ▶ `-g`—Essentially, ignore all clock differences and set the time.
- ▶ `-p`—PID file.
- ▶ `-f`—Drift file. This file allows `ntpd` to track the frequency of clock drift, and if it does not exist at `ntpd` startup, it will be created.

Although `ntpd` is capable of using keys to validate servers to clients, Mac OS X does not currently press this capability into service.

The `ntpd` daemon uses a sophisticated algorithm to determine the interval at which it polls external time servers. A machine typically starts with a short 64-second interval and gradually increases the polling to 1024 seconds (approximately 17 minutes).

In all, NTP is a very straightforward service. When `launchd` loads the NTP plist, it waits for network interfaces to be available and performs clock correction. This behavior testifies to how important this service is—Apple wants it to run flawlessly.

Troubleshooting

The DNS system can fail in subtle and not-so-subtle ways; however, it is typically the administrator that fails the DNS system. First and foremost, zone records must remain accurate and in sync with reality. Dropping sensitive files on the wrong host because DNS mismapped a name (enabled by a common ID and password on all internal systems) can be a serious problem. Possibly more frustrating is a DNS record that simply points nowhere, leaving no route to a host. Troubleshooting DNS involves both knowledge of the system, and testing and sleuthing work. Follow log files, look for clues, and *test*.

Testing at the Server

When DNS issues arise, the easiest place to start troubleshooting is often at the DNS server itself. If things are not right there, the client has no chance of retrieving correct information, or any information at all.

Access a root shell on the primary DNS server—or, the server that clients query—using direct login or Secure Shell (SSH). Use the ps command to check whether named is running:

```
# ps ax | grep named
16029   ??   Ss     0:04.17 /usr/sbin/named -f
```

(and yes, the process is named and not bind.)

If named is not running, see the next section, "Checking the Logs and the Process," for further troubleshooting steps. If it is running, ensure that you can actually perform lookups:

```
dig @127.0.0.1 www.example.com
```

If all of this works as expected, the issue is most likely with the client or the network—perhaps a firewall or router ACL that is preventing access sits between the client and DNS server. If a client uses Dynamic Host Configuration Protocol (DHCP) for configuration, ensure that the DHCP server is also supplying a (correct) DNS server.

Checking the Logs and the Process

There are many reasons that named may refuse to start, but only one place to look: the logs to /Library/Logs/named.log. Unfortunately, Server Admin sometimes gives DNS the green light, even though named is *not* running. The most common reason for named to not start up properly is bad syntax in one of the configuration files. While you cannot predict what this bad syntax will be, the following is an example:

```
15-Mar-2008 12:32:28.710 loading configuration from '/private/etc/named.conf'
15-Mar-2008 12:32:28.713 /etc/dns/publicView.conf.apple:31: zone '100.168.192.
in-addr.arpa': already exists previous definition: /etc/dns/publicView.conf.apple:23
15-Mar-2008 12:32:28.713 reloading configuration failed: failure
15-Mar-2008 12:32:28.715 shutting down
15-Mar-2008 12:32:28.715 stopping command channel on 127.0.0.1#54
15-Mar-2008 12:32:28.716 no longer listening on 127.0.0.1#53
15-Mar-2008 12:32:28.716 no longer listening on 192.168.100.16#53
15-Mar-2008 12:32:28.723 exiting
```

The log shows exactly what the problem is (zone '100.168.192.in-addr.arpa': already exists previous definition: /etc/dns/publicView.conf.apple:23) and where to look (/etc/dns/publicView.conf.apple, line 31). Interestingly, this log comes from a server that had never been hand-edited, therefore Server Admin miswrote the file.

You may also see a line like this in your log:

```
15-Mar-2008 12:36:29.632 checkhints: view com.apple.ServerAdmin.DNS.public:
L.ROOT-SERVERS.NET/A (199.7.83.42) missing from hints
```

This is telling you that the root server cache (/var/named/named.ca) has a bad entry—in this case, for L.ROOT-SERVERS.NET—and needs updating. Update this file as shown earlier in "Configuring DNS Services."

On a server that acts as a secondary DNS server, you may see this in the named.log file:

```
1-Feb-2008 17:53:02.588 zone radiotope.com/IN/com.apple.ServerAdmin.DNS.public:
refresh: failure trying master 10.10.10.12#53 (source 0.0.0.0#0): operation canceled
```

For some reason, the DNS server could not contact the master to load the zone. Its own network interface may be down, the master may be down, or a network issue may be causing the failure. The problem caused by this lack of connectivity is that a secondary DNS server will continue to serve DNS requests from its cached copy of the zone, which now may be out of sync with the master and giving incorrect results.

Checking the Configuration File Syntax

This step is an extension of the previous troubleshooting tip, "Checking the Logs and the Process." The BIND config file syntax is exacting and sometimes nonintuitive. If there has been any hand-editing, double-check edits if BIND will not load a particular zone or pick up its changes, or if it will not load at all.

Syntax errors will be pointed out in the named.log file.

Testing the Client Service

If all of the above tests come back clean, the issue is most likely on the client side. Simple things to check include the following:

▶ Is the client making requests of the *correct* name server?

▶ Is DHCP pushing out the correct name server?

- ▶ Is a DNS server entry set at all?
- ▶ Does the client have a stale entry in its cache?

The last point is important: Just like DNS servers, clients cache results. This way, once an entry is looked up, further requests do not need to take up resources on the server. However, if DNS is updated after a client caches the result, the two will be out of sync. Typically this does not cause a problem, but sometimes the issue raises its head. A client can flush its local cache with dscacheutil:

```
# dscacheutil -flushcache
```

If these suggestions do not work, you should investigate whether the DNS server set on the client is actually reachable. Use the dig utility to test lookups from the client:

```
$ dig www.example.com

; <<>> DiG 9.4.1-P1 <<>> www.example.com
;; global options:  printcmd
;; Got answer:
;; ->>HEADER<<- opcode: QUERY, status: NOERROR, id: 63675
;; flags: qr rd ra; QUERY: 1, ANSWER: 1, AUTHORITY: 2, ADDITIONAL: 1

;; QUESTION SECTION:
;www.example.com.               IN      A

;; ANSWER SECTION:
www.example.com.        172741  IN      A       208.77.188.166

;; AUTHORITY SECTION:
example.com.            172741  IN      NS      a.iana-servers.net.
example.com.            172741  IN      NS      b.iana-servers.net.

;; ADDITIONAL SECTION:
a.iana-servers.net.     10080   IN      A       192.0.34.43

;; Query time: 71 msec
```

```
;; SERVER: 192.168.100.12#53(192.168.100.12)
;; WHEN: Mon Mar 17 22:48:15 2008
;; MSG SIZE  rcvd: 113
```

There are two important parts here: that an answer is returned in the ANSWER SECTION, and the server that answered the question (in the statistics section at the bottom of the output). If the output of dig is too dense, you can use the +short flag:

```
$ dig www.example.com +short
208.77.188.166
Alternatively, use nslookup:
$ nslookup www.example.com
Server:        192.168.100.12
Address:       192.168.100.12#53

Non-authoritative answer:
Name:   www.example.com
Address: 208.77.188.166
```

The Non-authoritative answer line simply means that a server other than the server authoritative for this zone provided the results.

Many services that depend on DNS require that both forward and reverse DNS entries resolve correctly. You can test the forward lookup using dig or nslookup, and the reverse using host or dig:

```
$ dig www.radiotope.com +short
69.55.239.95
$ host 69.55.239.95
95.239.55.69.in-addr.arpa domain name pointer www.radiotope.com.
```

Checking NTP

Like all network-bound services, connectivity is typically the biggest issue. Ensure that firewall rules—host- or network-based—are not blocking access to NTP servers. NTP uses UDP port 123 for both client and server operation.

ntpd logs all information using the syslog facility, an important place to check if ntp is not behaving as expected.

The ntpd daemon stays running at all times. Use the ps command to check the ntpd daemon running status.

If the daemon is running, the ntpq (NTP query) command can be used. The rv command displays the state of the local clock:

```
$ ntpq -c rv
assID=0 status=06f4 leap_none, sync_ntp, 15 events, event_peer/strat_chg,
version="ntpd 4.2.2@1.1532-o Mon Sep 24 01:42:27 UTC 2007 (1)",
processor="Power Macintosh", system="Darwin/9.2.0", leap=00, stratum=3,
precision=-20, rootdelay=100.756, rootdispersion=43.373, peer=26021,
refid=17.254.0.27,
reftime=cb8afd96.e1abf593  Tue, Mar 18 2008 22:48:54.881, poll=10,
clock=cb8afee5.537b3508  Tue, Mar 18 2008 22:54:29.326, state=4,
offset=-4.128, frequency=23.587, jitter=0.855, noise=1.765,
stability=0.060, tai=0
$ ntpq -c rv
assID=0 status=06f4 leap_none, sync_ntp, 15 events, event_peer/strat_chg,
version="ntpd 4.2.2@1.1532-o Mon Sep 24 01:42:27 UTC 2007 (1)",
processor="Power Macintosh", system="Darwin/9.2.0", leap=00, stratum=3,
precision=-20, rootdelay=100.756, rootdispersion=43.373, peer=26021,
refid=17.254.0.27,
reftime=cb8afd96.e1abf593  Tue, Mar 18 2008 22:48:54.881, poll=10,
clock=cb8afee5.537b3508  Tue, Mar 18 2008 22:54:29.326, state=4,
offset=-4.128, frequency=23.587, jitter=0.855, noise=1.765,
stability=0.060, tai=0
```

Similarly, the pe command displays information about the peers that ntpd is contacting:

```
$ ntpq -c pe
     remote           refid      st t when poll reach   delay   offset  jitter
==============================================================================
*time1.apple.com 17.106.100.13    2 u   721 1024  367   92.074   -4.128   0.855
```

What You've Learned

This chapter covered two services that are critical to a network infrastucture: DNS and NTP. The following points should be clear:

▶ DNS provides a name-to-IP address and IP address-to-name mapping.

▶ Many services rely upon DNS, particularly Open Directory, Kerberos, and email.

▶ DNS provides a map of hosts on a network, so it is important to secure a DNS server properly. This can be accomplished by limiting zone transfers or via firewall protection.

▶ NTP is relied upon to keep system clocks in time with each other.

▶ Kerberos uses NTP to prevent replay attacks and synchronize authentication services.

▶ NTP is important to an administrator for any timestamps—file system, database, and log entries—which allow correlation of events across systems.

References

▶ Internet Systems Consortium: http://www.isc.org

▶ Mac OS X Server, Network Services Administration, v10.5: http://images.apple.com/server/macosx/docs/Network_Services_Admin_v10.5.pdf

▶ Albitz, Paul and Liu, Cricket, *DNS and BIND* (O'Reilly Media, Inc., 6th edition, 2006)

▶ NTP home page: http://www.ntp.org

▶ Network Time Protocol (Version 3) Specification, Implementation and Analysis: RFC 1305

Review Quiz

1. What is the name of the daemon that runs the DNS service in Mac OS X?

2. What function does a DNS A record perform?

3. What is the name and full path of the configuration file for named?

4. Are there any security issues in exposing an internal DNS server to the public Internet?

5. Why is NTP important for daily administration?

6. Why is NTP important to Kerberos?

7. Which are the most accurate set of NTP servers?

8. Which port and protocol does the NTP service use?

Answers

1. named is the daemon that runs the DNS service in Mac OS X.

2. An A record maps a name to an IPv4 address, allowing a forward lookup.

3. /etc/named.conf is the name and full path of the configuration file for named.

4. Security issues in exposing an internal DNS server to the public Internet include making available a list of valid hostnames and IP addresses to the network, if zone transfers to everyone are not disabled. Also, potential bugs in BIND can be exploited to compromise a computer. If a DNS server is exposed in error, queries from public sources will consume resources and compete with other services at your site.

5. With multiple machines, it is important to be able to correlate system events accurately.

6. Kerberos uses the time on each machine to prevent replay attacks. By default, Kerberos authentication fails if clocks differ by 5 minutes or more.

7. The servers that make up strata 0 are the most accurate NTP sources.

8. The NTP service listens on UDP port 123.

6

Time   This lesson takes approximately 45 minutes to complete.

Goals   Learn how to control access via technological means

Learn the different firewall options in Mac OS X

Learn how to use the RADIUS service to require authentication to
Apple AirPort wireless access points

Chapter 6

Controlling Access to Resources

Never before has security been so critical when administrating a system. All network-connected systems are constantly being probed and attacked, sometimes intentionally and sometimes unintentionally. Attacks can come from both internal and external sources. This chapter focuses on mitigating and controlling access with network-level controls.

These controls consist of Mac OS X firewalls designed to block access and Remote Authentication Dial In User Service (RADIUS), a client-server protocol used to authenticate and account for entry at given access points.

Configuring Firewall Service

The term *firewall* originated prior to the digital firewalls that technologists have come to know. Originally, the term was used to describe a fireproof wall designed to contain fire from spreading, such as from a car engine into the passenger section. Computer firewalls share similar qualities, as they work to contain improper network packets from breaching a host or network perimeter.

Mac OS X has two firewalls: IP Firewall (`ipfw`) and the Application Level Firewall (ALF). While `ipfw` is available in both Mac OS X and Mac OS X Server, only Mac OS X Server has a graphical user interface for the service, as well as the Adaptive Firewall, which can add and remove firewall rules based on network events.

> **NOTE** ▶ Technically, the `ipfw` program is now in its second generation, and some-times is called `ipfw2`. It consists of both the `ipfw` and `ip6fw` programs for restricting IPv4 packets and IPv6 packets, respectively. It is generally referred to as `ipfw`, as it will be in this text.

Mac OS X Server v10.5 contains a host-based firewall service. Based on `ipfw` software developed by Berkeley Software Distribution (BSD), it is a traditional stateful packet firewall (a stateful firewall keeps track of the state of network connections traveling across it). The Adaptive Firewall is new to Leopard Server. While most documentation makes this seem like a second firewall, the Adaptive Firewall is really just a monitor that creates and disables rules in the `ipfw` firewall as needed. The behavior that currently calls the Adaptive Firewall into action is 10 failed login attempts. Such behavior blocks the requesting IP address for 15 minutes—an action that makes brute-force password guessing virtually impossible.

Accessing the Firewall Setup

You can access the main firewall setup through Server Admin.app. The Address Groups tab in the Settings pane enables you to logically group addresses and create address ranges to which you can then apply rules.

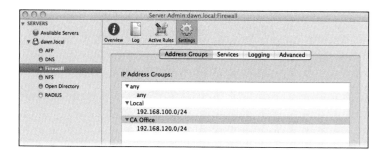

Clicking the Add (+) button at the bottom of the Server Admin window allows you to add new groups; click the pencil button to edit existing groups.

The Services tab defines the rules in place for a given address group.

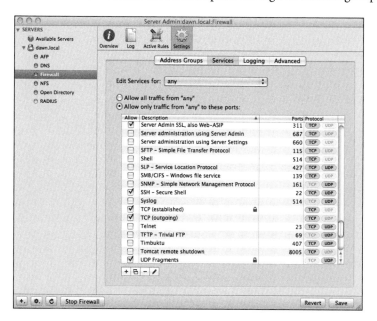

By default, all traffic is allowed out and only Apple administrative ports and established traffic are allowed in. Established traffic is traffic that has validly been sent out and is receiving a reply. Established traffic may receive reply traffic on ports that are closed, but because the firewall software tracks established traffic, use of the ports is allowed for established traffic streams.

The Services tab contains a long list of predefined services, any of which may be activated for a given address group. If the service or port range needed has not been predefined, it is easy to add a custom service. Clicking the Add (+) button brings up a dialog box that allows you to define a custom service to be added to the list.

If you are not sure which port to add for a given service, you can get that information from several places. You can find well-known services in the /etc/services file on your local computer. Use grep to filter out terms:

```
$ grep -i quake /etc/services
quake       26000/udp  # quake
quake       26000/tcp  # quake
```

NOTE ▶ Two good sources to refer to when determining port numbers are Apple and the Internet Assigned Number Authority (IANA).

For Apple services: http://docs.info.apple.com/article.html?artnum=106439

For general services: http://www.iana.org/assignments/port-numbers

Clicking the Active Rules button in the toolbar displays the currently active rules for all rule sets and address groups.

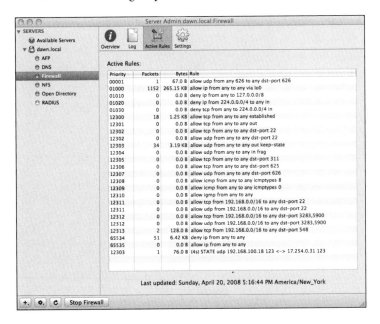

As mentioned earlier in "Configuring Firewall Service," the firewall service in Mac OS X Server is built atop ipfw, a kernel-based application. You can also control ipfw via the same-named command-line program. Unlike Mac OS X Server, in Mac OS X the command-line ipfw program is the only interface available.

An easy way to verify firewall rules is to list them. This list corresponds to the list in the Active Rules pane in Server Admin. With ipfw, use the list verb:

```
# ipfw list
01000 allow ip from any to any via lo0
01010 deny ip from any to 127.0.0.0/8
01020 deny ip from 224.0.0.0/4 to any in
01030 deny tcp from any to 224.0.0.0/4 in
12300 allow tcp from any to any established
12301 allow tcp from any to any out
12302 allow tcp from any to any dst-port 22
12302 allow udp from any to any dst-port 22
12303 allow udp from any to any out keep-state
12304 allow tcp from any to any dst-port 53 out keep-state
12304 allow udp from any to any dst-port 53 out keep-state
12305 allow udp from any to any in frag
12306 allow tcp from any to any dst-port 311
12307 allow tcp from any to any dst-port 625
12308 allow udp from any to any dst-port 626
12309 allow icmp from any to any icmptypes 8
12310 allow icmp from any to any icmptypes 0
12311 allow igmp from any to any
65534 deny ip from any to any
65535 allow ip from any to any
```

In the Server Admin Settings pane, under the Advanced tab, you can set stealth options and create custom rule sets for the firewall service. Stealth options drop denied packets rather than sending the requesting computer an error message.

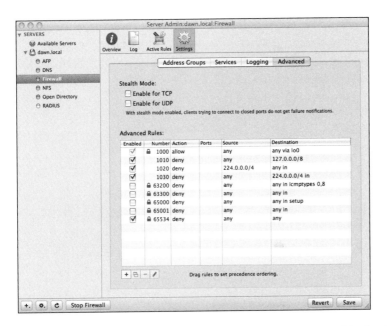

Once you have completed setup and testing, you should enable the Stealth Mode option for both TCP and User Datagram Protocol (UDP), which makes the job for attackers much more difficult because clients trying to connect to closed ports will not receive failure notifications.

The rules in the Firewall Settings Services pane operate with the rules shown in the Advanced pane. Usually, the broad rules in the Advanced pane block (or open) access for all ports. These broad, lower-priority (higher-numbered) rules apply after the rules in the Services pane.

The rules created in the Services pane open access to specific services. Higher in priority, Services rules take precedence over those created in the Advanced pane. For most normal uses, using the Advanced pane to open access to designated services is sufficient.

If you create multiple rules in the Advanced pane, the rule number determines the precedence for a rule. This number corresponds to the order of the rule in the Advanced pane. You can reorder rules in the Advanced pane by dragging them up or down in the list. If necessary, you can add more rules using the Advanced pane.

Although Server Admin treats the firewall as a service, it does not implement the firewall by a running process like other services. Implementation is simply a set of behaviors in the kernel, controlled by the `ipfw` and `sysctl` tools. To start and stop the firewall, Server Admin sets a switch using the `sysctl` tool. Use the `sysctl` tool to enable the firewall as follows:

```
$ sysctl -w net.inet.ip.fw.enable=1
```

You can also disable the firewall by changing the setting to `0`:

```
$ sysctl -w net.inet.ip.fw.enable=0
```

Regardless of this setting, the rules loaded in the firewall remain. But they are ignored when the firewall is disabled.

You can also use the `ipfw` command-line program to manipulate firewall rules. This is practical when working remotely, over `ssh`, or when a scripted solution is needed.

As an example rule, imagine the following scenario: An Xserve with multiple network interfaces—physical or virtual—is running AFP for file access. The security team decides that AFP should only be available on the subnets that it is serving. AFP does not have the control to specify which interface it binds to. However, you can use the built-in firewall, `ipfw`, to block AFP on the unwanted ports. For example, to block AFP on the `en0` interface, you can use the following command to add the appropriate rule:

```
ipfw add deny dst-port 548 via en0
```

The keywords to `ipfw` are as follows:

▶ `add` Denotes adding a rule

▶ `deny` Indicates what type of rule

▶ `dst-port` Denotes which port the rule affects and is specified by number or service name

▶ `via` Applies rules to packets arriving via the specified interface or IP address

If a rule number is not specified, `ipfw` will assign a default number to the added rule. You may want to specify this rule number yourself, because the firewall evaluates rules in a sequential order. When a default rule number is assigned, it will be done in such a way that the rule becomes the last rule, prior to the default rule. The following command adds an equivalent AFP blocking rule; however, it specifies the rule number (6000).

The command lists the destination port by service name (`afpovertcp`) and gives an IP address, rather than an interface name:

```
ipfw add 6000 deny dst-port afpovertcp via 10.10.15.68
```

If a rule is incorrect or no longer needed, you can remove it with the `del` (delete) command, as follows:

```
ipfw del 6000
```

Using Firewall Log Files

The firewall sends log messages to /var/log/ipfw.log. A sample follows:

```
Apr 17 09:41:17 server17 servermgrd[58]: servermgr_ipfilter:ipfw
config:Notice:Flushed IPv6 rules
Apr 17 09:41:19 server17 servermgrd[58]: servermgr_ipfilter:ipfw
config:Notice:Enabled firewall
Apr 17 09:41:24 dawn ipfw[1940]: 1040 Deny TCP 10.1.17.2:49232 10.1.17.200:548
in via en0
Apr 17 09:41:59 dawn ipfw[1940]: 1040 Deny TCP 10.1.17.2:49232 10.1.17.200:548
in via en0
Apr 17 09:42:31 dawn ipfw[1940]: 1040 Deny TCP 10.1.17.2:49232 10.1.17.200:548
in via en0
Apr 17 09:43:31 dawn ipfw[1940]: 100 Accept TCP 10.221.41.33:721 192.168.12.12:515
in via en0
```

Each entry follows a similar form:

▶ Time of entry: In this sample, it is `Apr 17`....

▶ Hostname: In this sample, it is `dawn`.

▶ Process name and ID: Here it is `ipfw[1940]`.

▶ The log message. The first two lines in this sample simply state that the firewall is starting and enabled.

For the firewall itself, each message follows this pattern:

▶ Matching rule number. Why the firewall took this behavior.

▶ Action. The action taken—Deny, Accept, and so on.

▶ Protocol. Which protocol this affected (TCP, UDP, and so on).

▶ Source. The source IP address of packet.

▶ Destination. The destination IP address of packet.

▶ Interface. On which network interface this packet appeared. In the example, it is
    `in via en0`, but it could also be `lo0` (loopback), `en1`, and so on.

You can fine-tune logging from the Server Admin graphical user interface (Settings >
Logging) or the `serveradmin` command-line utility. For example, to log all allowed packets,
you can make the following `serveradmin` call:

```
serveradmin settings ipfilter:logAllAllowed = yes
```

Configuring Firewall Files

In Mac OS X Server, the firewall is a service that can be configured by administrators.
In contrast, Mac OS X does not support the firewall directly; the `ipfw`-based firewall has
no graphical user interface, but users can manipulate it via the command line. However,
Mac OS X does contain the Application Level Firewall, which you can configure using the
Security Preference pane. This topic shows you how to configure both services.

Mac OS X Server uses several files for its `ipfw`-based firewall. The following configuration
files are stored in /etc/ipfilter:

```
-r--r--r--@  1 root wheel   281 Apr 17 12:56 ip6fw.conf.apple
-r--r--r--  1 root wheel     0 Apr 17 12:33 ip6fwstate-on
-rw-r--r--  1 root wheel 41219 Apr 17 12:56 ip_address_groups.plist
-r--r--r--  1 root wheel 38243 Sep 23 2007 ip_address_groups.plist.default
-rw-r--r--  1 root wheel  1874 Sep 23 2007 ipfw.conf
-r--r--r--@  1 root wheel  1353 Apr 17 12:56 ipfw.conf.apple
-r--r--r--  1 root wheel  1874 Sep 23 2007 ipfw.conf.default
-r--r--r--  1 root wheel     0 Apr 17 12:33 ipfwstate-on
-r--r--r--  1 root wheel   632 Sep 23 2007
standard_services.plist.default
```

Server Admin writes to these configuration files. Note that:

▶ IPv6 and IPv4 rules are kept in separate files.

▶ Any files with a name ending in "state-on" exist only if the service is running. They are flags used at boot time to indicate if the firewall should be enabled.

▶ The plist files contain information presented in Server Admin. They are well commented, and you can customize services and addresses seen in Server Admin. For example, if you have a custom application that communicates with other servers on a particular port, you can add an entry to this file so that this service appears in the list of ports that may be selected with a checkbox.

▶ The *.apple files are edited by servermgrd. Changes made in these files risk being overwritten by changes in Server Admin and may render Server Admin unable to manage the firewall service. You can make changes in other configuration files, such as ipfw. conf. Rules added to ipfw.conf will be loaded into ipfw at start time. The ipfw.conf file lists rules in the same format as rules added with the ipfw command line, minus the ipfw command itself. For example:

```
add 03000 allow tcp from any to any http
```

When added to ipfw.conf, rule 3000 is appended to the rule list, allowing HTTP on any interface. In addition, two premigration files may exist if the server was upgraded to version 10.5 from an earlier version.

As the earlier section, "Using Firewall Log Files," states, the Mac OS X Server ipfw logs messages to /var/log/ipfw.log. The Mac OS X Server Adaptive Firewall is configured by and uses several files:

▶ /etc/af.plist lists Adaptive Firewall preferences.

▶ /var/db/af/whitelist contains addresses that will not be blocked.

▶ /var/db/af/blacklist contains addresses that will always be blocked.

▶ /System/Library/LaunchDaemons/com.apple.afctl.plist contains the launchd plist.

Do not edit the whitelist and blacklist files manually. Rather, you should use the command-line utility afctl to manipulate these files. The Apple Event Monitoring daemon, emond, performs the actual monitoring and spurs the Adaptive Firewall into action. While emond is an off-limits subsystem, the man page claims that "emond accepts events from various services, runs them through a simple rules engine, and takes action." One of its rules is /etc/emond.d/rules/AdaptiveFirewall.plist.

This rule is activated on too many failed login attempts.

The Mac OS X Application Level Firewall also contains configuration files that affect its behavior. The Application Level Firewall is configured using the Security Preference pane.

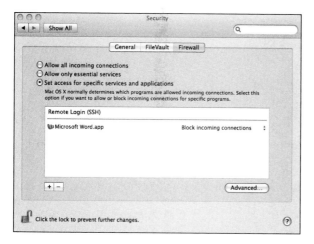

The Application Level Firewall can also be configured using the command line. The socketfilterfw program, which resides in /usr/libexec/ApplicationFirewall, can query and configure the Application Level Firewall. There is no man page for socketfilterfw, but a usage statement can be printed when using the -h switch.

By default, Application Level Firewall is set to allow all incoming connections. When configured to "Set access for specific services and applications," Application Level Firewall offers two choices for any given application: "Allow incoming connections" and "Block incoming connections."

The Application Level Firewall logs its activity at /var/log/alf.log when logging is enabled in the dialog box.

A sample log snippet follows:

```
Apr 29 16:16:00 dhcp-172-26-94-100 Firewall[38]: Deny Microsoft Word data in from
192.168.92.234:52684 uid = 0 proto=17
```

You can set the Application Level Firewall state from the command line using the `defaults` command to alter preferences:

```
defaults write /Library/Preferences/com.apple.alf globalstate -int 1
```

In this command, the integer passed is one of the following:

▶   0 = Off

▶   1 = On for specific services

▶   2 = On for essential services

For more on the `defaults` command, see "Defaults" in Chapter 9, "Automating Systems." The files that comprise the Application Level Firewall are as follows:

▶   The main preference file, /Library/Preferences/com.apple.alf.plist

▶   The executable files in /usr/libexec/ApplicationFirewall

Configuring RADIUS

RADIUS is a client-server protocol for authenticating users at RADIUS-enabled access points. It also provides accounting by logging usage as users supply required credentials. The service included in Mac OS X Server was designed with Apple AirPort base stations in mind, but other devices that support RADIUS, such as firewalls and third-party wireless access points, can use it too. Configuring the service consists mainly of configuring RADIUS devices.

RADIUS ties into Open Directory and Password Server to grant authorized users access to the network through a RADIUS device. When a user attempts access, the device communicates with the RADIUS server using the Extensible Authentication Protocol (EAP) to authenticate the user. Users are given access if their user credentials are valid and they are authorized to pass through the device.

Using RADIUS

You can access RADIUS through Server Admin and its graphical user interface. To configure RADIUS, follow these steps:

1   Enable the service in Server Admin and then choose one of the following options:

▶ Use Server Admin: Click the Configure RADIUS Service button in the Overview pane to display an assistant that walks you through the process of setting up Apple AirPort base stations.

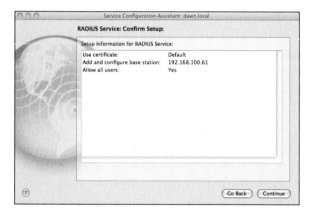

▶ Use AirPort Admin: Configure RADIUS from an AirPort base station using AirPort Admin. Choose the Access tab and fill in the appropriate values.

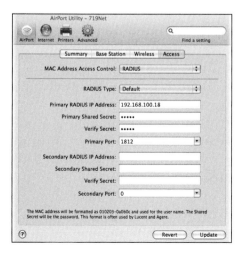

By default, all users with Open Directory accounts will be authenticated successfully.

NOTE ▶ Only AirPort base stations with firmware version 2.0.4 or greater are supported. The original Graphite base station is not among the supported models. Also, a maximum of 64 base stations can be added to the RADIUS service.

2   To limit which users and groups are allowed, use Server Admin to create a system access control list (SACL):

▶   Click the server name in Server Admin and click the Access tab.

▶   Choose "For selected services below," and click RADIUS.

▶   Select the "Allow only users and groups below" option.

▶   Click the Add (+) button at the bottom of the user list to display a list of users and groups that can be dragged into the list. Only the users in this list can authenticate to the RADIUS service.

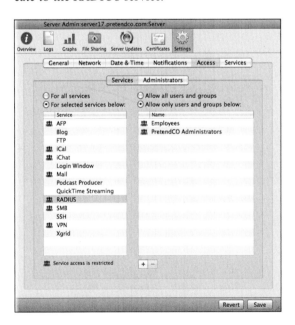

3   To connect wirelessly on a client machine:

▶   Choose the base station from the AirPort menu and choose WPA2 Enterprise from the pop-up menu.

▶   Fill in the correct user name and password corresponding to Open Directory.

▶   Choose the correct certificate generated by the server.

▶   Click Join to make the connection.

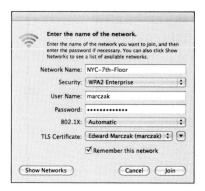

Remember that the user name and password supplied are the user's Open Directory credentials. The shared secret is not a password for authentication, nor does it generate encryption keys to establish secure tunnels between nodes. It is a token that the key management systems use to trust each other. The shared secret must be entered on the server or a base station, but not on an end-user computer.

Using RADIUS Configuration and Log Files

The RADIUS service relies on a directory of configuration files. It also logs its activity to two log files. The RADIUS service is built entirely on the open source FreeRADIUS project and uses the same configuration files and log files.

As an addition to the FreeRADIUS project, Apple created the modules necessary to authenticate via Open Directory. This fact distinguishes the FreeRADIUS version supplied by Apple from a stock FreeRADIUS download.

The first important file is the launchd plist file. The RADIUS service is started and managed by launchd, which uses the /System/Library/LaunchDaemons/org.freeradius.radiusd.plist file.

The RADIUS service depends on several files for its runtime configuration, all of which are stored in /etc/raddb.

RADIUS service logging occurs in two places:

▶ /Library/Logs/radiusconfig.log records configuration changes, such as adding or removing a device.

▶ /var/log/radius/radius.log documents regular activity.

For more information, see the man page for radiusd. (For information on using man pages, see "Getting Help" in Chapter 9, "Automating Systems.")

Troubleshooting

Both the firewall and RADIUS services discussed in this chapter require little setup or in-depth knowledge. Of course, this workhorse quality makes it a little more complicated when things do not run as expected, especially with the firewall service.

The firewall service requires planning. You should make one change at a time and ensure that it has the intended effect. Too many changes at once make it difficult to locate the source of a problem. Documenting changes is key. If there are several administrators who can make changes to the firewall rules, it is imperative that each be kept current with the actions of others.

If rules look like they should be working, but they are not, and time is not an issue, a packet sniffer will allow you to view the problem from the inside. Mac OS X ships with the popular open source tcpdump packet sniffer. tcpdump can print information in real time for a quick determination, or it can write its dump to a file for later, offline analysis. To dump all packets passing through the en0 interface to stdout, use the following commands:

```
# tcpdump -i en0
tcpdump: verbose output suppressed, use -v or -vv for full protocol decode
listening on en0, link-type EN10MB (Ethernet), capture size 96 bytes
06:42:37.514597 IP server.example.com.ssh > 72.14.228.89.11667: P
3011092458:3011092650(192) ack 3151495640 win 33312 <nop,nop,timestamp 1488505430
575729407>
```

```
06:42:37.523288 IP 72.14.228.89.11667 > server.example.com.ssh: .
ack 0 win 65535 <nop,nop,timestamp 575729408 1488505364>
06:42:37.589744 IP 72.14.228.89.11667 > server.example.com.ssh: .
ack 192 win 65535 <nop,nop,timestamp 575729409 1488505430>
06:42:37.637216 IP comproxy2.example.net.53730 > 192.168.1.1.9090:
UDP, length 74
06:42:37.760644 arp who-has 192-168-232-92.in-
addr.arpa.example.com tell 192-168-232-1.in-addr.arpa.example.com
06:42:38.137423 IP comproxy2.example.net.53730 > 192.168.1.1.9090:
UDP, length 74
06:42:38.320315 arp who-has 69-55-228-118.in-
addr.arpa.johncompanies.com tell 69-55-228-1.in-
addr.arpa.johncompanies.com
^C
316 packets captured
349 packets received by filter
0 packets dropped by kernel
```

Press Control-C to stop the capture. Each line displays the time that the packet was received, the protocol, the source of the packet, its destination, and, optionally, any set flags. To limit the tcpdump capture to a specific IP address, specify the host in the tcpdump command:

```
# tcpdump -i en0 host 192.168.55.72
```

Perhaps even more useful when troubleshooting a firewall problem is limiting the capture to a specific port—port 80 in this example:

```
# tcpdump -i en0 port 80
```

You can also negate a filter with the not keyword. For example, if you are troubleshooting remotely via Secure Shell (SSH), the SSH traffic that makes up your session is typically noise. Furthermore, you can combine filters with the and conditional. The following command listens for all traffic from the host at 192.168.55.8, but filters out traffic on port 22:

```
# tcpdump -i en0 host 192.168.55.8 not port 22
```

Sometimes, analyzing tcpdump on the fly is not enough. For deeper analysis, you can write dumps to a file and analyze them offline with a more powerful program, such as the open source Wireshark. For deeper analysis, you can also increase the size of the packet capture. By default, tcpdump captures only the first 96 bytes of each packet. For a deeper look, you should capture the entire packet. To capture all traffic of unlimited packet size and write it to a file, you can use the -s (size) and -w (write) switches:

```
# tcpdump -i en0 -s0 -w server_trace.pcap
```

The -s0 ("ess zero") designates unlimited packet size, and the -w switch in this example writes all capture data to the file server_trace.pcap. In most cases, all that you are looking for on a server is any activity getting through the firewall, or to the local interface. The more detailed traces are typically more helpful from the client side. In a worst-case scenario, you can document and back up the current firewall rule set, and then flush the current rules entirely. Then you can add half of the rules back in at a time, starting the firewall service each time that you introduce a new set of rules. Incrementally adding back rules will make it easier to determine which rule is causing the undesired behavior.

When working remotely with the firewall service, it is critical that you make available another way to enter the system, or configure a "dead-man's switch" that disables the firewall after a period of time. An example of an alternate path would be a secondary interface—physical or virtual—that is not affected by the firewall or has different rules applied. This alternate can include a virtual private network (VPN) interface. A dead-man's switch can be as simple as one line. The following line waits 90 seconds, and then stops the firewall completely, ensuring that access is unrestricted:

```
# sleep 90; sudo serveradmin stop ipfilter
```

This tactic can be useful when making a potentially access-stopping change.

If you become completely lost with the firewall configuration, you may want to back it up and start from scratch. For instructions on resetting the firewall to default values, see "Resetting the Firewall to the Default Setting" in the Apple Network Services Administration document at: http://images.apple.com/server/macosx/docs/Network_Services_Admin_v10.5_2nd_Ed.pdf.

The RADIUS service depends on both certificates and a shared secret (essentially a password or passphrase). If only certain devices are not working as expected, double-check their shared secret. You can easily reset the device and re-add it, if necessary. If the problem is more widespread, check the certificate being handed out. Did it expire or become corrupted? You can manage certificates in Server Admin by choosing the server and clicking the Certificates tab. Finally, RADIUS depends on these default ports for communication:

▶ Port 1812—RADIUS

▶ Port 1813—RADIUS Accounting

If these ports are blocked between any RADIUS device and the server, authentication at that device will not be possible. Note that the ports are configurable by changing the appropriate value in the /etc/raddb/radiusd.conf file.

For both firewall and RADIUS services, if the issue seems to be service-level, first check the log files. (For the location of log files, see "Using Firewall Log Files" and "Using RADIUS Configuration and Log Files" in this chapter. The Application Level Firewall logs its activity at /var/log/alf.log; see "Configuring Firewall Files.") Increase logging levels when necessary. You can change these levels with the graphical user interface, or, in some cases, via the command line. The RADIUS service can log useful extra information with the following directives:

```
# radiusconfig -setconfig log_auth yes
# radiusconfig -setconfig log_auth_goodpass yes
# radiusconfig -setconfig log_auth_badpass yes
```

Good server backup is critical. Most of the configuration files reside somewhere in the /etc hierarchy. Simply by practicing good backup habits, these key files will be preserved, and can be restored if needed. (For more on key configuration files, see "Configuring Firewall Files" and "Using RADIUS Configuration and Log Files" in this chapter.)

What You've Learned

This chapter discusses two network-level methods of protecting and controlling access to resources. You have learned the following:

▶ Mac OS X and Mac OS X Server contain a built-in stateful packet firewall that keeps track of the state of network connections traveling across it. The packet firewall is based on the open source `ipfw` project.

▶ Mac OS X Server runs a service called `emond` that monitors bad login attempts. Ten consecutive incorrect login attempts cause `emond` to use the Adaptive Firewall to inject a rule into `ipfw`, blocking it entirely for 15 minutes.

▶ The Mac OS X Server packet firewall uses rules to make decisions on which packets to allow or deny. You can modify these rules using the Server Admin.app graphical user interface, or the `ipfw` command-line tool. `ipfw` logs its messages in /var/log/ipfw.log.

▶ The RADIUS service in Mac OS X provides network-level authorization and accounting. RADIUS is based on the open source FreeRADIUS. Apple has provided the ability to allow FreeRADIUS to authenticate accounts in Open Directory.

▶ Mac OS X contains an Application Level Firewall. Unlike a traditional stateful firewall, Application Level Firewall grants or denies access to specific applications.

▶ `tcpdump` is an excellent utility to use when troubleshooting a service that is not connecting and a firewall is a suspected reason.

Review Quiz

1. What is the stateful firewall that is built into Mac OS X and Mac OS X Server?

2. When enabling the default set of firewall rules in Mac OS X Server, which traffic is allowed?

3. What is the primary way the Mac OS X Application Level Firewall differs from `ipfw`?

4. Why is `tcpdump` such a good utility for troubleshooting the firewall configuration?

5. When using the RADIUS service, how can use of wireless base stations be restricted to a certain group of users?

Answers

1. The IP Firewall, `ipfw`, is the stateful firewall built into Mac OS X and Mac OS X Server.

2. By default, all traffic is allowed out, and only Apple administrative ports and established traffic is allowed in.

3. The Application Level Firewall uses the application generating or receiving traffic in the decision-making process about which traffic to let through. `ipfw` strictly uses ports, not knowing which application is behind the traffic.

4. When used on the server side, `tcpdump` enables you to see whether traffic is making it past the firewall and arriving at the application layer. On a client, it lets you know whether traffic is being generated and accepted on the remote end.

5. Use Server Admin to apply a system access control list (SACL) to the RADIUS service.

Part 3   Administration

7

Time   This lesson takes approximately 60 minutes to complete.

Goals   Learn the different classifications of accounts in Mac OS X

Learn how to disable hardware via altering drivers

Learn about public key encryption

Learn how to work with digital certificates

Learn how to grant additional privileges using the authorization database

Learn to alter file system permissions via POSIX permissions, flags, and ACLs

Chapter 7

Securing Access to Resources

To provide deep protection, Mac OS X Server security is built on layers of defense. Various methods safeguard the system by authorizing whether a user or computer has the right to perform a restricted operation, and authenticating (that is, verifying) the identity of an account or service. These system-level methods of security complement the network-level methods discussed in Chapter 6, "Controlling Access to Resources."

Features for securing access to resources exist at all system levels, from hardware and the operating system to services and networks. Several subsystems, such as services that are running and the file system, comprise system-level methods and offer additional ways to control end users.

These various system-level security methods include the following:

▶ Hardware—A firmware password (also known as an *OpenFirmware* password) application helps prevent people who access your hardware from gaining root-level access to your computer files.

▶ Secure authentication protocols—Kerberos and public-key encryption secure the authentication process.

▶ Secure networking—A firewall, along with digital certificates and encryption, help protect resources and communication.

▶ Secure applications—Encryption in Keychain and FileVault helps prevent intruders from using your applications and viewing data on your computer.

▶ Operating system—Portable Operating System Interface (POSIX) permissions and access control lists (ACLs) help secure access to files.

About Authentication and Authorization

Authentication and authorization, while similar, handle two separate aspects of the security model.

Authentication is the process of verifying the identity of an account or service. You are accustomed to authenticating at the login window when the computer first boots. Sometimes, though, applications and operating system components carry out their own authentication. An account is authorized in some manner using *credentials*—most commonly, a user name and password pair. However, there are other methods for authenticating accounts, including digital keys and two-factor authentication, such as using "smart cards." This book covers only passwords and keys. For information on two-factor authentication and Mac OS X–compatible solutions, see http://www.cryptocard.com.

Authorization is the process by which an entity, such as a user or a computer, obtains the right to perform a restricted operation. Authorization can also refer to the right itself, for example, an account authorized to run a certain program. Authorization typically involves first authenticating the entity and then determining its permissions.

About Mac OS X Accounts

Each object and action in Mac OS X takes place in the context of an account. Mac OS X has four types of accounts, as follows:

▶ Standard users have full permission over their own home directory, but are restricted from the rest of the system. They have read-write access to files that they place in /Users/Shared and /tmp.

▶ Admin users can configure the OS, and have broader access to system directories, such as /Applications. Admin users can override most limitations on the system, and have near-complete control. Only trusted users should be granted admin-level privileges.

▶ There is only one root user, and it is not constrained by many of the normal limitations in Mac OS X. The root account is not prompted or initially restrained by the hurdles placed in front of admin-level users. See "Enabling and Disabling the Root Account" in the following section for more information.

▶ A system account is used by services rather than end users in Mac OS X, which requires that all actions be associated with an account. A system account is not a full account with a home folder or login password. It is preinstalled by Apple, or created by the software that requires it.

Enabling and Disabling the Root Account

For security considerations, the root account is disabled in Mac OS X. In contrast, Mac OS X Server keeps root enabled by default. On either platform, root can be enabled or disabled. You can use the dsenableroot command to enable or disable the root account. An admin-level user simply needs to run the command and answer the prompted questions when asked:

```
$ dsenableroot
username = marczak
user password:
root password:
verify root password:
dsenableroot:: ***Successfully enabled root user.
```

The password for the root account will be set to the password supplied. You can set the -d switch to disable the root account:

```
$ dsenableroot -d
username = marczak
user password:
dsenableroot:: ***Successfully disabled root user.
```

Mac OS X Server uses the root account while creating an Open Directory replica. If disabled in OS X Server, root must be re-enabled during the replica creation process. Once the replica is created, root can be disabled.

Protecting Hardware

Protecting hardware is as important, if not more so, than each of the other security methods described in this chapter. Sadly, protecting hardware is often an afterthought. Servers act as a central repository for large amounts of data, making them, or more specifically their storage, desirable targets. High-profile news stories have highlighted the plight of companies that do not protect their mobile devices, such as laptops, while out of the office.

If someone can physically access a computer, it can always be compromised. Given physical access, unauthorized users can install malicious software or various event-tracking and data-capturing services.

To protect hardware, use as many layers of physical protection as possible:

▶ Restrict access to rooms containing computers that store or access sensitive information. Provide room access only to individuals who must use those computers. If possible, lock the computer in a secure container when it is not in use, or bolt or fasten it to a wall or piece of furniture.

▶ Take special care with storage units—hard drives, tapes, USB Flash drives, and so on. Lock or secure this hardware. If users can install your storage device on another system, they can bypass any safeguards that you have set up. If you cannot guarantee the physical security of a storage device, consider using encryption: FileVault for home folders, or encrypted disk images for other data.

▶ If you have a mobile device, keep it secure. Lock it up or hide it when it is not in use. When in transit, never leave it in an insecure location.

► Consider buying an attaché case or computer bag with a locking mechanism, and lock the equipment in when you are not using it.

► Be aware that a computer left unattended and logged in can be a security risk. To protect your computers from being used when on and unattended, enable a password-protected screen saver.

Disabling Hardware

If your company policy requires it, hardware components such as wireless features and microphones can be physically disabled (but only by an Apple Certified Technician). Physically disabling hardware may not be practical in all circumstances.

You can also disable hardware by removing the software driver, because the operating system interfaces with hardware via kernel extensions (.kext files). Removing kernel extensions does not permanently disable the components, and you will need administrative access to restore and reload them. Disabling hardware by removing the software driver is not as secure as physically disabling the hardware, but is more secure than disabling it through system preferences.

Kernel extensions are stored in /System/Library/Extensions. You can disable the following hardware by removing or *stubbing* the listed extensions:

AirPort:

► AppleAirPort.kext

► AppleAirPort2.kext

► AppleAirPortFW.kext

Bluetooth:

► IOBluetoothFamily.kext

► IOBluetoothHIDDriver.kext

Audio:

► AppleOnboardAudio.kext

► AppleUSBAudio.kext

► AudioDeviceTreeUpdater.kext

▶ IOAudioFamily.kext

▶ VirtualAudioDriver.kext

External iSight camera:

▶ AppleUSBVideoSupport.kext

▶ Apple_iSight.kext

External mass storage devices:

▶ IOUSBMassStorageClass.kext

▶ IOFireWireSerialBusProtocolTransport.kext

Simply dragging these files to the Trash will suffice to remove the extension. Even more secure is to provide stubs for these files (empty files with the same name as the folder being replaced) and to lock them, which will prevent future updates from adding newer versions back. If you have trashed a file, remember to trash it again after applying any system update. In either case, you should also remove the contents of the Cache directory and immediately restart the system.

Xserve hardware also has the ability to lock FireWire and USB ports. The physical key on the front panel engages and disengages this lock. However, keyboard and mouse devices can be excepted in software, using the toggle in the Security Preference pane of the Xserve.

Using Hardware Passwords

Any Leopard-compatible Macintosh is capable of setting a hardware password, using OpenFirmware for PowerPCs or Extensible Firmware Interface (EFI) for Intel-based machines. When enabled, hardware password protection blocks the ability to do the following:

▶ Use the C key to start up from an optical disc.

▶ Use the N key to start up from a NetBoot server.

▶ Use the T key to start up in Target Disk Mode (on computers that offer this feature).

▶ Use the D key to start up from the Diagnostic volume of the Install DVD (Intel only).

▶ Start up a system in single-user mode by pressing the Command-S key combination during startup.

▶ Reset the parameter RAM (PRAM) by pressing the Command-Option-P-R key combination during startup.

▶ Start up in verbose mode by pressing the Command-V key combination during startup.

▶ Start up in Safe Boot mode by pressing the Shift key during startup.

In addition, hardware password protection requires the password to use the Startup Manager, accessed by pressing the Option key during startup.

To enable a hardware password, start from the Leopard installation DVD and choose Utilities > Firmware Password Utility. Select the option to "Require password to change Open Firmware settings"; then type and verify the password, and click OK.

You can disable a forgotten hardware password by powering down the hardware, changing the RAM configuration (for example, removing 2 GB from a 4 GB machine), and rebooting. This procedure works for all Macintosh machines except the first-generation MacBook Air, which contains no user-serviceable RAM (the chips are soldered to the motherboard). If you forget a hardware password for a MacBook Air, contact your local Apple authorized service center.

Authenticating Accounts

Authentication is the process of identifying an account or service, and verifying its right to perform a restricted operation. Mac OS X uses several different methods of authentication, along with separate subsystems. All system utilities tie into directory services to verify credentials.

For example, imagine a server with Open Directory accounts and a FileMaker Pro server for custom databases. Users can authenticate to Application Level Firewall and Secure Shell (SSH) using their Open Directory credentials; however, accessing FileMaker Pro databases will require an entirely different set of credentials. Even if user names are kept the same between systems, each technically has two separate sets of credentials.

Using sudo

Many traditional UNIX administrators are accustomed to logging in as and working with a root account. However, Mac OS X administrators are discouraged from doing so, because root can bypass normal access restrictions in most cases. Root is normally disabled in

Mac OS X, but it is still possible to effectively authenticate as a root-level account without using the actual root account. The sudo tool allows granting rights to users and groups to run programs that they may not have access to otherwise. Using sudo, you can grant a user the ability to run one specific program with root privileges, all the way up through gaining a root-level shell to work in.

sudo uses the /etc/sudoers file as a configuration file to determine which accounts can gain elevated privileges. You should always use the visudo program to edit the sudoers file, because the program performs locking and syntax checks upon saving. The general format of sudoers is formulaic. Following is an example of a typical entry in the sudoers file:

```
%itops                  ALL = /bin/mkdir, /bin/chmod, /bin/chown
```

The percent sign (%) indicates that the rule applies to a group (in this case, itops). The ALL designation refers to a machine group, checked by host name. In this case, the group is allowed regardless of the machine name ("all machines"). Finally, the entry specifies the commands that this group can use with the sudo command, to run with root-level privileges. As a member of the itops group, you could create a new directory in a protected area by using sudo and supplying the account password:

```
$ sudo mkdir /usr/sbin/extras
```

See the sudoers man page for more ways of granting rights with sudo; for instructions on using man pages, see "Getting Help" in Chapter 9.

Setting Password Policies

Open Directory supports several password policy rules. These are available globally in Server Admin or per user in Workgroup Manager. You can also set the policy on the command line using the pwpolicy tool.

To view the current policy settings, use the -getGlobalPolicy flag:

```
$ pwpolicy -getglobalpolicy
```

You may find the settings easier to read if you run them through tr:

```
$ pwpolicy -getglobalpolicy | tr ' ' '\n'
```

This converts spaces to new lines and lists each policy on its own line.

pwpolicy lists each policy. To change a policy, use the -setGlobalPolicy switch with a space-delimited list of policies to set. For example, to set the minimum number of characters for a password and disallow the password from matching a user ID, you would issue the following command:

```
$ pwpolicy -a diradmin -n /LDAPv3/127.0.0.1 -setglobalpolicy "minChars=6
passwordCannotBeName=1"
```

This command will enact policies against a server's Open Directory (LDAP) database. The -n switch specifies the node to operate on. You will also need to authenticate as a directory administrator (in this example, diradmin).

Using PAM

A pluggable authentication module (PAM) is a mechanism that originated on the Linux platform. Apple has ported PAM to Mac OS X because Mac OS X uses several open source applications that rely on PAM for authentication. PAM uses *libraries* and *modules* that describe which credentials are allowed and valid for a particular service. Of special importance are the Apple-specific authentication methods that Apple has added to its implementation of PAM, which allow PAM to authenticate accounts stored in Open Directory.

PAM service definitions are stored as a configuration file or files in /etc/pam.d. These configuration files define the connection between applications (services) and the pluggable authentication modules that perform the actual authentication tasks. When a PAM-aware privilege-granting application starts, it activates its attachment to the PAM application programming interface (API). This activation performs numerous tasks—most importantly, reading the configuration files in the /etc/pam.d/ directory. These configuration files list which PAMs will do the authentication tasks required by this service, and how the PAM API should behave if individual PAMs fail.

PAM Management Groups

PAM separates the tasks of authentication into four independent management groups: account, authentication, password, and session. These management groups carry out different aspects of a typical user's request for a restricted service:

▶ account provides account verification types of service: Has the user's password expired? Is this user permitted access to the requested service?

▶ `authentication` establishes that the user is who they claim to be. Typically, this is via some challenge-response request that the user must satisfy, such as, "If you are who you claim to be, please enter your password." In place of standard approaches to authentication, you can give PAM greater flexibility by substituting one of the many ways to prove identity, such as the use of smart cards and biometric devices, for passwords.

▶ `password` updates authentication mechanisms, such as standard UNIX password-passed access.

▶ `session` covers tasks that should be done prior to a service being granted and after it is withdrawn. Examples include maintaining audit trails and unmounting the user home directory. These tasks provide both an opening and closing hook for modules to affect the services available to a user.

One service of particular significance that relies on PAM is SSH. The configuration file that PAM uses is/etc/pam.d/sshd. The contents of a sample configuration file are as follows:

```
# sshd: auth account password session
auth      required    pam_nologin.so
auth      optional    pam_afpmount.so
auth      sufficient  pam_securityserver.so
auth      sufficient  pam_unix.so
auth      required    pam_deny.so
account   required    pam_securityserver.so
password  required    pam_deny.so
session   required    pam_launchd.so
session   optional    pam_afpmount.so
```

PAM Rules
Each line of the preceding sample code represents a *rule* for PAM to follow when authenticating a user for this service. The contents of each line are broken down into the following fields:

▶ Type is the management group to which a rule corresponds. It is used to specify with which of the management groups the module is to be associated. Valid entries are `account`, `auth`, `password`, and `session`, as described in the earlier section, "PAM Management Groups."

▶ Control specifies the behavior of the PAM API if the module fails to authenticate. Valid control values are as follows:

requisite: Failure of the PAM module results in the authentication process immediately being terminated.

required: Failure of the PAM module ultimately causes the PAM API to return failure, but only after the remaining modules have been invoked.

sufficient: Success of the PAM module satisfies the authentication requirements of the stack of modules. (If a prior required module has failed, the success of this one is ignored.)

optional: The success or failure of this module is important only if it is the only module in the stack associated with this service and type.

▶ module-path: Either the full filename of the PAM to be used by the application (if it begins with a /), or a relative pathname from the default module location of /usr/lib/pam/. You can also supply modules, on a per-module basis, with arguments to influence their behavior.

Using SSH and Digital Key Pairs

SSH is a valuable tool, used to access a shell on a remote machine. The SSH shell is designated "secure" because all network traffic between the client station and the SSH server is encrypted, which stops eavesdroppers on the network from capturing traffic and reading its contents. SSH can use passwords and Kerberos for authentication, as well as a form of public-key encryption that calls for *key pairs*.

Key-pair authentication enables you to log in to an SSH server without having to supply a password, and can be more secure than password authentication. The key-pair method requires that you have the private-key file and know the password that lets you access that key file. Password authentication alone can be compromised without needing a private-key file.

> **NOTE** ▶ Don't confuse key-pair authentication with Kerberos authentication, which takes place for the SSH service if you are using an Open Directory user account and have already logged in. A valid Kerberos ticket also will let you log in without supplying a password.

Here is how the process works:

1   A private and a public key are generated by the user (see "Generating a Key Pair" in this chapter). Each key pair is associated with a user name to establish that user's authenticity. When a user attempts to log in, the user name is sent to the remote computer.

2   The remote computer is sent the user's public key by the client SSH program.

3   A challenge is then sent by the SSH server to the user based on that individual's public key.

4   Using the private portion of the key pair to decode the challenge, the user verifies his or her identity.

5   Once the challenge is decoded, the remote computer logs in the user without requiring a password.

Generating a Key Pair

To generate the identity key pair, use the ssh-keygen command on the local computer:

```
$ ssh-keygen -t dsa
```

When prompted, enter a filename to save the keys in. By default, the public and private key files will be stored in the user home directory, inside the .ssh subdirectory. Enter a password followed by password verification (empty for no password). A sample session looks like this:

```
Generating public/private dsa key pair.
Enter file in which to save the key (/Users/Alice/.ssh/id_dsa): frog
Enter passphrase (empty for no passphrase):
Enter same passphrase again:
Your identification has been saved in frog.
Your public key has been saved in frog.pub.
The key fingerprint is:
2a:3c:6a:9d:3d:37:8b:e5:c9:5a:ad:00:b5:b6:a7:56 user@example.com
```

The key-pair process creates two files. Your *identification* or *private key* is saved in one file (~/.ssh/id_dsa) and your public key is saved in the other (~/.ssh/id_dsa.pub). The key *fingerprint*, which is derived cryptographically from the public key value, is also displayed. This secures the public key, making it difficult to duplicate.

> **NOTE** ▶ A server's SSH key is /etc/ssh_host_key.pub. Back up this key in case you need to reinstall your server software. Once your server software is reinstalled, you can retain the server identity by putting the key back in its folder.

Append a copy of the contents of the resulting public key to the .ssh/authorized_keys file in the user's home folder on the remote computer. The next time you log in to the remote computer from the local computer, you will not need to enter a password.

The /etc/ssh/sshd_config file that configures an SSH server's behavior has two parameters relating to handling authentication. The `PubkeyAuthentication` parameter can be set to yes or no to allow or disallow the use of public keys, respectively. To disallow passwords and only use public-key authentication, set the `PasswordAuthentication` to no.

Updating SSH Key Fingerprints

The first time you connect to a remote computer using SSH, the local computer prompts for permission to add the remote computer's fingerprint to the user's ~/.ssh/known_hosts file. A message like this appears:

```
The authenticity of host "server1.pretendco.com" can't be established.
RSA key fingerprint is f8:0e:37:53:74:f1:dd:cd:5a:a4:1d:b3:57:a9:a6.
Are you sure you want to continue connecting (yes/no)?
```

The first time you connect, you have no way of knowing if this is the correct host key. Most people simply respond "yes." The host key is then inserted into the ~/.ssh/known_hosts file for comparison in later sessions. Make sure that this is the correct key before accepting it. If at all possible, distribute the host key either through Secure FTP (SFTP), encrypted email, downloading, or personally, so that users can be sure of the identity of the server.

When you try to connect later, a warning message may appear about a man-in-the-middle attack (a third computer that sits in between the client and server and captures all SSH traffic), possibly because the key on the remote computer no longer matches the key stored on the local computer. Mismatched keys can occur in these circumstances:

▶   The SSH configuration on either the local or remote computer is changed.

▶   The server has been reinstalled.

▶   The remote machine has changed its IP address since the last time you connected. The IP address can change on networks using Bonjour names and DHCP.

To connect again, first figure out why the key on the remote computer has changed. Then delete the entries corresponding to the remote computer that you are accessing (which can be stored by both name and IP address) from the ~/.ssh/known_hosts file. Be aware, however, that removing an entry from the known_hosts file bypasses a security mechanism that would help you thwart imposters and man-in-the-middle attacks.

Using Certificates for Authentication

Like digital key pairs, digital certificates are another form of public-key encryption, and another method of authenticating a user.

Mac OS X Server supports many services that ensure encrypted transfer of data, which is facilitated by certificates. To generate and maintain certificates of identity, Mac OS X Server uses a Public Key Infrastructure (PKI) system. PKI allows two parties in a data transaction to be authenticated to each other, and to use encryption keys and other information in identity certificates to encrypt and decrypt messages traveling between them. You can think of certificates almost like a driver's license. When you are asked to show identification, others believe the information presented on your driver's license because the Department of Motor Vehicles (DMV) has certified it. If you make your own license, it would be viewed as suspect. The DMV in this example plays the role of a public certificate authority (CA) in a digital certification infrastructure.

To encrypt data transmission for mail, web, directory, and other services, Mac OS X Server uses Transport Layer Security (TLS) technology. TLS technology relies on a PKI system for secure data transmission and user authentication. It creates an initial secure communication to negotiate a faster, secret key transmission. TLS is the successor to SSL and remains similar in implementation. It is common to see references to SSL/TLS, denoting the similarity.

Before you can use SSL in the Mac OS X Server services, you must create or import the certificates—easily done with Server Admin. You can create your own self-signed certificate, generate a Certificate Signing Request (CSR) to send to a CA, or import a certificate previously created with OpenSSL. Each installation of Mac OS X Server v10.5 also includes a unique, self-signed certificate.

Server Admin has various features that make it easy to manage SSL certificates: Certificate Manager, for creating, using, and maintaining identities for SSL-enabled services; and the Certificate Assistant application, which allows you to issue and sign certificates as a CA.

About Public Key Infrastructure

It's helpful to understand how PKI works as well as the terminology it uses.

Public and Private Keys

Within PKI, two digital keys are created: the public key and the private key. These keys are mathematically linked in such a way that data encrypted with one key can only be decrypted by the other, and vice versa. The public key can (and should) be distributed to other communicating parties. In contrast, the private key is just that: private to the owner and not meant to be distributed to anyone. It is often encrypted by a passphrase.

Table 7-1 summarizes the capabilities of public and private keys.

Table 7-1   Comparision of Capabilities of Private and Public Keys

Public Keys Can	Private Keys Can
Verify the signature on a message coming from a private key.	Digitally sign a message or certificate, claiming authenticity.
	Decrypt messages that were encrypted with the public key.
Encrypt messages that can only be decrypted by the holder of the corresponding private key.	Encrypt messages that can only be decrypted by the corresponding private key.

As an example, if a user named Bob distributes his public key, user Alice could use it to encrypt a message and send it to him. Only Bob is able to decrypt and read the message because only he has his private key. In this scenario, Alice still has to verify that the key that is supposedly from Bob is really from him. Suppose a malicious user posing as Bob sent Alice his own public key. The malicious user would then be able to decrypt Alice's message, which might have been intended for Bob only.

To verify that it's really Bob who is sending Alice his public key, a trusted third party can verify the authenticity of Bob's public key. In SSL parlance, this trusted third party is known as a certificate authority. The CA signs Bob's public key with *its* private key, creating a certificate. Now, anyone can verify the certificate's authenticity using the CA's public key.

Public Key Certificates

Public keys are often contained in certificates. A user can digitally sign messages using his or her private key, and another user can verify the signature using the public key contained in the signer's certificate, which was issued by a CA within the PKI.

A public key certificate (sometimes called an *identity certificate*) is a file in a specified format (Mac OS X Server uses the x.509 format) that contains the following:

▶ The public-key half of a public-private key pair.

▶ The key user's identity information, such as a person's user name and contact information.

▶ A validity period (how long the certificate can be trusted to be accurate).

▶ The URL of someone with the power to revoke the certificate (its "revocation center").

▶ The digital signature of either a CA or the key user.

Certificate Authorities (CAs)

A CA is an entity that signs and issues digital identity certificates claiming trust of the identified party. In this sense, it is a trusted third party between two transactions.

In x.509 systems, CAs are hierarchical in nature, with CAs being certified by CAs, until you reach a "root authority." The hierarchy of certificates is always top-down, with a root authority's certificate at the top. A root authority is a CA that is trusted by enough or all of the interested parties, so that it does not need to be authenticated by yet another trusted third party.

A CA can be a company that, for a fee, signs and issues a public-key certificate stating that the CA attests that the public key contained in the certificate belongs to its owner, as recorded in the certificate. In a sense, a CA is a digital notary public. A user applies to the CA for a certificate by providing identity and contact information, as well as the public key. A CA must check an applicant's identity, so that users can trust certificates issued by that CA to belong to the identified applicant.

Identities

Identities, in the context of the Mac OS X Server Certificate Manager, are the combination of a signed certificate for both keys of a PKI key pair. The system keychain makes identities available to the various services that support SSL.

Self-signed certificates are certificates that are digitally signed by the private key of the key pair included in the certificate. Each installation of Mac OS X Server v10.5 includes a unique, self-signed certificate. This is done in place of a CA signing the certificate.

By self-signing a certificate, you are attesting that you are who you say you are. No trusted third party is involved.

Using Certificate Manager

Server Admin features Certificate Manager to help you create, use, and maintain identities for SSL-enabled services. Certificate Manager integrates management of SSL certificates in Mac OS X Server for all services that allow their use.

Certificate Manager allows creation of self-signed certificates and CSRs to obtain a certificate signed by a CA. The certificates, either self-signed or signed by a CA, are accessible by the services that support SSL.

Identities that were previously created and stored in SSL files can also be imported into Certificate Manager, where they are accessible to all the services that support SSL. Certificates are stored in the system keychain, located at /Library/Keychains/System.keychain.

Certificate Manager displays the following for each certificate:

▶   The domain name for which the certificate was issued.

▶   Its dates of validity.

▶   Its signing authority, such as the CA entity. If the certificate is self-signed, it reads "Self-Signed."

Certificate Manager in Server Admin does not allow you to sign and issue certificates as a CA, nor as a root authority. However, you can perform these functions with Certificate Assistant; see "Creating a CA Using Certificate Assistant" later in this chapter.

Requesting a Certificate from a Certificate Authority

Certificate Manager helps you create a CSR to send to your designated CA. To request a signed certificate:

1   Open Server Admin.

2   In the Server list, select the server for which you are requesting a certificate.

3   Click Certificates.

4   Click the Add (+) button.

5   Fill out all identity information.

6   Click the Done button.

7   Follow the onscreen directions for requesting a signed certificate from your chosen CA.

8   Click Done.

9   Click the preferences Gear button and choose Generate Certificate Signing Request (CSR). When the CA replies to the email, it includes the signed certificate in the email text.

10   Click the preferences Gear button and choose Add Signed Certificate.

11   From your CA certificate email, copy the characters from ==Begin CSR== to ==End CSR== into the text box. Then click OK.

12   Click Save.

Creating Self-Signed Certificates

Whenever you create an identity in Certificate Manager, you also create a self-signed certificate. First you specify the key size (512 to 2048 bits), and Certificate Manager creates a public-private key pair at the specified key size in the system keychain, as well as the corresponding self-signed certificate.

At the same time that Certificate Manager creates the self-signed certificate, it generates the CSR. The CSR is not stored in the keychain, but is written to disk at /etc/certificates/ cert.common.name.tld.csr, where `common.name.tld` is the Common Name of the certificate that was issued.

To create a self-signed certificate, follow steps 1 through 11 of the procedure in "Requesting a Certificate from a Certificate Authority"; in Step 12, save the request to the CA.

Importing Certificates

In Certificate Manager, you cannot create self-signed and CA-issued certificates, but you can import previously generated SSL certificates and private keys. The items are stored in the list of identities and are available to SSL-enabled services.

Follow these steps to import an existing SSL certificate:

1   Open Server Admin.

2   In the server list, select the server into which you are importing a certificate.

3   Click Certificates.

4   Click the preferences Gear button and choose Import Certificate.

5   In the Certificate File field, enter the existing certificate's filename and path. Alternatively, click Browse and locate your certificate file.

6   In the Private Key File field, enter the existing private key filename and path. Alternatively, click Browse and locate your private key file.

7   In the Certificate Authority File field, enter the existing certificate authority filename and path. Alternatively, click Browse and locate your certificate authority file.

8   Enter the private key passphrase.

9   Click Import.

Modifying Certificates

After a certificate is created and signed, you should not have to do much more with it. Certificates are editable only in Server Admin. Only self-signed certificates can be changed; CA-signed certificates cannot be changed. Certificates should be deleted if they have expired, if their contents (such as contact information) are no longer correct, or if you believe the key pair has been compromised in some way.

You can modify all the fields of a self-signed certificate, including domain name, private key passphrase, private key size, and so on. If the identity was exported to disk from the system keychain, it must be exported again after editing.

Follow these steps to edit a certificate:

1   Open Server Admin.

2   In the Computers & Services list, select the server with the certificate you are editing.

3   Click Certificates.

4   Select the Certificate Identity to edit. You can edit only self-signed certificates.

5   Click the Edit button.

6   Modify the certificate settings.

7   Click Save.

Follow these steps to delete a certificate:

1   Open Server Admin.

2   In the Computers & Services list, select the server with the certificate you are deleting.

3   Click Certificates.

4   Select the Certificate Identity to delete.

5   Click the Delete (–) button to delete the certificate.

6   Click Save.

Configuring Certificates via the Command Line

To modify certificates via the command line, you have several choices in command-line utilities. Because certificates are stored in keychains, keychain manipulation utilities such as security and systemkeychain can manipulate certificates as well as other keychain entries. Also, certtool exists as a certificate-specific utility that manipulates keychains to import certificates, create key pairs, create certificates, and create CSRs.

The security tool is capable of importing, exporting, and verifying certificates in keychains. Additionally, it can add certificates to the list of trusted certificates. For example, to import a Privacy Enhanced Mail (PEM) certificate into the current user's default keychain, use the security import command:

```
$ security import ~/mailcert.pem -f pem
```

The systemkeychain command only manipulates the system keychain. This is significant because system certificates are stored in the active system keychain. For example, to create a new, empty keychain and establish it as the primary system keychain, the following command can be issued:

```
# systemkeychain -C
```

The unlocking of the designated system keychain is automatically handled by the system. If a password is specified after the -C switch, the keychain can be unlocked with that password; otherwise, the keychain has no password and can only be unlocked by the system.

The certtool is often used to import certificates into a keychain—either a user keychain or system keychain. For example, to import the certificate certificate.pem into the current user's mycerts keychain file, use the following command:

```
$ certtool i certificate.pem k=~/Library/Keychains/mycerts c
```

The i command specifies an import operation, and the k command specifies the keychain to operate on. In this example, the k command is followed by the c option, which causes the keychain to be created if it does not already exist.

For more information on command-line certificate manipulation, see the respective man page for each utility.

Configuring Services to Use Certificates

The following services can be configured to use certificates to protect data transfer:

▶ iCal (via the web service)

▶ iChat

▶ Mail

▶ Open Directory

▶ RADIUS

▶ VPN

▶ Web

The process for enabling certificate use is similar across all services: Use the Server Admin Settings tab to specify a certificate to use for the service. For example, to enable the iChat service to use an SSL certificate for encryption, do the following:

1 Open Server Admin.app.

2 Choose the iChat service in the list of services from the enabled services on the left of the Server Admin window.

3 Choose the Settings icon in the toolbar.

4 On the General tab of the Settings page, change the SSL Certificate drop-down menu from No Certificate to the certificate that you want to use.

Each installation of Mac OS X Server v10.5 includes a unique, self-signed certificate that can be used with the services listed above.

Creating a Certificate Authority to Sign Certificates

If your server must communicate using SSL with external computers that are out of your control, you should purchase SSL certificates from a well-known CA. Once you have obtained the certificates, configuring the services is the same, whether the certificates were purchased from a vendor or signed by your own CA.

If you are setting up an internal network and only need to encrypt local traffic, set up a CA to sign SSL certificates for the internal network. While the security is only as good as the security of the CA, in many cases this is sufficient to enable encrypted communication between a web or mail server and their clients.

The basic steps to set up an internal SSL-encrypted network are as follows:

▶   Create a CA. You can use either Certificate Assistant or the command line.

▶   Use the CA to sign the certificates that the servers will use.

▶   Distribute the CA certificates to client systems.

Creating a CA Using Certificate Assistant

The Certificate Assistant application included in Mac OS X Server allows you to sign and issue certificates both as a CA and as a root authority. (You can use these corresponding CA-issued and self-signed certificates in Certificate Manager by importing them.) You can also use Certificate Assistant to create a CA, as described in the following procedure.

Certificate Assistant is located in /System/Library/CoreServices/ and is available as a menu item in the Keychain Access application.

It is critical that you perform this procedure on a secure computer. The security of your certificates depends on the security of the CA. Make sure that the computer is physically secure and not connected to any network.

To create the CA using Certificate Assistant, follow these steps:

1   Open Certificate Assistant and click Continue.

2   Select Create a Certificate Authority (CA).

3   Deselect "Certificate will be self-signed (root)."

Selecting this option creates a self-signed root certificate authority, which is often used for testing purposes in place of certificates signed by proper CAs.

4   Fill out the certificate information.

The common name is the fully qualified domain name (FQDN) of the server that uses SSL-enabled services. The validity period is the number of days the certificate is valid.

5   Click Continue.

6 Choose an issuer for the certificate. An issuer signs the certificate that you are going to create. Click Continue.

7 Select the key size (2048 bits, by default) and algorithm (RSA, by default) used to create your key pair for the CA. Click Continue.

8 Select the key size (2048 bits, by default) and algorithm (RSA, by default) that specify the public and private key-pair information for users of this CA when they request a certificate. Click Continue.

9 Set the Key Usage Extension (KUE) for this CA. Deselect "This extension is critical" if it is safe for the software using the certificate to ignore the extension if unrecognized; otherwise, if the software does not recognize a critical extension, the certificate will be rejected. Click Continue.

These extensions identify the security capabilities of the CA certificate and how it can be used. For example, a certificate can be created to sign emails, but not to encrypt them.

10 Set the Key Usage Extension for users of this CA, if required. Click Continue.

11 Set the miscellaneous extensions for this CA by selecting the following options and then clicking Continue:

▶ "Include Basic Constraints extension (Extension is always critical)" to indicate whether the certificate is a CA and the maximum allowable depth of the certificate chain.

▶ "Use this certificate as a certificate authority."

▶ If required, "Include Subject Alternate Name extension" for this CA. This allows the CA to use additional names for the certificate subject and provides for flexible controls.

12 Set the miscellaneous extensions for the users of this CA, if required, by selecting "Include Basic Constraints extension (Extension is always critical)" and "Use this certificate as a certificate authority."

13 Select "Include Subject Alternate Name extension," if required for the users of the CA. Click Continue.

14 Specify a location for the certificate by choosing a keychain where the certificate will be stored. Click Continue.

15 Create a CA configuration file by entering the name of the CA configuration file. This file can be used by others to easily request a certificate from you.

16 Select "Make this CA the default," if necessary. Click Continue. Your CA is then created and is ready to issue certificates.

Creating a CA from the Command Line

You can also create a CA from the command line.

Again, it is critical that you perform this procedure on a secure computer. The security of your certificates depends on the security of the CA. Make sure that the computer is physically secure and not connected to any network.

To create the CA using the openssl command, follow these steps:

1 Enter the following in Terminal.app to create a certificate directory:

```
$ cd /usr/share
```

```
$ sudo mkdir certs
```

```
$ cd certs
```

2 Generate a key pair with the openssl command:

```
$ sudo openssl genrsa -des3 -out ca.key 2048
```

This command generates a Triple Data Encryption Standard (Triple-DES) encrypted RSA public-private key pair named ca.key. The length of the key in bits is 2048. On creating the key, OpenSSL asks for a passphrase for it. Use a strong passphrase rather than a single-word password, and keep it secure. A compromise of this passphrase undermines the security of your entire certificate system.

Storing the CA Private Key

Remember, the CA private key should remain *private*. For added security, you can store the keychain containing the private key on removable media, to keep the CA private key unavailable when connected to the network.

Signing a Newly Created CA

After the key pair is created, the public key is signed to create an SSL certificate that can be distributed to other systems. Later, when you sign other server certificates with your CA private key, any client can then use the CA's SSL certificate (containing its public key) to verify those signatures. When a CA signs a server's certificate with its private key, it means that it is vouching for the authenticity of those certificates. Anyone who can trust the CA can then trust any certificate the CA signs.

To sign the newly created CA's public key to produce a certificate for distribution, use this command:

```
$ sudo openssl req -new -x509 -days 365 -key ca.key -out ca.crt
```

When prompted, enter a strong passphrase for the key, as well as these fields:

▶ Country Name

▶ Organizational Unit

▶ State or Province Name

▶ Common Name

▶ Locality Name (city)

▶ Email Address

▶ Organization Name

Fill out these fields as accurately as possible; leave blank those that do not apply. You must fill in at least one field.

This command sequence creates a self-signed certificate named ca.crt, using the keys in ca.key, which is valid for a year (365 days). You can set the limit for a longer period of time, for less security. The issue of security is similar to changing passwords regularly. You must find a balance between convenience and security.

Creating Folders and Files for SSL

When signing certificates, SSL looks for keys and related information in directories specified in its configuration file openssl.cnf, which is found in /System/Library/OpenSSL/.

To create the directories and files where SSL expects to find them by default, use this code:

```
$ cd /usr/share/certs
$ sudo -s
$ mkdir -p demoCA/private
$ cp ca.key demoCA/private/cakey.pem
$ cp ca.crt demoCA/cacert.pem
$ mkdir demoCA/newcerts
$ touch demoCA/index.txt
$ echo "01" > demoCA/serial
```

Now the CA is ready to sign certificates for servers, enabling encrypted communication between servers and clients.

Distributing Server Certificates to Clients

Mac OS X Server ships with certificates only from well-known commercial CAs. If you are using self-signed certificates, a warning pops up in most user applications saying that the certificate authority is not recognized. Other software, such as the LDAP client, simply refuses to use SSL if the server CA is unknown. To prevent this warning, your CA certificate must be exported to every client computer that will be connecting to the secure server.

To distribute the self-signed CA certificate, follow these steps:

1   Copy the self-signed CA certificate (the file named ca.crt) onto each client computer. This is preferably distributed using non-rewritable media, such as a CD-R. Using non-rewritable media prevents the certificate from being corrupted.

2   Double-click the ca.crt icon where it was copied onto the client computer; this action opens the Keychain Access tool.

3   Add the certificate to the X509Anchors keychain using Keychain Access. This can also be performed using the certtool command in Terminal:

```
$ sudo certtool i ca.crt k=/System/Library/Keychains/X509Anchors
```

Now, any client application that checks against the system's X509Anchors keychain (such as Safari and Mail) recognizes any certificate signed by your CA.

Authorizing Accounts

Authorization defines whether an account is allowed to perform an action. Each object and action in Mac OS X takes place in the context of an account. Each time an action is performed, such as a file being accessed, Mac OS X checks to verify that the account performing the action is permitted to do so.

Authorization takes place at many levels, from login to service access and file access.

Editing System Rights

Certain Mac OS X services use a policy database to determine account capabilities. This information is stored in a single file: /etc/authorization. The authorization file contains two halves. The first half contains *rights*, or the level of permission to be granted. The rights are applied when conditions from *rules*, detailed in the second half, are met.

One example of this in action is the screensaver. When configured to require a password to be dismissed, it uses a right in /etc/authorization to determine the rules to allow unlocking.

When presented with an authorization dialog box, you can determine the right being requested using the disclosure triangle for Details. In the case of unlocking a screensaver, the right is system.login.screensaver. The existing rule in the policy database (/etc/authorization) allows the owner and any administrator to unlock the screensaver. You can add to or edit the policy database, to allow an additional rule or modify an existing one.

Altering the policy database is a good way to give certain users or groups admin-like rights without giving full admin accessibility to a machine. Be aware, however, that /etc/authorization is a system file, and that you should make a backup before making changes and work only on a copy. Also be aware that /etc/authorization may get updated along with a system update, so keep good backups of this file if you are relying on customized changes.

The existing system.login.screensaver right from the database follows:

```
<key>system.login.screensaver</key>
  <dict>
      <key>class</key>
      <string>rule</string>
      <key>comment</key>
      <string>The owner or any administrator can unlock the screensaver.</string>
```

```
        <key>rule</key>
        <string>authenticate-session-owner-or-admin</string>
    </dict>
```

The right contains a `rule` key, specifying which rule it will follow. In this case, the right is `authenticate-session-owner-or-admin`. Traveling further down the file reveals the rule details:

```
    <key>authenticate-session-owner-or-admin</key>
      <dict>
          <key>allow-root</key>
          <false/>
          <key>class</key>
          <string>user</string>
          <key>comment</key>
          <string>Authenticate either as the owner or as an administrator.</string>
          <key>group</key>
          <string>admin</string>
          <key>session-owner</key>
          <true/>
          <key>shared</key>
          <false/>
      </dict>
```

As this example shows, the group admin and the session owner both allow the rule to successfully authorize.

To alter the behavior of the screensaver unlocking mechanism, you can modify /etc/authorization. Since other applications use this database, it is best to add a right and rule, rather than alter any existing entries. Create a copy of the `authenticate-session-owner-or-admin` rule, and place it directly beneath the original. Rename the rule `authenticate-session-owner-or-itops` by changing the `<key>` value. Additionally, allow the group `itops` in the rule. It should look like the following:

```
    <key>authenticate-session-owner-or-itops</key>
      <dict>
          <key>allow-root</key>
          <false/>
```

```
        <key>class</key>
        <string>user</string>
        <key>comment</key>
        <string>Authenticate either as the owner or as an administrator.</string>
        <key>group</key>
        <string>itops</string>
        <key>session-owner</key>
        <true/>
        <key>shared</key>
        <false/>
    </dict>
```

Now, go back to the `system.login.screensaver` right, and edit it to use the rule that you just created. Change the value for the rule key to read:

```
<key>rule</key>
        <string>authenticate-session-owner-or-itops</string>
```

This change allows anyone in the `itops` group to unlock the screensaver.

Setting File Permissions

Files and folders are protected by setting permissions that restrict or allow user access.

(It is important to note these distinctions in terminology: "Permissions" refers only to the permission settings applied to a file. "Privileges" refers to the combination of ownership and permissions.)

Mac OS X Server supports two methods of setting file and folder permissions:

▶   Portable Operating System Interface (POSIX) permissions—standard for UNIX operating systems.

▶   Access control list (ACL) permissions—used by Mac OS X, and compatible with Microsoft Windows NTFS.

ACLs use POSIX in their process of verifying file and folder permissions. The process that ACL uses to determine whether an action is allowed or denied includes checking specific rules called access control entries (ACEs). If none of the ACEs applies, then standard POSIX permissions are used to determine access.

Setting POSIX Permissions

Mac OS X Server bases file permissions on POSIX standard permissions, such as file ownership and access. Every share point, file, or folder has read, write, and execute permission defined for three different categories of users (owner, group, and everyone).

There are four types of standard POSIX access permissions that you can assign to a share point, folder, or file: Read & Write, Read Only, Write Only, and None.

Viewing POSIX Permissions

Apple Training Series: Mac OS X Server Essentials v10.5 taught you how to use Server Admin and the Finder to set and view permissions. Shell-based tools provide more concise and accurate ways to query and manipulate permissions. To view the permission of folders or files, use the ls command with the -l ("ell") switch:

```
$ ls -l
total 500
drwxr-xr-x 2 alice alice  68 Apr 28 2006 Artwork
-rw-r--r-- 1 alice alice 43008 Apr 14 2006 file.txt
```

The POSIX permissions can be interpreted by reading the 10 bits in the first column of this listing.

In the preceding example, the Artwork directory has the POSIX permissions of drwxr-xr-x and has an owner and group of alice. The d of the POSIX permissions signifies that Artwork is a directory. The first three letters after the d (rwx) signify that the owner has read, write, and execute permission for that folder. The next three characters, r-x, signify that group has read and execute permission. The last three characters, r-x, signify that all others have read and execute permission.

Occasionally, you will see a t instead of an x for others' privileges on a folder used for collaboration. This t is sometimes known as the "sticky bit." Enabling the sticky bit on a folder prevents people from overwriting, renaming, or otherwise modifying other people's files. This is something that can become common if several people are granted rwx access. The sticky bit being set can appear as t or T depending on whether the execute bit is set for others. If the execute bit appears as t, the sticky bit is set and has searchable and executable permissions. See the sticky man page for more information; see "Getting Help" in Chapter 9 for instructions on using man pages.

Modifying POSIX Permissions

After you determine the current POSIX permission settings, you can modify them using the chmod command:

```
$ chmod g+w file.txt
```

This adds write permission for the group owner to file.txt.

Setting Flags

Flags can protect files and folders. These flags override standard POSIX permissions and can be used to prevent the system administrator (root) from modifying or deleting files or folders. Use the chflags command to enable and disable flags. The flag can only be set or unset by the file's owner or an administrator using sudo. To display flags set on a folder, use the ls command with the -o switch:

```
$ ls -lo MyFolder
-rw-r--r-- 1 alice alice uchg 0 Mar 1 07:54 MyFolder
```

In this example, the flag settings for a folder named MyFolder are displayed. The uchg, or "unchangeable," flag is set.

You can modify flags using the chflags command. This is equivalent to the Locked checkbox in a Finder's Get Info window. To lock a file or folder using flags, specify the uchg argument to the chflags command:

```
$ sudo chflags uchg MyFolder
```

In this example, the folder named MyFolder is locked. To unlock the folder, change uchg to nouchg.

For more information, see the chflags man page; see "Getting Help" in Chapter 9 for instructions on using man pages.

Setting ACL Permissions

For greater flexibility in configuring and managing file permissions, Mac OS X implements ACLs. An ACL is an ordered list of rules that control file permissions. Each ACE refers to a user or group, and grants or denies a set of permissions. In cases where a user and a group exist with the same name, you can specify the type by adding the "user:" or "group:" prefix, respectively. The rules specify the permissions to be granted or denied to a user or group, and how these permissions are propagated throughout a folder hierarchy.

To determine whether an action is allowed or denied, Mac OS X considers the ACEs in order. The first ACE that applies to a user determines the permission, and no further ACEs are evaluated. If none of the ACEs applies, then standard POSIX permissions determine access.

The `chmod` command has been extended to add and manipulate ACLs for files and folders. To set ACL permissions for a file, use this command:

```
$ chmod +a "joe allow read" file.txt
```

This command adds the specified ACE to the file file.txt. Group permissions can be handled in a similar manner:

```
$ chmod +a "admins allow delete" file.txt
```

To deny access to a file or folder, add a deny rule:

```
$ chmod +a "mikeg deny write" file.txt
```

View ACL permissions using the `ls` command with the `-e` switch:

```
$ ls -le file.txt
-rw------- 1 ajohnson admin 43008 Apr 14 2006 secret.txt
 0: joe allow read
 1: mikeg deny write
 2: admins allow delete
```

When using `chmod` to apply an ACL to a directory, existing files inside do not receive the applied ACEs. Use the `chmod -R` switch to recursively copy ACEs through a directory structure. New files and directories put in the directory do not inherit ACEs applied to the parent unless the `file_inherit` or `directory_inherit` permissions, or both, are applied. For example, to ensure that the files from the group sales inherit the same permissions applied to the New_Clients directory, you could add the following ACE:

```
$ chmod +a "sales allow file_inherit,directory_inherit" New_Clients
```

Now, any new files or directories created in the New_Clients directory by users in the sales group will inherit the same permissions that are applied to the New_Clients directory.

For more information, see the `chmod man` page; see "Getting Help" in Chapter 9 for instructions on using `man` pages.

Altering Initial File Permissions

Every file or folder has POSIX permissions associated with it. When you create a new file or folder, the umask setting determines the initial POSIX permissions applied. The umask can be altered for files and folders created in the shell.

The default umask setting of 022 removes group and other write permissions. The umask is applied by removing the corresponding bits from full permissions (777). For example, if you change the umask setting to 027, files and folders can still be read and run by group members, but cannot be accessed in any way by others. If you want to be the only user who can access your files and folders, set the umask to 077.

The umask setting affects only the initial POSIX permissions that have been applied. They may be changed later with the chmod command.

To change the current umask value, use the umask command:

```
umask 027
```

This change affects any new files created in the shell. To keep a particular behavior between new shells, add the umask command to your ~/.bash_profile file.

Setting Service Access Privileges

Service access control lists (SACLs) allow you to add another layer of access control on top of standard and ACL permissions. SACLs are a powerful method of controlling access to services on a server. You should use SACLs to authorize services only to specified users and groups, and apply them to each service early in its life.

SACLs are stored in a group record in the directory. You can manipulate these records with dscl. The GroupMembership and GroupMembers attributes control the SACL for a given service. GroupMembership lists a user or group short name, and GroupMembers lists a user or group GeneratedUID. For example, to add the group Shell_Users to the SACL for SSH, you need the following two commands:

```
$ dscl -u admin . append /groups/com.apple.access_ssh GroupMembership Shell_Users
$ dscl -u admin . append /groups/com.apple.access_ssh GroupMembers 98162A2C-49D7-
488E-8B70-182790889E10
```

The first command lists the group by short name, while the second command appends the group's Globally Unique ID (GUID) to the GroupMembers attribute. Both commands require authentication, with the appropriate credentials supplied partially with the -u switch (user name) and partially on the command line when prompted.

To display the members in a SACL, read the GroupMembership attribute from the specified group. For example, to list the members of the SSH SACL, use the following command:

```
dscl . read /groups/com.apple.access_ssh GroupMembership
```

To remove a member of a SACL group, use dscl to remove the appropriate values. For example, to remove the Shell_Users group added earlier, use the dscl delete command:

```
$ dscl -u admin . delete /groups/com.apple.access_ssh GroupMembers 98162A2C-49D7-
488E-8B70-182790889E10
$ dscl -u admin . delete /groups/com.apple.access_ssh GroupMembership Shell_Users
```

Another method of displaying SACLs is possible with the serveradmin command-line tool. To display possible administrative SACL names or the list details, respectively, use the following commands:

```
# serveradmin settings info:adminControlListNames
# serveradmin settings info:adminControlLists
```

To display possible SACL names or their contents, respectively, use the following commands:

```
# serveradmin settings info:accessControlListNames
# serveradmin settings info:accessControlLists
```

You also use SACLs in Workgroup Manager and Server Admin when creating limited, or "junior," administrators.

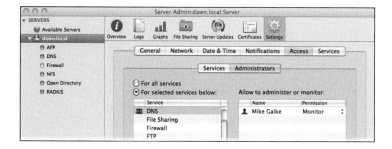

In Server Admin, under the Access > Administrators tab, individual services can be assigned users and groups, which can either administrate or only monitor them.

To add or remove a user or group from the monitoring groups, use `dscl` to manipulate the appropriate `com.apple.monitor` group. For example, to add a user to the DNS SACL for monitoring, use the following commands:

```
$ dscl -u admin . append /groups/com.apple.monitor_dns GroupMembership mgalke
$ dscl -u admin . append /groups/com.apple.monitor_dns GroupMembers 228CC345-E0DD-
4591-B536-5733167821E9
```

Workgroup Manager also has the feature to give certain users and groups administrative control over other users and groups. This is also handled via directory record entries.

Encrypting Files

Encryption uses a key to transform plain text information so that it is unreadable to anyone without the decryption key. Encryption can protect both information on disk and information in transit over a network.

Using FileVault

Mac OS X Server includes FileVault, which can encrypt your home folder and all the files contained within it. You should enable FileVault on mobile computers and on any other machines whose physical security cannot be guaranteed.

Enabling FileVault copies all data from your home folder into an encrypted home folder—a sparse-bundle disk image that uses AES-128 encryption. After copying, FileVault erases the unencrypted data.

The home folder's sparse format allows the image to maintain a size proportional to its contents, which can save disk space. When files are removed from a FileVault-protected home folder, the space is reclaimed on logout.

If you insecurely delete files before using FileVault, those files are still recoverable after activating it.

By default, FileVault insecurely erases the unencrypted data. You should enable the secure erase option when enabling FileVault on a home directory, so that your unencrypted data is securely erased. When initially enabling FileVault, you also can securely erase free space using Disk Utility or the `diskutil` shell tool. The following command will securely erase free space on the boot drive with one pass of random data:

```
# diskutil secureErase freespace 1 /
```

See the `diskutil` `man` page for other secure erase options; see "Getting Help" in Chapter 9 for instructions on using `man` pages.

FileVault does not encrypt or protect files transferred over the network or saved to removable media. However, you can create an encrypted disk image separate from FileVault that can protect files outside the home directory. If you mount these encrypted images over a network link, all data transmitted over the network will be encrypted with AES-128 encryption. See "Encrypting Disk Images" later in this chapter for more information.

To set up FileVault, you should create a master password. If you forget your login password, you can use the master password to recover encrypted data. If you forget both your login password and your master password, you cannot recover your data. Consider sealing your master password in an envelope and storing it in a secure location. You can also use Password Assistant to help create a complex master password that cannot be easily compromised.

Setting a FileVault Master Keychain

You can set a FileVault master keychain to decrypt any account that uses FileVault to encrypt data. You should set a FileVault keychain to ensure that data is not lost in the event of a forgotten password. If you forget the FileVault account password, which is used to decrypt encrypted data, you can use the FileVault master keychain to decrypt the data.

To create the FileVault master keychain, set a master password using the Security Preference pane in System Preferences. This creates a keychain called FileVaultMaster.keychain located in /Library/Keychains/.

The FileVault master keychain now contains both a FileVault recovery key (self-signed root CA certificate) and a FileVault master password key (private key). You should delete the private key from FileVaultMaster.keychain, after backing it up. This ensures that even if someone is able to unlock the FileVault master keychain, that person would be unable to decrypt the contents of a FileVault account because no FileVault master password private key is available for the decryption.

Centrally Managing FileVault

Once you modify the FileVault master keychain, you can distribute it to all of your network computers. Distribution is done by transferring FileVaultMaster.keychain to the desired computers in one of these ways: using Apple Remote Desktop, executing a distributed installer on each computer, scripting using various techniques, or just including it in the original disk image if your organization restores systems with a default image. Copying the FileVaultMaster.keychain file to target computers provides network management of any FileVault account created on any computer with the modified FileVaultMaster.keychain located in the /Library/Keychains/ folder. These computers indicate that the master password is set in Security preferences.

When a new user account is created and the modified FileVault master keychain is present, the public key from the FileVault recovery key is used to encrypt the dynamically generated AES 128-bit symmetric key. The latter key is used for the encryption and decryption of the encrypted FileVault disk image.

To decrypt the encrypted disk image, the FileVault master password private key is required to decrypt the original dynamically generated AES 128-bit symmetric key. The user's original password continues to work as normal. However, it is assumed that you are using the master password service because the user has forgotten the password, or the organization must perform data recovery from a user's computer.

Encrypting Disk Images

Encrypted disk images are a perfect way to transport data on external media, save files to removable media, and protect files on shared systems.

FileVault does not protect files transmitted over the network or saved to removable media. However, Mac OS X Server includes utilities for encrypting disk images. Using a server-based encrypted disk image provides the added benefit of encrypting all network traffic between the computer and the server hosting the mounted encrypted disk image.

You can create a read-write or sparse image to encrypt and securely store data. A read-write image takes up the entire space that was defined when the image was created. For example, if the maximum size of a read-write image is set to 10 GB, then that image will take up 10 GB of space even if it contains only 2 GB of data. A sparse image will only take up the amount of space containing data in the image. For example, if the maximum size of a sparse image is 10 GB and the data contained in it is only 2 GB, it will occupy only 2 GB of space.

Creating an encrypted image from existing data copies the data from an unprotected area into the encrypted image. If the data is sensitive, it is better to create the image prior to creating the documents, because the working copies, backups, or caches of files would all be created in the encrypted storage from the start.

To create a new encrypted disk image, use `hdiutil`. The following is an example that creates a 1 GB sparse image named `secure_files.sparseimage`:

```
hdiutil create -size 1G -encryption -type SPARSE -fs HFS+ secure_files.
```

A sparse image can expand as data in the image grows. To create a fixed-size image, simply leave off the `-type SPARSE` switch.

You can also create a disk image from the contents of an existing folder. This is accomplished with the `hdiutil -srcfolder create` subcommand. Here's an example command that creates an encrypted disk image named `sales_2008.dmg` from an existing folder named `2008`:

```
hdiutil create -encryption -srcfolder /Volumes/Sales/2008 -fs HFS+ sales_2008
```

Troubleshooting

Typically, authentication and authorization are set once and then forgotten about. As with most other topics in this book, if problems occur, you should look first in the logs. However, determining which log to look in can be a bit perplexing. Most subsystems log to /var/log/system.log when running into problems. Authorization issues are logged to /var/log/secure.log. When an SSH session fails to authorize, log lines such as the following are entered into secure.log:

```
May 3 12:24:16 dawn com.apple.SecurityServer[35]: Failed to authorize right system.
login.tty by client /usr/sbin/sshd for authorization created by /usr/sbin/sshd.
May 3 12:24:16 dawn sshd[79271]: error: PAM: Authentication failure for illegal user
baduser from example.com
May 3 12:24:16 dawn sshd[79271]: Failed keyboard-interactive/pam for invalid user
baduser from 10.10.149.201 port 34348 ssh2
```

Additionally, some services offer verbose output on their connection status. Using SSH as an example, the SSH client offers the -v switch for use when diagnosing problems:

```
$ ssh -v dawnadmin@dawn.radiotope.com
OpenSSH_4.7p1, OpenSSL 0.9.7l 28 Sep 2006
debug1: Reading configuration data /etc/ssh_config
debug1: Applying options for *
debug1: Connecting to dawn.radiotope.com [192.168.100.18] port 22.
debug1: Connection established.
debug1: identity file /Users/marczak/.ssh/identity type 0
debug1: identity file /Users/marczak/.ssh/id_rsa type -1
debug1: identity file /Users/marczak/.ssh/id_dsa type -1
debug1: Remote protocol version 2.0, remote software version OpenSSH_4.5
debug1: match: OpenSSH_4.5 pat OpenSSH*
debug1: Enabling compatibility mode for protocol 2.0
debug1: Local version string SSH-2.0-OpenSSH_4.7
debug1: SSH2_MSG_KEXINIT sent
debug1: SSH2_MSG_KEXINIT received
debug1: kex: server->client aes128-cbc hmac-md5 none
debug1: kex: client->server aes128-cbc hmac-md5 none
debug1: SSH2_MSG_KEX_DH_GEX_REQUEST(1024<1024<8192) sent
debug1: expecting SSH2_MSG_KEX_DH_GEX_GROUP
debug1: SSH2_MSG_KEX_DH_GEX_INIT sent
debug1: expecting SSH2_MSG_KEX_DH_GEX_REPLY
debug1: Host 'dawn.radiotope.com' is known and matches the RSA host key.
debug1: Found key in /Users/marczak/.ssh/known_hosts:15
debug1: ssh_rsa_verify: signature correct
debug1: SSH2_MSG_NEWKEYS sent
debug1: expecting SSH2_MSG_NEWKEYS
debug1: SSH2_MSG_NEWKEYS received
debug1: SSH2_MSG_SERVICE_REQUEST sent
debug1: SSH2_MSG_SERVICE_ACCEPT received
debug1: Authentications that can continue: publickey,password,keyboard-interactive
debug1: Next authentication method: publickey
debug1: Trying private key: /Users/marczak/.ssh/id_rsa
```

```
debug1: Trying private key: /Users/marczak/.ssh/id_dsa
debug1: Next authentication method: keyboard-interactive
```

The output lists each step in the transaction—if keys are located and tried, key exchanges attempted, and so on. If SSH prints alerts about a man-in-the-middle attack or a mismatched IP address, make sure that the machine you are connecting to is valid. These messages are often printed when computers are assigned addresses via DHCP. Servers using static IP addresses should never change, but maintenance may inadvertently remove keys. If this happens, administrators must communicate this to users.

Unlike Linux systems, it is rare that PAM files are modified on Mac OS X. However, given problems, PAM issues are logged to /var/log/secure.log.

Digital certificates tend to have issues in two places: on importing a CA-issued certificate and expiration. When accepting a certificate from a certificate authority, not all authorities issue them with UNIX systems in mind. Also, email programs can alter the line endings that are so important to the process. When you import a certificate, system.log may receive lines like the following:

```
[error] mod_ssl: Init: Pass phrase incorrect (OpenSSL library error follows)
[error] OpenSSL: error:0D07207B:asn1 encoding routines:ASN1_get_object:header too long
```

Ensure that the text file being imported has UNIX line endings—line feed (0x0A)—not DOS CRLF or Mac CR (0x0d). Command-line utilities like xxd offer a hexdump of a text stream that can be useful for decoding this information.

Another issue occurs when a certificate is already in use, but a session starts displaying errors. This typically happens when the certificate expires.

You can determine information about a certificate and whether it has expired in several ways. The easiest way is if the certificate is being used for a web server. Connect with a web browser, such as Safari, and click the lock icon in the upper right corner to display information about the certificate in use.

The resulting display clearly shows the expiration date.

If the certificate is being used with other services, however, `openssl` is the best multiuse utility. The most general purpose command is `s_client`. `openssl` will connect to an SSL-protected service and return heaps of information regarding the certificates—too much to print here. For example, to connect to an SSL-enabled Internet Message Access Protocol (IMAP) server, you can use the following command:

```
$ openssl s_client -connect smtp.example.com:993
```

The output will contain information about the certificates returned, including expiration information. You can use this information to determine whether an expired certificate is causing problems. The output also provides an interactive session where you can issue commands to the service that you have connected to. If you are only after the certificate information, press Control-C to end the session and return to the command prompt. If the certificate has expired, follow the instructions in "Creating Self-Signed Certificates" earlier in this chapter to generate a new certificate.

Finding problems in the authorization realm depends primarily on the service in question. File system privileges are a good example.

While POSIX permissions are fairly simple, ACLs can get out of hand quickly if not managed properly. Using groups in ACEs, rather than individual users, is one way to simplify the amount of entries on the system, and allows management at a higher level.

If a set of permissions is ever an issue, use the Server Admin Effective Permissions Inspector (EPI). To view the Effective Permissions Inspector, open Server Admin, click the server that mounts the file system, and click the File Sharing button in the toolbar. Click the preferences Gear button and choose Show Effective Permissions Inspector from the pop-up menu.

Choose a share point, or browse the file system for files and folders. Drag the user name from the user list into the EPI window. The EPI will composite all permissions applicable to this user for the file in question, and report on their ultimate permissions.

What You've Learned

This chapter addresses some of the most fundamental reasons why administrators exist. Not just anyone can walk into a company and rifle through filing cabinets and access any document they like. Doors and filing cabinets are locked and only appropriate people are given keys. Company policy should define what and when to lock, and system administrators enforce those policies via technology. Mac OS X provides broad means to do so. Specific points to understand about this process are as follows:

▶ Authentication is the process of identifying credentials for an account. Authorization processes determine an account's right to perform a specific operation.

▶ Credentials may be supplied as a name and password combination, two-factor authentication (ID/password plus smartcard), or public-key ID certificates.

▶ Physically protecting systems is equally as important as the digital barriers. Given physical access to a machine, it can always be compromised.

▶ Hardware can be disabled in software by removing or stubbing the kernel extensions that interface with specific hardware.

▶ A hardware password (also known as an "OpenFirmware password") can prevent modifications to parameter RAM and block most startup keys.

▶ PAMs, or pluggable authentication modules, use libraries and modules to determine if supplied credentials are valid for a specific service. Apple has created both libraries and modules that tie into Apple-specific technology, such as Password Service that integrates services into the Mac OS X single sign-on model.

▶ SSH provides a secure remote shell. All data is encrypted between the SSH client and SSH server. As credentials, SSH can use traditional name and password pairs, or digital key pairs. `ssh-keygen` generates an identity key pair. Connecting to an SSH server records its public key, or "fingerprint," in the account's ~/.ssh/known_hosts file.

▶ Another form of PKI exists in Mac OS X in the form of SSL certificates. Mac OS X Server contains a Certificate Manager in Server Admin, while Mac OS X can manage certificates via the `openssl` command. Both platforms contain Certificate Assistant, which can generate CA files. A CSR is required for a public CA to be able to sign a self-generated certificate.

▶ If your company chooses to run an internal CA, you must distribute the root certificate to internal clients for them to trust the certificate. The certificate must be imported into the system's X509Anchors keychain.

▶ The /etc/authorization file represents the Mac OS X policy database. It defines rights and rules. Most authorization attempts utilize the policy database to determine if an action is authorized. This file can be modified to grant greater or lesser rights to users.

▶ Mac OS X uses both POSIX permissions and ACLs to determine access rights for file objects. Access control lists are made up of a series of rules called access control entries (ACEs). Each ACE is evaluated in order, and the first to match applies. If no ACE applies, the POSIX permissions are enforced.

▶ chmod is used to set both POSIX and ACL permissions on files and folders. ls is used to view permissions—POSIX or ACL—applied to files and folders.

▶ Service access control lists (SACLs) are a method of defining which users and groups have access to a given service. Definitions for SACLs are simple groups in a directory service. These can be manipulated from the shell using dscl.

▶ Encryption transforms plain text information into a version that is unreadable to anyone without the decryption key.

▶ The Mac OS X FileVault uses an encrypted disk image to protect an entire home directory via AES-128 encryption. Setting a FileVault master password creates a keychain called FileVaultMaster.keychain located in /Library/Keychains/. New FileVault accounts created on a computer with this keychain in place will also include the capability for recovery using the master password.

▶ hdiutil can create plain or encrypted disk images. Encrypted disk images can be used to protect files and folders outside of FileVault, particularly those on removable or portable storage.

Review Quiz

1. What is the definition of authentication?

2. What is the definition of authorization?

3. What is the command-line utility used to enable the root user on an out-of-the-box installation of Mac OS X?

4. What is the command-line utility used to enable the root user on an out-of-the-box installation of Mac OS X Server?

5. What command should be used to edit the sudoers file?

6. The contents of which file should be copied to a remote host to provide key-based authentication for the SSH protocol?

7. Which file contains the system's authorization database?

8. Which command-line utility is used to set file system ACLs?

9. Where are certificates stored?

10. Which command-line tool creates disk images, including encrypted disk images?

Answers

1. Authentication is the process of identifying the identity of an account or service.

2. Authorization is the process by which an entity gains the right to perform a restricted operation.

3. `dsenableroot`

4. The root user is enabled by default on Mac OS X Server, so there is no need to enable it after a default installation.

5. `visudo`, because it checks the syntax of the file upon save.

6. The user public key, typically ~/.ssh/id_rsa.pub, or ~/.ssh/id_dsa.pub.

7. The authorization database is contained in the /etc/authorization file.

8. The `chmod` command sets file system ACLs.

9. Certificates are stored in a keychain file.

10. The `hdiutil` command manipulates disk images and can create encrypted disk images.

8

Time
This lesson takes approximately 90 minutes to complete.

Goals
Learn the details of the Apple System Logger and the logging infrastructure used in Mac OS X

Understand the predefined log levels and facilities used by `syslogd`

Learn the tools available for viewing data in log files

Learn the tools available for monitoring system activity

Learn monitoring tools specific to Xserve hardware

Learn about methods of notification

Learn to create reports containing important system properties

Chapter 8

Monitoring Systems

No computer system can simply be set up and then forgotten. The best case is that a device will need only occasional attention. In the case of modern servers providing one or more services to users, an administrator must regularly monitor the services and system to ensure that resources are performing adequately. In a larger system, it is also important to monitor production systems for underutilization. This chapter teaches administrators the logging and monitoring structure and utilities in Mac OS X.

NOTE ▶ All utilities in this chapter need root-level access to run unless specified otherwise.

Using the System Log and ASL

A log file is a chronological recording of activities. Traditionally, UNIX-based systems ran syslogd, the system logging daemon. The syslogd daemon is responsible for receiving messages and logging them in an appropriate text-based log file.

While you can still use traditional log-viewing methods, it is important to understand and use the Apple-supplied tools. Apple has created a completely custom system, and a system that respects prior methods of logging. Thanks to this, previous logging utilities and methods from other UNIX-like systems will continue to work. Apple has taken the traditional logging system and modified it in some subtle and some not-so-subtle ways. Improvements to the Apple-based syslogd and Leopard syslog since their debut in v10.4 address criticisms of that early version.

Veteran administrators coming from other UNIX-based platforms may not even realize that Mac OS X runs the Apple System Logger (ASL). The evidence is in the man page for syslogd:

```
SYSLOGD(8)              BSD System Manager's Manual              SYSLOGD(8)


NAME
     syslogd -- Apple System Log server
```

Apple usurped the syslogd name with a completely custom logging agent. Rather than immediately logging to various text-based log files, ASL logs to a binary database of log messages. This data store is located at /var/log/asl.db. The database can be viewed and manipulated with the syslog command. Again, ASL and its database system is unique to Mac OS X.

The structure of ASL borrows from the past, but adds features on top. The syslogd daemon accepts and processes log messages. *Modules* of syslogd can accept messages using various sources, such as the syslog application programming interface (API) and User Datagram Protocol (UDP) sockets from other syslog-capable devices. These messages are accepted and written to the ASL database. They are then also written to various traditional log files based on rules. Unlike traditional logs, the ASL database is treated as a real database. Rather than the data store being rolled and compressed, old log messages are pruned and cleaned in place by the syslogd daemon. The cleaning is also rule-based, respecting the type and severity of the log entry. For example, login entries are retained longer than some other log types.

About Log Levels and Facilities

Once ASL accepts a log message, besides logging it in /var/log/asl.db, it will also respect the traditional syslog system by writing plain-text messages into the files specified in /etc/syslog.conf. By default, messages are sent to files in the /var/log directory.

The syslog.conf file routes log messages to appropriate log files based on *log level* and *facility*. The log level is also called the *severity*. Basically, that means "How important is this message? Is it simple information, or is it considered an emergency?" The facility categorizes which subsystem the message applies to, using both predefined and user-definable labels. The log level is one of the following eight predefined values:

Table 8-1   Log Level Values

Value	Definition
Debug (level 7)	Message that contains information normally of use only when debugging a program
Info (level 6)	Informational message
Notice (level 5)	Condition that is not an error, but that may need special handling
Warning (level 4)	Cautioning message
Error (level 3)	Error
Critical (level 2)	Serious condition, such as a hard drive error
Alert (level 1)	Condition that needs immediate attention, such as a corrupt database
Emergency (level 0)	A panic condition

The built-in facilities are auth, authpriv, cron, daemon, kern, lpr, mail, mark, news, syslog, user, uucp, and local0 through local7. The local0 through local7 facilities are available for use at an administrator's discretion. For example, as a site, you may decide that all log information from internal intrusion detection systems (IDSs) use local5. This way, it's easy to correlate all IDS information.

The combination of a facility and level is called a *selector*. In the syslog.conf file, a dot separates the selector facility and level. Sample entries from /etc/syslog.conf illustrate this. For example, this entry denotes that messages of the facility mail and of log level crit should be written to the log file /var/log/mail.log:

```
mail.crit                       /var/log/mail.log
```

This entry directs messages in the ftp facility of *any* level—indicated by the wildcard asterisk character—to the /var/log/ftp.log file:

```
ftp.*                             /var/log/ftp.log
```

Semicolons separate multiple selectors on the same line:

```
auth.info;authpriv.*;remoteauth.crit  /var/log/secure.log
```

The "at" symbol (@) sends log entries to a host specified by name or IP address. The remote host must accept remote syslog messages:

```
*.*                   @yew.radiotope.com
```

You can use multiple definitions of the same selector, which allow routing the same message to separate destinations:

```
local5.*                        /var/log/firewall.log
local5.*                        @yew.radiotope.com
```

To enable a Mac OS X v10.5 Server (or plain old Mac OS X) to accept remote syslog messages and become a central log server, the launchd plist file for ASL must be edited. Edit /System/Library/LaunchDaemons/com.apple.syslogd.plist and remove the comments (the opening ‹!-- and closing --›) from around this block of XML:

```
<key>NetworkListener</key>
<dict>
        <key>SockServiceName</key>
        <string>syslog</string>
        <key>SockType</key>
        <string>dgram</string>
</dict>
```

Then, with a root-level account, issue the following commands:

```
#launchctl unload /System/Library/LaunchDaemons/com.apple.syslogd.plist
#launchctl load /System/Library/LaunchDaemons/com.apple.syslogd.plist
```

Now, set up a client to test with. Edit a client machine's /etc/syslog.conf file to include the following line (substituting the DNS name or IP address for "server.name.here"):

```
user.*                          @sever.name.here
```

Use launchctl to restart syslogd. Then use logger to send the message into ASL:

```
$logger test
```

This produces the following line in /var/log/system.log:

```
Mar 21 12:51:58 192.168.100.163 Jack-Kerouac marczak[5429]: test
```

and the following in asl.db:

```
Fri Mar 21 12:51:58 192.168.100.163 Jack-Kerouac marczak[5429] <Notice>: test
```

Alternatively, you can use the Apple-specific syslog command to send messages:

```
syslog -s -r yew.radiotope.com -l 2 "This is a test"
```

The -s flag directs syslog to send a message, -r sends the message to the remote server that follows, and -l specifies the log level. The test message is enclosed in quotes. The result looks like this in system.log:

```
Mar 21 12:52:31 192.168.100.163 Jack-Kerouac.local syslog[5431]: This is a test
```

and this in asl.db:

```
Fri Mar 21 12:52:31 192.168.100.163 Jack-Kerouac.local syslog[5431] <Critical>: This
is a test
```

About Log Formats

The log formats, by default, differ only in the display of a log level. It is important to be able to read logs properly. As an example, here is a breakdown of the preceding log message:

`Fri Mar 21 12:52:31`—The date and time that this message was logged, using the local time of the `syslog` server and displayed in 24-hour clock format

`192.168.100.163`—The IP address of the host generating the message

`Jack-Kerouac.local`—The host name of the device generating this message

`syslog[5431]`—The name and process ID (PID) of the process that sent this message

`<Critical>:`—The severity of the message

`This is a test`—The actual log message

All of the preceding lines are valid for log files that route through ASL and `syslogd`. An interesting fact about logs, however, is that they are simply text files. Applications are free to ignore `syslogd` and simply append log entries to the file of their choice. As an example, Apache—the web server at work in Mac OS X—does just this. It writes its logs to /var/log/apache2/access_log on its own, with no help from `syslogd`. Samba, the process responsible for providing file services to Server Message Block (SMB) clients, also writes logs without sending entries into `syslogd`. Similarly, many Apple processes write their logs to /Library/Logs. Finally, an application is absolutely free to write entries to both a file of its choice and `syslogd`. (Samba can also do this, but is not configured by Apple to log in this manner.) While services that create their own logs are free to come up with a completely custom logging format, most are very similar to the format just described.

Reading Log Files

Mac OS X provides various ways to read log files. First is the GUI-based Console.app. Second, on Mac OS X Server, is another graphical user interface-based utility, Server Admin.app (referred to simply as Server Admin). Finally, several tools are available in your favorite shell.

Console.app has steadily improved, version by version. It provides quick and easy access to all major log files on the system, and is an excellent exploratory tool. Clicking the Show

Log List icon in the toolbar will reveal the list, as shown in the following Console.app screen shot:

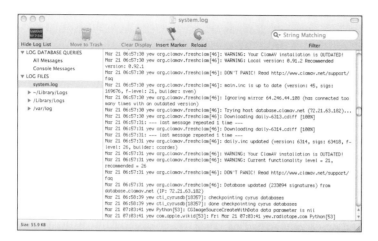

Console.app can insert a line of text, a "marker," into its display to make tracking sections of a log easier. These markers do not get written back into the actual log file. One downside to Console.app is that it does not update the display as the log file itself is updated. To see the current state of a log file before it's refreshed on its own, click the Reload button in the toolbar. A nice upside to Console.app, however, is the ability to search, by plugging in a search term. All log lines in the current log that have a non-case-sensitive match are displayed. You can perform advanced searches, basing queries on log text, sender facility, and more, by choosing File > New Log Database Query. This query can also be saved to the Console.app sidebar for quick access.

Server Admin also has a feature for viewing logs. Clicking the Logs icon displays logs related to the selected server or service, as shown here:

Server Admin lets you select a file by a descriptive name, and also shows the full path to the log file in a breadcrumb trail on top of the log itself. Like Console.app, Server Admin periodically refreshes the view of the log file and has the ability to search.

Finally, there are many shell tools that allow an administrator to view log files, including syslog, which is the only real way to interact with asl.db. The asl.db file is also the only file that syslog works with—you cannot use syslog to monitor arbitrary log files. Traditional utilities such as tail, grep, and less continue to be of use for the remainder of the text files on the system (which really comprise everything besides asl.db itself).

Typing syslog by itself will print out the entire contents of the asl.db datastore, which is typically of little use. The syslog utility, however, can do much better. Entries in asl.db are stored in raw key-value pairs, and syslog can query based on this scheme. For example, to view all entries sent by mDNSResponder, issue this command:

```
syslog -k Sender mDNSResponder
```

Multiple -k flags are ANDed together. If one wishes to see mDNSResponder messages only from the past four hours, use the following:

```
syslog -k Sender mDNSResponder -k Time ge -4h
```

The syslog man page contains full details and examples for querying the datastore.

Finally, syslog can follow the log store as it changes. The -w switch causes syslog to wait for changes:

```
syslog -w
```

Any new entries to asl.db are quickly written to the syslog output (typically the Terminal, unless redirected).

The best way to watch files, other than asl.db, as they change is the tail utility. The command is simple:

```
tail -f file.log
```

The tail utility will output the last 10 lines of the file and then follow it—by printing out any changes that occur to the log file.

In a similar fashion, less will follow log files and much more. To load a file into less, simply enter the filename:

```
less /var/log/system.log
```

Scroll through the file using the Up and Down arrow keys. Control-F and Control-B scroll forward and back a page, respectively. More importantly, you can search in a file by pressing the forward slash [/], and then typing a regular expression to match. Matches will then be highlighted through the file. Press N to go to the next match. Shift-N jumps to the previous match. Even better, pressing Shift-F will act like `tail` and follow the current file. Unlike `tail`, though, previous search results are still active in `less`, and matches on new lines are also highlighted. This is a great way to pick out patterns in a log file.

Creating a Monitoring Policy

As a system administrator, you should help your company come up with a monitoring policy. Monitoring log files is only useful if you have a plan to take action when you are made aware of an issue. A response should be planned as much as possible, and not decided on casually when faced with an issue. It is also important to know what to monitor and what not to monitor.

When creating a monitoring policy, compile a list of services and devices that require monitoring, and determine how and where it will be logged. Check with your legal department to determine if there are sources that need monitoring and logging. Also, determine if there are any systems that should *not* be monitored or logged.

A monitoring policy should contain the following sections:

▶ Purpose: Describe the purpose of providing monitoring

▶ Scope: Describe who and what this policy applies to

▶ Policies: List all the monitoring and logging areas

▶ Retention: Length of time that logs will be kept

▶ Response: What actions will occur when a problem is detected

Use Google to find sample monitoring policies, such as those listed on http://www.comptechdoc.org/independent/security/policies/server-monitoring-policy.html. Seeing samples of other policies can help you hone your work.

When crafting the retention portion of the policy, understand that Mac OS X has a built-in system to clean logs. The `newsyslog` program handles log maintenance. Logs are first rolled—compressed and renamed with a numeric suffix that denotes the order. Logs at the end of the rotation are deleted to save disk space.

The `newsyslog` program is configured using the /etc/newsyslog.conf file. This configuration file informs `newsyslog` when to roll a log, based on time or size, how to protect the newly rolled archive (through permissions), and how many compressed versions to keep.

Just as important as planning how to monitor is planning responses to problems encountered via monitoring or notifications. This section of the policy should include a list of issues, each with the following subsections:

▶   Contact: Who to contact when this issue presents itself, and contact methods (phone, email, and so on).

▶   Method: Is someone required to be onsite, or is it acceptable to work remotely?

▶   Documents: Pointers to documents that aid in a resolution.

▶   Response time: How quickly does the problem need to be resolved?

▶   Testing: How to ensure that the problem is resolved.

Overall, a monitoring policy helps a business think through how to manage log assets. From an IT perspective, monitoring provides alerting, but also data about the frequency of issues. Recognizing these trends will help plan future needs. From a business perspective, certain log assets may be helpful to mine data from, but there may also be legal implications to which logs to keep and which to destroy after a certain period of time. Work with your company's legal department if you are not sure.

Using Tools and Utilities

The value of log files cannot be disputed, but log files do not complete the entire picture of system activity. There are many other activities and statistics that do not appear in log files, such as network utilization, open file count, memory use, CPU load, and more.

Each of the components in a system affects the overall performance.

One of the most common components to monitor is CPU, with the primary question being "How busy is it?" There are actually two ways to view this. Contrary to many people's view, CPU usage is a sign of a healthy system. CPUs should not sit idle. Typically, it is not so much the percentage of CPU usage that you should be worried about, but rather the load average. That is not to say that percentage of CPU usage is not an important statistic. While a CPU should be in use, it should not be used needlessly. Small, poorly planned applications, typically looping tightly in code, can drain a CPU, and those processes need to be identified.

top, CPU Percentage, and Load Averages

The first utility to reach for is top, a console-based (text) process monitor that will refresh its output and sort by various criteria. Its goal is to show you the "top" processes according to your sort. It does not give you every statistic possible, but understanding the data it presents is crucial to understanding what is happening with your system.

The top utility will primarily display data about processes in user space. It also displays system CPU utilization and process 0—called kernel_task—that gives information about the kernel. You won't see this in a standard ps listing. The kernel_task process begins during the boot sequence, called into existence as one of the kernel's first jobs (see the xnu kernel source, available from http://developer.apple.com/opensource/).

When running with the default settings, top displays a list of processes, sorted by descending process ID, with associated statistics about each. Besides each individual process, you'll see a dashboard of statistics, similar to the following:

```
Processes:  129 total, 3 running, 122 sleeping... 438 threads        22:12:18
Load Avg:  0.71,  0.95,  0.95    CPU usage: 17.39% user, 10.00% sys, 72.61% idle
SharedLibs: num =    8, resident =   63M code,  412K data, 4280K linkedit.
MemRegions: num = 27913, resident = 1302M +   19M private,  289M shared.
PhysMem:  354M wired, 1319M active,  763M inactive, 2436M used,  1627M free.
VM: 16G + 371M   567026(0) pageins, 106583(0) pageouts
```

The first line displays how many processes the Berkeley Software Distribution (BSD) UNIX layer currently is responsible for, the number of processes that are active, how many are idle, the total number of threads (remember that each process is further broken down into threads of execution), and the current time.

On the next line is the statistic of load average. Explanations for the load average range from fairly straightforward to very complex. First, the load average metric appears in several places: the top utility, the uptime command, the output from w, and more. One thing remains constant: As in the example above, three numbers appear. They are the 1-minute, 5-minute, and 15-minute load averages—the result of the number of jobs in the run queue, or the load on the system. Some say it's the most important metric, and some say it's of little use. In either case, you have to know the system in question, and load average is just another data point for your investigation.

Load average is not solely CPU usage. It also encompasses disk I/O and network-bound processes. It is not just an average—it is a time-based damped average. In short, a load average of 0 means you have a completely idle system (not unheard of, but rare). A load average of 1 means that your CPU is handling things fine—there is a 1:1 ratio of instructions in the run queue to the CPU processing them. Less than 1 means that you have more headroom to spare, and more than 1 means that the system could benefit from a more powerful single processor, or multi-core processors to handle the load. It is situation-dependent, and will mean different things depending on the use of the system: A machine acting solely as a database server—even under heavy use—will have a completely different load average pattern than a file server or a shell server. So, while somewhat confusing, load average is certainly not a useless metric. Watch it, and learn the patterns from your system or systems.

Following load average is CPU usage. Don't panic when the CPU load rises. It's the job of Mac OS X to make sure that the CPU is getting used. There is no sense in having a CPU if you're not going to put it to work. The values displayed in the example show CPU usage segmented into user processes, system use, and percent idle. You're likely to see these numbers jumping about as the CPU does its job. Even though you may run a basic user space program such as, say, iTunes, the kernel still has to work keeping track of all the resources used by the application. These values are affected by everything the CPU needs to handle—running applications, processing interrupts (think video cards, network interfaces, and so on), moving memory around, and more. Once again, you need to learn the patterns of the system that you're monitoring. In conjunction with the load average metric, you can get a good idea if processes are suffering or flourishing with the CPU usage statistics.

The next line after CPU usage summarizes statistics about shared libraries. Basically, a shared library is a set of code that multiple programs use in common. For example, the Secure Sockets Layer (SSL) libraries contain routines that are useful to many other programs. You don't want each of those programs to have to implement its own SSL routines, nor do you want each to use memory on loading its own copy. So, they all can load the precompiled libssl and use its proven routines. To pull this off, multiple applications are able to share the code.

The MemRegions line lists the number and size of allocated memory regions. This is broken down into private (library and non-library) components and shared components.

The PhysMem line is just what you'd expect: the breakdown of physical memory allocation. "Wired" memory is active memory that cannot be moved out of real RAM; it's *wired down*. The *active* and *inactive* portions add up to how much memory is used. "Used" plus "free" equal the total RAM in your machine. Like CPU usage, these RAM statistics are often misinterpreted. Don't panic when free RAM is low; that's just the way Mac OS X works. About the only time free RAM is high is just after booting up. However, as Mac OS X runs over time, it starts to fill RAM for different purposes. It doesn't release RAM into the free pool immediately after a program is finished with it; rather, it then becomes "inactive." Mac OS X keeps this data available in case it needs it. If not, and it really needs more real RAM for some task, it first purges the inactive memory to make room. Mac OS X has a sophisticated and effective memory management scheme that shuffles pages of memory out to disks, wires them down, caches memory, and frees it as needed.

The final line in the example displays statistics about virtual memory. The VM statistic does not refer to virtual memory as simple swapping to disk. The first statistic on that line represents the entire virtual address space currently in use. You can match this number by adding up everything in the VSIZE column. VSIZE is a fairly useless statistic under Mac OS X because Mac OS X always gives applications a generous virtual address space to work in. But VSIZE gives you a good sense of the total address space in use, or about how much RAM you would really need if Mac OS X had no virtual address space.

Finally, you'll see pageins and pageouts statistics. A pagein happens when a page is copied from "swap" (or the "backing store") into main memory. A pageout occurs when memory is written to the backing store. Unlike older methods, Mac OS X pages rather than swaps. In earlier systems, a program was either fully in main memory or was swapped out entirely. Mac OS X, on the other hand, can take pages—4k blocks—of RAM and get them out of the way, or pull them back in as needed. A pager is responsible for moving pages in and out of RAM. A page-fault occurs when the system looks for something that should be in core memory but doesn't find it. A page-fault then causes the pager to read the appropriate page or pages from the backing store and into core memory. What does top have to say about all of this?

The top utility simply displays the current number of pageins and pageouts requested by a pager. These counts are shown as the total number, followed by the recent counts in parentheses. The recent counts are the number of pageins or pageouts in the last 1 second for the respective counter. These are important values to watch. Normally, these are 0—especially for pageouts. If you're watching top, and the number of recent pageouts stays above 0, your system is short on real RAM. The count of pageouts will rise occasionally. However, if you're witnessing a surge of pageouts over a long period of time, your system is thrashing—the system spends more time paging in and out than actually accomplishing any real work. If you see your pageouts keep creeping up, the course for system improvement is to increase the RAM in your machine.

To get more specific and detailed information about VM statistics, use the vm_stat command. This simple tool gives grand-total and interval-based statistics regarding the VM system, such as free and wired pages and pagein and pageout totals. See the man page for further information on the vm_stat command.

Besides the dashboard for top, the lower half of the display looks similar to this:

PID	COMMAND	%CPU	TIME	#TH	#PRTS	#MREGS	RPRVT	RSHRD	RSIZE	VSIZE
405	Safari	33.3%	8:50:53	19	618+	3762	348M+	44M	345M+	1009M+
8438	top	12.8%	0:01.67	1	19	34	1512K	200K	2104K	19M
213	Terminal	2.8%	52:39.76	3	102	1007	23M	22M	27M	417M
0	kernel_tas	1.3%	3:00:21	60	2	753	13M	0	233M	299M
70	WindowServ	0.9%	66:39.06	5	479	1482	13M	102M	115M	515M
7799	Mail	0.3%	21:58.11	13	342	608	93M	52M	136M	565M
7625	Microsoft	0.3%	1:43.14	5	120	670	132M	36M	181M	624M
196	SystemUISe	0.2%	4:31.74	13	482	519	8732K	17M	15M	380M
573	DashboardC	0.2%	23:20.40	4	105	158	2732K	11M	6328K	334M
8134	diskimages	0.1%	0:11.71	3	70	59	5128K	10M	7212K	39M
260	screen	0.1%	2:14.24	1	11	56	8308K	400K	8240K	45M

This sample is sorted by %CPU, issued with top -u. This makes the process area of top dynamic, always sorting the highest CPU-using tasks to the top. The columns are described as follows:

- ▶ PID—The BSD process ID

- ▶ Command—The name of the program or application bundle

- ▶ %CPU—The percentage of CPU cycles used during top's refresh interval for this process, including both kernel and user space

- ▶ Time—CPU time used by this process since launch, in minutes:seconds:hundredths format

- ▶ #TH—Number of threads in use by this process

- ▶ #PRTS—Number of machine ports used by the process

- ▶ #MREGS—The number of memory regions this process has allocated

- ▶ RPRVT—The amount of resident private memory—probably the best of these statistics to determine how much real memory a program is using

- ▶ RSHRD—The amount of resident shared memory used

- ▶ RSIZE—Resident memory size

- ▶ VSIZE—The total address space allocated to the program

There are other switches to top that will alter the number of columns and amount of information displayed. See the top man page (type man top) for more information.

The -l switch turns on logging mode, which makes top noninteractive—it just dumps its output raw to stdout. You can tell top how many times it should output. A value of 0 causes top to loop until you interrupt it by pressing Control-C. For example, top -l 0 -u -n 15 is useful to find issues when waking from sleep (too much happens before you can open a terminal and run anything to record the activity): Run top with the -l switch before putting a machine to sleep. This way, there will be a record of what happens on wake.

Other System Monitoring Utilities

Similar information to that gleaned from top can be obtained from Activity Monitor.app, a GUI-based utility, installed by default in the Utilities directory and shown in the following illustration. The CPU and System Memory tabs display identical information as seen in top, presented in the section "top, %CPU, and Load Averages."

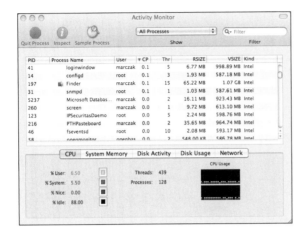

The Disk Activity tab displays statistics for system disk I/O, such as total amount read and written, and transactions per second. Similar data can be found using the command iostat. The main difference is that iostat can break down these statistics for individual devices. See the iostat man page (type man iostat) for more information.

The Disk Usage tab displays disk capacity statistics on a given device. You can also get this information using the df command-line utility. Passing in the -h ("human readable") and -t ("type") switches can produce nice results:

```
# df -h -t hfs
Filesystem      Size   Used  Avail Capacity  Mounted on
/dev/disk0s2   200Gi  177Gi  23Gi    89%     /
/dev/disk1s2   558Gi  315Gi 243Gi    27%     /Volumes/Data
/dev/disk2s2    40Gi   15Gi  25Gi    38%     /Volumes/Users
```

In this example, -t hfs limits the output to devices that are hierarchical file system (HFS) formatted (the default Macintosh file system). In the category of disk access, Activity Monitor also can display the open files (and network ports) of a running process. Double-clicking the process row in the process list displays a detail window, as shown here, for the Open Files and Ports tab.

You can also get a report of this information from a shell by using the lsof command. When you pass the -p switch and the PID of the process in question, lsof will limit its output to files related only to that process's files:

```
# lsof -p 5684
COMMAND    PID    USER    FD   TYPE    DEVICE  SIZE/OFF      NODE NAME
Firewall  5684  marczak  cwd   DIR      14,2      1258         2 /
Firewall  5684  marczak  txt   REG      14,2     43008  12653878 /usr/libexec/
ApplicationFirewall/Firewall
Firewall  5684  marczak  txt   REG      14,2   1059776  12653820 /usr/lib/dyld
Firewall  5684  marczak  txt   REG      14,2 132886528  12758680 /private/var/db/dyld/
dyld_shared_cache_i386
Firewall  5684  marczak   0r   CHR       3,2       0t0  88316804 /dev/null
Firewall  5684  marczak    1  PIPE  0x6fa91f4     16384
Firewall  5684  marczak    2  PIPE  0x6fa91f4     16384
Firewall  5684  marczak  43u  unix 0x100c9088       0t0            ->0x10d96330
```

Consult the lsof man page (type man lsof) for its many more useful abilities. Of course, the list of files that a process has open is dynamic.

A complementary tool to lsof is fs_usage. The fs_usage tool can display file system activity in real time, system-wide, or limited to a certain process or type of activity. Running fs_usage with no parameters includes the activity of all processes (except the current fs_usage process, Terminal, telnetd, sshd, rlogind, tcsh, csh, and sh—but this behavior can be overridden). The fs_usage tool can also filter its output based on certain criteria. For example, to view just the network activity for any processes named "Mail," fs_usage could be invoked with the following flags:

```
# fs_usage -w -f network Mail
```

(Remember: UNIX treats just about everything as a file—including network sockets. This is how fs_usage monitors network activity.) Being able to view file system activity as it occurs can help determine which configuration file an application is reading or writing as it runs. For example, to watch all files accessed by Microsoft Word as it runs, you can run the following command:

```
# fs_usage -f filesys "Microsoft Word"
```

Finally, the Network tab in the Activity Monitor displays statistics about systemwide network activity. This includes total packets and data sent and received, and packets and data per second. You can get this information in a shell using the `netstat` command. Once again, the command-line version can provide per-interface details. When given the -b and -I switches, `netstat` provides totals for a given interface:

```
# netstat -b -I en1
Name  Mtu   Network      Address          Ipkts Ierrs     Ibytes    Opkts Oerrs
Obytes  Coll
en1   1500  <Link#6>     00:17:f2:e6:eb:d9 27181164 2455107 14894908477 24950784      0
7706401964    0
en1   1500  Jack-Keroua fe80::217:f2ff:fe 27181164     - 14894908477 24950784      -
7706401964    -
en1   1500  192.168.100  192.168.100.163 27181164     - 14894908477 24950784      -
7706401964    -
```

When also used with the -w ("wait") switch, `netstat` provides statistics at the given interval:

```
# netstat -b -I en1 -w 2
          input       (en1)        output
   packets errs    bytes    packets errs    bytes colls
        0    1       0         6    0       234    0
        0    0       0        12    0       468    0
        0    2       0        12    0       372    0
        0    2       0         6    0       186    0
        0    3       0         6    0       186    0
```

Pressing Control-C stops the output. The -a flag will show the state of all sockets and, as a result, can be used to detect a process that is listening on the network but not generating any network activity.

To delve deeper into network traffic, the `tcpdump` utility can display and capture the IP packets that are arriving and leaving on a given interface. To view all traffic on the en0 interface, run `tcpdump` with the following flags:

```
# tcpdump -s0 -v -i en0
```

The -s0 switch instructs tcpdump to capture the entire packet (because, by default, only 68 bytes of each packet are captured); -v causes verbose output; and -i en0 makes tcpdump watch the interface named en0.

You may notice that a lot of data scrolls by on your screen. Consider two options. One is that your terminal has a scroll-back option; use it. Alternatively, tcpdump will line buffer its output when using the -l (ell) switch, which enables the output to be piped into a pager, such as less, in order to scroll through at your own pace.

The tcpdump utility can also write its output to a file with the -w switch. This is useful in three ways. First, it allows you to play back the file and inspect it at your own pace. Use the tcpdump -r switch to denote a file to read. Second, many other utilities read the output of tcpdump. (tcpdump is based on the libpcap packet capture library. Any program that works with libpcap files—often just shortened to "pcap"—will read a file created with tcpdump.) Other programs may perform additional analysis or allow you to visualize the results (such as the excellent Wireshark application). Last, having tcpdump output in file form allows you to send the file to someone else who may be able to help you interpret it.

Instruments and DTrace

Completely new to Leopard, a single utility can sum up just about everything mentioned so far: Instruments. Instruments can dynamically examine currently running code—either user-based or OS-based. While Instruments is a very impressive utility, there are some caveats. First, it takes some learning to use the tool thoroughly and effectively. The second is more a matter of policy. Instruments is installed as part of the Apple Xcode developer tool environment. It is often considered a security risk to install developer tools—particularly compilers—on certain production equipment, because this enables an attacker to upload source code and compile it on the system. You must understand your company's policy and what is permissible, and the risks associated, before installing.

Instruments is based on the command-line utility dtrace. Both applications can collect disparate statistics and information about running processes on a given system. Instruments presents its results graphically, allowing you to visualize activity patterns and associations. While a full tutorial in using Instruments is beyond the scope of this book, a quick introduction is necessary and useful.

Installing Xcode also installs Instruments in the Xcode Applications directory (by default, /Developer/Applications). Launching Instruments provides templates for common scenarios, such as the File Activity template shown here:

Select the template and click Choose to display an empty trace window. From the Default Target menu in the toolbar, choose to trace a specific running application, launch an application, or follow all currently running processes. Then click Record to begin tracing; click it again to stop tracing. Here's an example of a short trace on Mail.app:

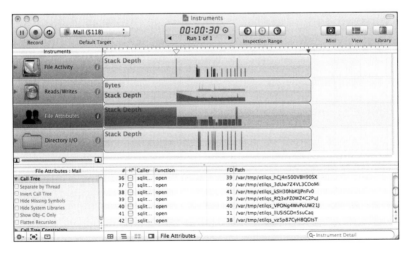

Due to the architecture of Instruments, unlike many other utilities, it hardly impacts the system that it's tracing. The dtrace utility—without which Instruments.app would not exist—can perform all of this instrumentation from a command-line shell, which presents its results textually. The dtrace utility uses its own command language called d to build probes. Instruments.app can build a d script based on the trace document currently set up, saving you from learning each aspect of the language. The dtrace utility can perform as a top replacement in one respect: finding which process is making the most system calls (and therefore being the "top" process). The following example, from a relatively short sample measured in seconds, asks dtrace to instrument syscall:::entry and aggregate on count per executable; dtrace will run until it receives the break signal (Control-C):

```
# dtrace -n syscall:::entry'{@[execname] = count()}'
dtrace: description 'syscall:::entry' matched 427 probes
^C

  openinfo                               2
  IPSecuritasDaem                        4
  socketfilterfw                         4
  syslogd                                4
  configd                                6
  openexec                               6
  pvsnatd                               11
  httpd                                 12
  DirectoryServic                       13
  mdworker                              13
  fseventsd                             18
  llipd                                 30
  screen                                32
  Finder                                36
  snmpd                                 39
  ntpd                                  42
  Terminal                              48
  dtrace                                48
  openmonitor                           51
```

```
SystemUIServer                              80
launchd                                    104
mds                                        105
WindowServer                               176
Mail                                       194
```

Leopard also includes dtruss, a shell script that is part of the dtrace toolkit by Brendan Gregg. dtruss leverages dtrace, but specifically prints details on system calls. Consider it the Leopard replacement for the now missing ktrace. As an example, to watch system call activity for an already running Mail process, run dtruss using the -n switch:

```
dtruss -n Mail
```

To run an application and monitor it, simply pass in the executable name:

```
dtruss uptime
```

The dtrace and dtruss man pages should be consulted for more information. Documentation for Instruments can be found in PDF form on disk at /Developer/ Documentation/DocSets/com.apple.ADC_Reference_Library.DeveloperTools.docset/ Contents/Resources/Documents/documentation/DeveloperTools/Conceptual/ InstrumentsUserGuide/InstrumentsUserGuide.pdf.

Xserve Tools

While Mac OS X Server will run—and run well—across different Macintosh hardware, one unit in particular stands out: the Xserve. In addition to high-availability features such as hot-swappable disk drives and redundant power supplies, an Xserve running Leopard brings a few more management methods to the mix.

Server Monitor.app (referenced here as Server Monitor) is exclusive to Mac OS X running on an Xserve, and allows you to monitor Xserve hardware status. When configured, with the addresses of one or more Xserves, colored status indicators appear in the main window, allowing a quick visual inspection, as shown here:

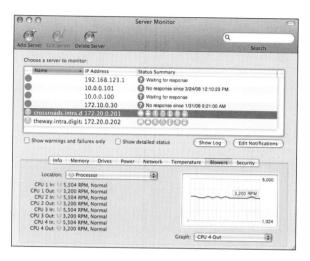

Server Monitor also allows access to the hardware's Lights Out Management (LOM) component. Essentially, LOM allows power management even when the server is powered off and no OS is running. This is accomplished over Ethernet and standard TCP/IP, using the XServe built-in network interface cards (NICs). NIC configuration for LOM is offered at initial OS install time, and can also be accessed using Server Admin. Choose Manage > Configure Local Machine to use the setup screen shown here:

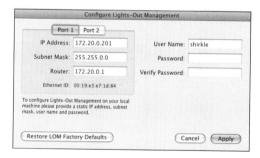

Lights Out Management can also be configured using the `ipmitool` command-line utility. Intelligent Platform Management Interface (IPMI) is a solution developed by Intel. The hardware responsible for implementing LOM is called a baseboard management controller (BMC). You can retrieve basic information about the BMC using `ipmitool`:

```
# ipmitool -U admin -a bmc info
Password:
```

```
Device ID                : 32
Device Revision          : 1
Firmware Revision        : 1.2.7
IPMI Version             : 2.0
Manufacturer ID          : 63
Manufacturer Name        : Apple Computer, Inc.
Product ID               : 1 (0x0001)
Device Available         : yes
Provides Device SDRs     : no
Additional Device Support :
    Sensor Device
    SDR Repository Device
    SEL Device
    FRU Inventory Device
    IPMB Event Receiver
    Chassis Device
Aux Firmware Rev Info    :
    0x01
    0x00
    0x27
    0x01
```

You can also gather the power-on hours (POH) of the chassis that the BMC is running on:

```
# ipmitool -U admin -a chassis poh
Password:
POH Counter  : 5633 hours total (234 days, 17 hours)
```

View more detailed information by requesting chassis status:

```
# ipmitool -U admin -a chassis status
Password:
System Power      : on
Power Overload    : false
Power Interlock   : inactive
Main Power Fault  : false
```

```
Power Control Fault   : false
Power Restore Policy : always-on
Last Power Event      :
Chassis Intrusion     : inactive
Front-Panel Lockout  : inactive
Drive Fault           : false
Cooling/Fan Fault     : false
```

Administrators have been known to not pay perfect attention to the LOM interface setup during initial Xserve install. As shown earlier, these values can be retrieved with Server Admin.app, but they can also be retrieved with `ipmitool`. The two interfaces on an Xserve are channels 1 and 2:

```
# ipmitool -U admin -a lan print 1
Password:
Set in Progress         : Set Complete
Auth Type Support       : NONE MD5 PASSWORD
Auth Type Enable        : Callback : MD5
                        : User     : MD5
                        : Operator : MD5
                        : Admin    : MD5
                        : OEM      :
IP Address Source       : Static Address
IP Address              : 192.168.70.12
Subnet Mask             : 255.255.255.0
MAC Address             : 00:19:E3:E7:70:E8
SNMP Community String   : public
IP Header               : TTL=0x40 Flags=0x40 Precedence=0x00 TOS=0x10
BMC ARP Control         : ARP Responses Enabled, Gratuitous ARP Enabled
Gratuitous ARP Interval : 127.0 seconds
Default Gateway IP      : 192.168.70.1
Default Gateway MAC     : 00:00:00:00:00:00
Backup Gateway IP       : 0.0.0.0
Backup Gateway MAC      : 00:00:00:00:00:00
RMCP+ Cipher Suites     : None
```

```
Cipher Suite Priv Max  : XXXXXXXXXXXXXX
                       :    X=Cipher Suite Unused
                       :    c=CALLBACK
                       :    u=USER
                       :    o=OPERATOR
                       :    a=ADMIN
                       :    O=OEM
```

See the `ipmitool` `man` page (type `man ipmitool`) for more information.

Other Monitoring Options

Other methods of monitoring are beyond the scope of this book, but you should be aware of them as options. Mac OS X v10.5 has a full, working SNMP implementation.

There are also third-party monitoring tools, from open source apps that you compile yourself through off-the-shelf commercial applications. Open source monitoring applications include Nagios, Swatch, Logwatch, and Tripwire. Commercial applications include Lithium, Intermapper, and Splunk. (There's a free version of Splunk, which, even with its limitations, may serve your site just fine.)

The easy lesson here is that monitoring Mac OS X can be done in many ways. You can choose the tools to use and can fit your monitoring strategy into just about any form necessary.

Setting Notifications

Systems must be able to detect problems and provide notification appropriately. There are two ways to accomplish this task: off-the-shelf applications and monitoring agents that are custom-written for the task.

As noted in the "Using Tools and Utilities" section, there are as many monitoring tools available as things to monitor. Often, problems with the system or subsystem that you are trying to monitor are well-known problems with ready solutions. Pure "system up" and "system down" monitoring and notification has been solved for some time now. Server Monitor and Server Admin even provide this functionality.

Server Admin has the more basic functionality of the two. The Settings pane for a server has a Notifications tab, shown in the following illustration. From here, you can configure two types of notifications: disk space monitoring and available software updates. When activated, and one or more valid email addresses supplied, the configured server will send an email when certain conditions are met. When configured, the configuration and rules for emond (the event monitoring daemon in Leopard) are put into place on the Xserve. A configuration file resides at /etc/emond.d/emond.conf, which informs emond how to use the rules it reads in at start, which are found in /etc/emond.d/rules/. Activating these notifications will in turn require Simple Mail Transfer Protocol (SMTP), so be aware and update firewall rules accordingly.

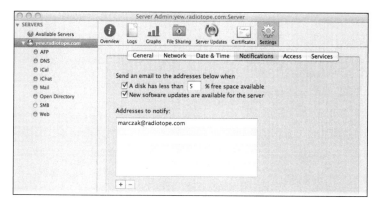

Server Monitor also can configure notifications, but will work only with an Xserve. Of course, this also allows for more detailed notifications. The notification configuration window of Server Monitor looks like this:

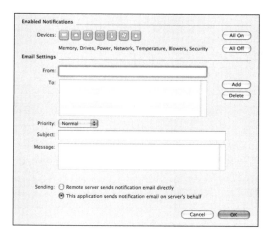

Unlike Server Admin, Server Monitor allows a custom subject and message to be configured. You can enable notifications for all hardware and sensors of an Xserve. You can configure Server Monitor in these two different ways to actually send the notification email:

▶   The option "This application sends notification email on server's behalf" enables
    Server Monitor itself to send the email message. This requires Server Monitor to be
    running to send the email; however, it also allows a centralized place to monitor several
    Xserves.

▶   The option "Remote server sends notification email directly" places the burden on the
    individual Xserve being configured. Specifically, this burden is on the hwmond daemon.
    Server Admin notifications are really just a nice front end to the hwmond configuration
    file. hwmond is launched at boot time by launchd, and controlled by the hwmond.plist
    file found at /System/Library/LaunchDaemons/com.apple.hwmond.plist. The hwmond
    file reads in /etc/hwmond.conf and /etc/hwmond.conf.SMART.

While the built-in tools are useful in smaller environments, their limitations come to light in larger environments. The Server Monitor "This application sends" option is generally a bad security practice because it leaves an administrative application open at all times, and relies on it to be running to send out notifications. Also, neither Server Admin nor Server Monitor have the ability to specify recipients of notifications; all users configured will receive all notifications.

Custom-Scripted Notifications

To provide notifications for situations that Server Admin and Server Monitor do not account for, you may consider an off-the-shelf product. No tool can anticipate every need and every situation. Off-the-shelf products may require custom-written scripts in order to take action. As an example, see "Creating Action Scripts" for the Lithium monitoring platform (http://docs.lithiumcorp.com/content/view/192/122/). Additionally, there are many opportunities to write scripts that monitor a system that do not require third-party applications.

These scripts can typically take the form of any scripting language, as long as the language can pass back a return code denoting success or failure. Another built-in method of monitoring is launchd. In Mac OS X v10.5, launchd contains a new key that automatically monitors a service: KeepAlive.

When `launchd` runs a plist with the `KeepAlive` key set to true, `launchd` will automatically restart the executable if it exits. Further enhancing this functionality are subkeys to `KeepAlive` that can determine if the program should actually be restarted under current conditions. See "launchd and launchctl" in Chapter 9 for more information and examples of `launchd` using the `KeepAlive` key.

Creating Reports

In many ways, reporting and documenting are just other forms of monitoring. This section covers two Mac OS X–specific methods of creating reports.

System Profiler.app, found in the Utilities directory, provides practically every detail about a system that you would need for a report. Of course, it would be impractical to visit every machine in an organization, run System Profiler.app, record the information, and move on. Therefore, Apple includes a command-line version of System Profiler.app: `system_profiler`.

`system_profiler` can retrieve any data about the system that it runs on that the GUI-based System Profiler.app can. Being text-based, it lends itself to easily moving that data to other sources, possibly as part of a script that can make other decisions. It can create plain, human-readable output, or XML output (which, of course, is also technically "human readable").

For a standard report, simply type:

```
system_profiler
```

To get the same data but create XML output, use the `-xml` switch.

`system_profiler` breaks its areas of reporting into separate data types, or groups. Not all data types or groups are reported on by default. To get an entire list of data types, use the `-listdatatypes` switch (output is truncated for space considerations):

```
system_profiler -listdatatypes
Available Datatypes:
SPHardwareDataType
SPNetworkDataType
SPSoftwareDataType
SPParallelATADataType
```

```
SPAudioDataType
SPBluetoothDataType
SPDiagnosticsDataType

...

SPApplicationsDataType
SPExtensionsDataType
SPFontsDataType
SPFrameworksDataType
SPLogsDataType
SPManagedClientDataType
SPPrefPaneDataType
SPStartupItemDataType
SPUniversalAccessDataType
```

Individual data types can be reported on simply by specifying them on the command line:

```
system_profiler SPHardwareDataType SPDiagnosticsDataType -xml
```

This reporting is much faster than forcing system_profiler to dump everything and then use grep to pick out an individual result. Combine the methods if needed:

```
system_profiler SPBluetoothDataType -detaillevel mini | grep Address
```

As the preceding example also shows, you can specify the level of detail with the -detail-level switch. Acceptable levels are mini, basic, and full.

With all of its options, system_profiler is an ideal tool to sporadically run on systems, or to use a login hook to extract system information and feed it to a central database. Thanks to the broad support for scripting languages in Mac OS X, this is easily achievable. Perl, Python, Ruby, and PHP all support calling external executable programs, and all have modules that talk to popular database engines. Finally, they all make ideal environments in which to make decisions in a login hook.

Another Apple creation suited for the task of reporting is Apple Remote Desktop (ARD). Unlike system_profiler, Apple Remote Desktop is not built into the system and must be purchased. Its capabilities extend beyond just reporting. This section, however, will only focus on its reporting capabilities.

If your credentials are authorized for a given machine or set of machines, you will be able to run a `system_profiler`-like report against one or all of the machines. Clicking the Report button in the ARD toolbar brings up a dialog box like this:

Once the report data has been collected, ARD displays a summary window with the data from all machines listed in a table, as shown here:

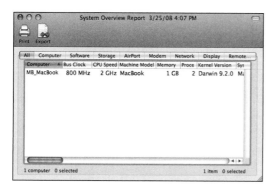

You can export this data as a tab-delimited or comma-delimited file by clicking the Export button in the toolbar of the report data window. The Save As dialog box then appears:

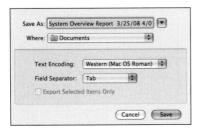

The tab-delimited or comma-delimited file can then be imported into other databases, such as MySQL or FileMaker Pro. This is useful for documentation, further analysis, and general reporting.

Troubleshooting

A section on troubleshooting may seem repetitive, because this entire chapter has in some way been about troubleshooting. Logs and other monitoring history are what you reach for in the event of a problem. However, even those tools can themselves have problems.

One problem that crops up is that no new entries are being written to the system log. The first troubleshooting step here is simple, but often overlooked. Is syslogd running? Use the ps (process status) command to find out. If it is not, use launchctl to relaunch syslogd:

```
launchctl load /System/Library/LaunchDaemons/com.apple.syslog.plist
```

If syslogd fails to stay alive, check the system log. Often, syslogd will write its failure reason to the log before exiting. If no message is written to the system log, check the crash log in /Library/Logs. If there is no indication of a syslogd crash, a disk scan may be in order.

If notifications are configured in any of the various ways discussed in this chapter, but you believe they are not being sent out, there may be a few points of failure. However, they mostly relate to email troubleshooting, because all of the methods discussed rely on standard SMTP. Issues to look for would include checking the server-side mail logs, ensuring that proper email addresses are being specified, checking whether any firewall or network issue is blocking SMTP traffic, and checking client-side issues such as notifications being trapped by a spam filter.

What You've Learned

The information in this chapter should remove all doubt about routine monitoring. Log files are the harbinger of upcoming system problems. Log files and information are generated 24 hours a day, every day, so it should also be clear that you need some type of automated monitoring solution. Thankfully, monitoring and notification solutions are built into the system, and custom methods of monitoring are relatively easy to create using built-in scripting languages and utilities.

▶   Logs are a critical part of monitoring and understanding a system.

▶   Apple has rewritten the traditional UNIX system logging daemon, `syslogd`, to include writing log entries to the asl.log database.

▶   Log messages are categorized by level and facility.

▶   There are many tools built into Mac OS X to read and monitor log files, such as Console.app, `syslog`, `tail`, and `less`.

▶   A monitoring policy helps a business determine what to monitor, who has access, how long to keep log files, and what the response to issues will be.

▶   Apple provides many tools along with Mac OS X to monitor the state of the system and its utilization. Some of these tools are specific to, and only work with, the Xserve hardware.

▶   There are many options for creating reports on systems running Mac OS X, including Apple Remote Desktop, `system_profiler`, third-party applications, and custom scripts.

Review Quiz

1. What is the name of the logging daemon used in Mac OS X?

2. How does the Apple System Logger (ASL) differ from traditional UNIX logging daemons?

3. What is the purpose of log levels and facilities?

4. Do all programs need `syslogd` to create logs?

5. Name two statistics to help determine CPU usage.

6. What is the graphical application that allows an administrator of an Xserve to send notifications when problems are detected with its hardware?

Answers

1. `syslogd` is the logging daemon used in Mac OS X.

2. ASL immediately writes all entries to a database at /var/log/asl.log. It is a binary file that can only be inspected using the `syslog` command-line tool or various interfaces.

3. Log levels and facilities help classify a log entry. The level determines the severity of the message, and the facility helps determine which subsystem sent the message. The Apple system logger can also route messages based on their level and facility designation.

4. Since a log file is simply text, a program is free to create its own method of logging and determine where to put that method on disk.

5. CPU percentage and load average are two statistics that help determine CPU usage.

6. Server Monitor.app is the graphical application that allows an Xserve administrator to send notifications when problems are detected with the hardware.

9

Time   This lesson takes approximately 90 minutes to complete.

Goals   Learn how automation through scripting benefits administrators

Learn about different automation technologies included with Mac OS X

Learn about launchd and its importance to Mac OS X

Learn how to convert legacy job control systems into launchd jobs

Chapter 9

Automating Systems

The graphical user interface of Mac OS X is highly regarded by many. You can accomplish almost everything by dragging a mouse pointer around the screen. Crucial for administrators, Mac OS X also contains scripting frameworks that allow for powerful *automation*: the automatic actions of systems, reducing or eliminating the need for human intervention.

Automation benefits many of the tasks involved in system administration. Automating your system spares an administrator from manually performing time-consuming tasks and raises quality as consistency is ensured. From manipulating user accounts to installing packages on thousands of machines, it's in an administrator's best interest to learn ways to automate these tasks.

Understanding Mac OS X Automation

Mac OS X is truly an automator's dream system. While many administrators know one or two technologies that Mac OS X offers for scripting and automation, few realize all of the possibilities.

The original Apple-created scripting language, AppleScript, is alive and well in Mac OS X, along with Automator, a new AppleScript-inspired tool. Automator allows you to automate tasks even if you are relatively inexperienced with scripting or programming. Mac OS X features many technologies that are well-known on other platforms: shell scripting; Perl and Python (discussed in this chapter); and PHP, Tcl, and Ruby. Any of these languages can call and be called by AppleScript.

Specifically, the following shells are included with the system:

▶   bash—The "Bourne-again" shell (the default shell)

▶   sh—A copy of the bash shell, which behaves like the original sh shell when called as sh

▶   csh—The C shell

▶   tcsh—The Tenex C Shell (enhanced csh)

▶   ksh—The Korn shell

▶   zsh—Similar to ksh (includes features from csh, tcsh)

▶   tclsh—Shell-like tool for the Tool Command Language (Tcl)

All shells are stored in the /bin directory except tclsh, which is in the/usr/bin directory.

All of these technologies differ in their specific approach, but share some overall similarities: Each scripting technology can interact with the user to some extent, use variables to store values, make decisions (called *flow control*), and perform an action one or more times (called *looping*).

A major addition to Mac OS X starting with v10.4 is launchd, a daemon responsible for starting up the system, starting jobs on a schedule or on demand, and handling shutdown. Leopard delivers the second revision of launchd, adding more capabilities. Unlike the scripting technologies just discussed, launchd is not a language and does not share the same capabilities; it is used to start scripts written in a scripting language. This chapter covers launchd separately from the other technologies.

Comparing Automation Technologies

You do not need to master every automation technology, but it helps to know the strengths and weaknesses of each when tackling certain problems. Because of the variety of capabilities, it's to your advantage to be familiar with several languages. For example, bash can quickly loop over shell commands to touch many directories, but is poor at taking advantage of Mac OS X application programming interfaces (APIs), which are native methods of the operating system to support requests from programs. While an exhaustive look at each scripting environment is beyond the scope of this book, this section introduces the most popular languages: bash, Python, and AppleScript.

Using bash

Unlike other scripting environments, bash is a scripting language *and* an interactive shell. By default, bash is what is running "inside" Terminal.app. Mac OS X has other shells, but bash is the default when creating a new account. The bash shell also will often be your interface when running executables written in any language, compiled or interpreted. For this reason alone, it is important to become familiar with working in bash. The bash shell excels at batching shell commands and at general automation. It is poor at database access, fast math, and lengthy programs. It is typically used to automate system maintenance.

When running Terminal.app, bash awaits your command at the prompt. By default, the prompt is a dollar sign ($) and a cursor that marks the point of insertion for typing. When you type a command and press Return, bash goes to work. First, bash locates the command, creates a subshell (this action is also called *forking*) in which to run the command, runs the command, and waits for completion. Administrators who repeatedly type the same commands to achieve a task now can put those commands into a file and make them executable. This file is called a *script*. When a script is run, it will execute all of the commands in the file. For example, if, as an administrator, you check disk capacity every morning by logging in and typing df -h, you could replace this action with a script. You can run the following sample script on a server to gather the disk capacity data and mail it to an email address:

```
#!/usr/bin/env bash

MAIL_ADDRESS="admin@pretendco.com"

df -t hfs -h > /tmp/diskcap.txt
mail -s "Disk Report" ${MAIL_ADDRESS} < /tmp/diskcap.txt
rm /tmp/diskcap.txt
```

This script nicely illustrates several features of the bash shell. When a script is run, it is evaluated line-by-line, in order, top to bottom.

The first line is the *shebang* line that informs the shell which interpreter to use when running this script. In this case, it's a bash script, so bash will find out that the commands should be run through bash itself.

Next, the script sets a *variable*. A variable is a name that stands for a value. In this case, MAIL_ADDRESS is assigned the value admin@pretendco.com. When a variable is created, just the name of the variable is used, and an equals sign (=) with no spaces on either side is used to assign a value. When the variable is referenced, a dollar sign is used to show that it's not to be taken literally.

The next line demonstrates *output redirection*. The df command is run (see "Determining Disk Utilization" in Chapter 4 for more information on df), and the greater-than symbol (>) captures any output destined for stdout and redirects it into the file listed: /tmp/diskcap.txt. The following line demonstrates *input redirection*. The mail command receives the contents of the file after the input redirection symbol, the less-than sign (<), and uses it as the body of the email.

The same line references the MAIL_ADDRESS variable. The bash shell basically replaces the name ${MAIL_ADDRESS} with its value *before* running the mail command. In a larger script, variables are critical to program maintenance and readability.

Finally, the script uses an rm command to remove the file that you created.

The script is typed into a regular text editor: TextWrangler, TextMate, and vi are all good choices. It is important that you save the file as plain text, and not in a word processing format like Microsoft Word. (Although Word can save in plain text, it's not the default format.)

Once you've saved the script in a file, you must make the script *executable*. This is accomplished using the chmod command:

```
chmod 770 name_of_script
```

You can then run the script by specifying a full or relative path to the new executable. If you're working in the same directory as the script, you must still provide the current directory. So, for a script named diskcap.sh, you would run it from the current directory with this command:

```
./diskcap.sh
```

Alternatively, you can specify the *fully qualified* or *absolute* path. If this file was saved in your home directory, and your user name is "bill", this command would be:

```
/Users/bill/diskcap.sh
```

Paths play an important role in the shell. A *path* generally refers to the on-disk hierarchy to find a particular folder or file. For example, the path to the Apache web server's configuration file, http.conf, is /etc/apache2.

The shell, when asked to run a program, will search a default set of locations. For this reason, you don't have to type the full path for certain commands. Consider the df command (see "Determining Disk Utilization" in Chapter 4). The command resides in the /bin directory. You don't need to type the *absolute* path, /bin/df, because the /bin directory is specified in the shell's *search* path. The bash shell looks at the directories specified in the $PATH shell variable, and searches each in turn, looking for the specified command. The first executable file found that is matched by name is run. That is, if two executable files with the same filename reside in different directories, both of which are in the search path, the first found is executed. If the shell does not find a match, it prints a "command not found" error:

```
$ commence_plan.sh
-bash: commence_plan.sh: command not found
```

You can find all current shell variables using the set command. The $PATH variable stores the current search path, which is easier to find when filtered out with grep:

```
$ set | grep ^PATH
PATH=/usr/bin:/bin:/usr/sbin:/sbin:/usr/local/bin:/usr/X11/bin
```

Another method of displaying an environment variable is to use echo:

```
$ echo $PATH
/usr/bin:/bin:/usr/sbin:/sbin:/usr/local/bin:/usr/X11/bin
```

A colon (:) separates each individual absolute path in the overall search path. When bash is asked to run an unqualified executable, each path listed in the $PATH variable will be searched by bash in order. For example, using the list shown in the preceding echo statement, bash would first search /usr/bin, and then /bin, then /usr/sbin, and so on. Each path in the example above ends in "bin" (but doesn't have to). In this case, bin is short for binary, and the directory where UNIX systems have traditionally stored binary (or compiled) executables. Nowadays, not every executable in a bin directory is actually a binary—often the executable will be interpreted scripts written in bash, Perl, or Python—but the spirit is the same.

The $PATH variable is an *environment* variable. An environment variable is a shell variable exported with the export keyword. A standard shell variable and an environment variable differ in subtle but important ways. When the shell runs a command, it forks off a subshell in which the command is run. Only environment variables are passed into, or *inherited* by, subshells. You can display current environment variables using the env command. Create a shell variable with a simple assignment:

```
$ color=blue
```

Use the export command to create an environment variable:

```
$ export city=NY
```

Combining bash and User Attributes

Closing the current shell, which happens after rebooting or exiting a shell intentionally, discards the shell and environment variables mentioned in the previous section. How are all of the variables set in the first place, and how can you set your own to affect your session?

The bash shell looks for certain files as it starts up. First, it looks for and executes /etc/profile, if the file exists. This affects all users logging in. After processing /etc/profile, bash processes the user-specific files in the current user's home directory, in the order ~/.bash_profile, ~/.bash_login, and ~/.profile. The bash shell reads and executes commands from the first file that exists and is readable. These files create the startup environment.

You should put systemwide variables and startup scripts into /etc/profile. But do not store password information in this file (for example, to run a program that needs a password passed to it on the command line); login shells need access to /etc/profile, so it's open for anyone to read.

You should place options specific to a user in one of the personal files in a user's home directory—typically ~/.bash_profile. The contents of these files are run at shell login, and can be used to set variables or run utilities. A common use of a ~/.bash_profile startup is to alter the default $PATH variable and set the shell prompt.

As an administrator, you'll need a root-level shell to view the profile scripts of other users. For example, if you need to look at the profile for the user "tim," use `cat` or `less` with `sudo`:

```
$ sudo less /Users/tim/.bash_profile
```

Getting Help

While there are many books, articles, and web tutorials about the `bash` shell, often you need help on-the-spot. The `bash` shell offers built-in help in the form of *man* pages. "man" is short for manual, and the "pages" in `man` contain information on individual commands and their options, including ways to influence the behavior of the `bash` shell itself. They even contain help on the `man` command (`man man!`).

Using `man` is as simple as typing the `man` command followed by the command for which you want help. For example, if you can't recall the multitude of switches that the `ls` command uses to format its output in a particular fashion, type the following and then press Return to fill your terminal with the `man` page:

```
man ls
```

You can use these navigation and search techniques:

▶ Navigate the page with the Up and Down arrow keys to move one line at a time.

▶ Press the Space bar to move forward one page at a time.

▶ Press Control-F and Control-B to move forward and backward one page at a time, respectively.

▶ Search for words by pressing the forward slash (/) and typing a pattern to search for. The pattern is actually a regular expression. When searching literally for any of the following characters, you must type a backslash (\) before the character (called *escaping* the character):

  ▶ Square bracket: [

  ▶ Backslash: \

  ▶ Caret: ^

  ▶ Dollar sign: $

  ▶ Dot: .

- ▶ Pipe: |

- ▶ Question mark: ?

- ▶ Asterisk: *

- ▶ Plus sign: +

- ▶ Parenthesis: ()

- ▶ Curly braces: {}

For example, to find "3.1", you would type 3\.1 to escape the dot.

To have man search for keywords across multiple man pages, use the -k switch:

```
$ man -k sort
radixsort(3), sradixsort(3) - radix sort
scandir(3), alphasort(3) - scan a directory
slapo-valsort(5)       - Value Sorting overlay
sort(1)              - sort lines of text files
texindex(1)           - sort Texinfo index files
top(1)               - display and update sorted information about processes
tsort(1)             - topological sort of a directed graph
(some output removed for space considerations)
```

Many of the options returned may seem similar to other options, or even have the same name. The number in parenthesis beside each name lists the *section* or the manual that it comes from. You can think of the section number as a chapter number, with each chapter being dedicated to one style of command. The sections are organized into the following categories:

1. General User Commands

2. System Calls

3. Library Routines

4. Special Files and Sockets

5. File Formats and Conventions

6. Games and Fun Stuff

7. Miscellaneous Documentation

8. System Administration

9. Kernel and Programming Style

You can use the section number to open a man page for a specific variant of a command. For example, when typing man -k open, you'll find both an open (1) and open (2).". To open the specific man page, tell man the section number:

```
man 2 open
```

This will display "open" from section 2, "System Calls," rather than "open" from section 1.

The individual man pages are simply individual files on the system disk. The man program knows where to find man pages via the $MANPATH shell variable. Much like the shell search path shown earlier, the $MANPATH variable contains a colon-separated list of file system paths in which to find man pages. To find the current list of man page locations, use set and then use grep to filter on MANPATH:

```
$ set | grep MANPATH
MANPATH=/usr/share/man:/usr/local/share/man:/usr/X11/man
```

The three paths in the example are the default locations where Mac OS X stores the man pages.

Finally, many commands will give help directly when called with the --help switch, or with no parameters:

```
$ man --help
man, version 1.6c

usage: man [-adfhktwW] [section] [-M path] [-P pager] [-S list]
           [-m system] [-p string] name ...

  a : find all matching entries
  c : do not use cat file
  d : print gobs of debugging information
(output removed for space considerations)
```

Having local man pages available can enable you to get help on-the-spot, rather than have to search for the answer in a book or on the web.

Employing Flow Control

Without flow control, a bash script is really a batch processor: It takes a list of commands and runs them one at a time in order. While that sequential approach can be useful, flow control allows your script to take different paths based on certain conditions. This directed approach makes a script much more powerful than a simple batching of commands. The flow control statements in bash allow a script creator to test for the presence of files, whether a program succeeded or failed, and compare variables. They also allow repeating sections of a script, called *looping*.

To test conditions, use an if statement. Here is the generic version:

```
if condition; then
  true branch
else
  false branch
fi
```

The else section is optional. Unlike many high-level languages that actually include tests for different variable types, bash only gives the illusion of doing so. All the if statement can test is a program's exit code. By convention, when a program exits, it passes a numerical value back to the program that started it—its *exit code*. In this case, that program is the bash shell itself. An exit code of 0 specifies success. Any other number denotes a warning or failure. The bash shell uses this exit code to determine which branch to take in an if statement. For example:

```
if grep -qi fail /var/log/syslog; then
echo "Failure conditions in the log"
fi
```

When grep runs, it will return an exit code to if. On finding the text in the file, grep is successful and returns a 0. If grep does not find the text it is looking for, or the file doesn't exist, it returns a non-zero result. With this success error code, if allows the echo statement to run and print its message.

The bash shell's test command, or [, can perform many different tests and return the result as an exit code. In this way, bash flow control allows almost arbitrary testing, beyond just exit-code testing. See the test man page for the full list of tests that bash can perform. (For information on using man pages, see "Getting Help" earlier in this chapter.)

Besides a binary yes/no in the if flow control, the for loop provides looping. A *loop* repeats the same section of code until a condition is met. Here is the generic for loop:

```
for variable in (list); do
 [commands to repeat]
done
```

The best way to describe bash's for loop is with an example:

```
for i in a e i o u; do
echo ${i}
done
```

Each pass through the loop assigns each letter in the list to the variable $i. The loop is complete when the elements in the list have been exhausted. The list can be generated at runtime. For example:

```
for i in `grep -l Edward *`; do
mv ${i} /Shared/ed_files/$1
done
```

In this example, the grep statement outputs a list of files that contain the string Edward. One at a time, the body of the loop moves the file specified to the /Shared/ed_files directory.

Using Alternate Shells

The bash shell is the default shell when creating a new user, but it's not the only option of the many popular shells bundled with Mac OS X. Users who want to change their shell probably know how to do so. But users may have reasons for wanting a particular shell. Someone may want to be set up with a particular shell from the start. Users who have upgraded to Mac OS X since v10.3, when tcsh was the default shell, and have kept their home directory intact, will still have the tcsh shell in effect. They may want to change over to bash.

It is simple to change the default shell in the various graphical user interfaces that alter user information. Additionally, Mac OS X includes the traditional UNIX chsh (change shell), which has been updated to change the shell information in the right place.

Users can update their own shell by invoking chsh. This example changes the current user's shell to /bin/csh:

```
chsh /bin/csh
```

As root, you can alter other users' shell preference. Use the -u switch to specify the user. The following example changes the user marczak to use /bin/zsh:

```
chsh -u marczak /bin/zsh
```

In Mac OS X, this information is stored in the user record in Directory Services, which can be read with dscl:

```
dscl localhost read /Search/Users/username UserShell
```

Using Mac OS X–Specific Commands

With foundations in traditional UNIX, Mac OS X also includes many Mac OS X–specific commands in the operating system. In many cases, using the Mac OS X–specific command is the only way you can script a solution. If you're coming to Mac OS X from another platform, you need to be aware of these methods. Always search man pages when looking for commands that alter system settings; see "Getting Help" in this chapter for more information.

defaults

The defaults command allows users to read and write entries from user defaults (preferences). Mac OS X stores user defaults in plists (property lists). Increasingly, these plist files are binary rather than plain text, making direct editing difficult. Each preference file is considered a domain. To read or write a value from a domain, use the read or write verbs, respectively. For example, to find the current defaults about the desktop background, you can read the information from the com.apple.desktop domain:

```
defaults read com.apple.desktop Background
```

To find a specific value, you can read an entire preference file:

```
defaults read com.apple.iChat | less
```

When a preference to change has been identified, you can use the write verb to write the key and value to the user defaults:

```
defaults write com.apple.iChat UseSingleChatWindow 1
```

If the specified key exists, it is overwritten. If it does not exist, it is created.

Machine-wide defaults can be altered using sudo and specifying the /Library/Preferences path:

```
defaults read /Library/Preferences/com.apple.loginwindow
```

User preferences typically appear in a program's preferences menu item. However, often options are not available through this menu—so-called *hidden preferences*. The defaults system allows administrators to script these changes, which can, in turn, affect many machines in an automated way. See the defaults man page for more options; for information on using man pages, see "Getting Help" earlier in this chapter.

systemsetup

The systemsetup command allows command-line scripting of most values in System Preferences. For example, to display the current boot disk, supply the -getStartupDisk switch:

```
$ systemsetup -getstartupdisk
/System/Library/CoreServices
```

You can find valid boot disks using the -listStartupDisks switch:

```
$ systemsetup -liststartupdisks
/System/Library/CoreServices
/Volumes/Server_Backup/System/Library/CoreServices
/Volumes/ServerAlt/System/Library/CoreServices
```

You can supply any of the values from the -listStartupDisks list to systemsetup and the -setStartupDisk switch:

```
# systemsetup –setstartupdisk /Volumes/Server_Backup/System/Library/CoreServices
```

Sometimes systemsetup and other ways of changing system preferences overlap. However, systemsetup is usually more efficient and may change values in several places with a single command.

networksetup

While Mac OS X contains the full breadth of traditional UNIX command-line utilities, some may not work as expected, especially when it comes to setting values. For instance, the ifconfig command works as expected to read information about a network interface. However, the Mac OS X automatic configuration system, configd, will override changes made with ifconfig. The networksetup command can alter all aspects of network interfaces and their properties in a way that Mac OS X expects. networksetup uses an interface's "friendly name" (the name presented in the Networking Preference pane, not the Berkeley Software Distribution [BSD] device name) because system labels are ephemeral and may change between boots.

To list the network services by name, use the -listAllNetworkServices switch:

```
# networksetup -listallnetworkservices
An asterisk (*) denotes that a network service is disabled.
Built-in Ethernet
*Built-in FireWire
*AirPort
*Bluetooth
FireWire
```

For example, to display current Domain Name System (DNS) servers for the Built-in Ethernet interface, use the -getDNSServers switch:

```
# networksetup -getdnsservers "Built-in Ethernet"
127.0.0.1
```

Other Mac OS X–Specific Commands

You should be aware of the following commands. Most of them are covered elsewhere in this book, but are included here for the sake of completeness.

system_profiler—Reports on system software and hardware configuration

dscl—Directory Services Command Line; reads and writes values relating to bound directory services

dsimport—Directory Services Import

osascript—Runs AppleScript commands and other OSA language scripts from the command line

`automator`—Starts Automator workflows from the command line

`lpadmin`—Along with other `lp` commands (`lp`, `lpc`, `lpinfo`, `lpmove`, `lpoptions`, `lppasswd`, `lpq`, `lpr`, `lprm`, and `lpstat`), allows printer queue querying, manipulation, and maintenance

Using Python

Python is a unique language that blurs the line between a scripting language and a full programming language. As many companies, including Apple, have adopted Python for their projects, this section presents the `bash` examples from this chapter in their corresponding Python code. These examples should help you understand what you're looking at if you ever need to investigate a Python script.

Python excels at just about everything. Many libraries are available that allow Python to access databases, create graphical user interface applications, and interact more closely with the system. When you first execute a Python file, it is compiled into an intermediary byte-code file. This format greatly speeds future executions. The only potential downside to Python is that not all system administrators know it, making code written in Python more difficult for others to maintain.

Python scripts should start with the following shebang (`#!`) line to denote the Python interpreter that should run the program:

```
#!/usr/bin/env python
```

Variables are straightforward assignments in Python. Just do it:

```
b=7
print b
```

To reference a variable, you need only its name, no dollar sign. Python specifies strings using single, double, or triple quotes (that is, three single quotes). Triple quotes allow multiline strings.

Rather than using braces or other keywords to denote the start and end of a block of code, Python relies on the indent level. Flow control statements use this fact to set the code. Here is a sample comparison (`if`) statement:

```
if name=="mike":
    print "Hello, Mike"
```

Python has several types of loops. One is a `while` loop; code repeats *while* a condition is true:

```
b=5
while b>0:
    print b
    b=b-1
```

Like `bash`, Python also has a `for` loop:

```
for i in range(1, 5):
print i
```

In Mac OS X, Apple has increased the use of Python in several ways. It is now a first-class language in Xcode, and can make Objective-C API calls. Python is a deep, object-oriented language that cannot be summed up in a short space. For more information, you can refer to many excellent books and sources of information on the subject.

Using AppleScript

AppleScript is the original scripting and automation language for Macintosh. Created by Apple in 1992, it is an English-like language, designed to be easy for beginners to learn. It is unique in many respects, not the least of which is that it is a graphical user interface scripting language. This means that is it designed to query and manipulate objects in the graphical user interface (remember that before Mac OS X, there was no command line in the Macintosh). This section will present the examples from the `bash` section in their AppleScript form as closely as possible.

AppleScript is tightly integrated with Mac OS X. As a graphical scripting language, it can interact with graphical user interface elements in ways that are more difficult or impossible for other languages to match. It is the closest thing to a native scripting language that Mac OS X has, and is easy for nonscripters to pick up. One downside is its comparatively slow speed of execution. Also, not all applications are AppleScript-friendly and they can be difficult to script. Finally, AppleScript is implemented as a component of the Open Scripting Architecture (OSA), which provides a standard and extensible mechanism for interapplication communication in Mac OS X.

Mac OS X includes the Script Editor application, found in Applications > AppleScript, designed to edit and execute AppleScript code.

Variables in AppleScript are assigned with the set keyword:

```
set theText to "Hello there!"
display dialog theText
```

With no shell environment, text output must be displayed in the graphical user interface in some manner. The display dialog function places a string in a dialog box with an OK button for dismissal. As with any other scripting language, flow control in AppleScript plays an important role.

The if conditional statement uses the then and end if keywords to denote the block of code to execute:

```
if the percent_free is less than 10 then
    display dialog "The startup disk is low on space!"
end if
```

Looping is accomplished with a repeat statement:

```
set wordList to words in "This short list"
repeat with currentWord in wordList
    display dialog currentWord
end repeat
```

This example displays a dialog box three times, each time with a word from the wordlist variable.

AppleScript can run shell scripts of any variety with its do shell script command. AppleScript code can also be called from the command line or a script using the osascript command. For example, to display a dialog box in the Finder with the text "Alert!," the following command could be used:

```
$ osascript -e 'tell application "Finder"' -e "activate" -e "display dialog
\"Alert!\"" -e 'end tell'
```

The osascript command can also run commands contained in a file. For example, to run the script file alert_me.scpt, the following command could be used:

```
$ osascript /path/to/alert_me.scpt
```

Finally, note that AppleScript is used extensively throughout the graphical Automator.app.

You can download the Apple AppleScript reference free from http://developer.apple.com/documentation/AppleScript/Conceptual/AppleScriptLangGuide/introduction/ASLR_intro.html.

Using launchd

To be familiar with Mac OS X, you must become familiar with launchd. An Apple-created technology, launchd is the master way to launch, monitor, and maintain jobs. It encompasses a wide range of system functionality previously handled by many separate subsystems. The launchd man page describes it as the "System-wide and per-user daemon/agent manager." Actually, launchd runs *everything*. As process ID number 1, launchd is responsible for tasks such as booting the system and running boot-time jobs, through launching applications run via a double-click in the Finder. It also makes the system more efficient in various ways.

About launchd

The impetus behind launchd was the combination of separate subsystems that made it difficult to choose a startup method and, for administrators, to manage jobs once they had been started.

In its first versions, Mac OS X (and NEXTSTEP before it) took a lot of time-tested UNIX technology verbatim. If you look on a computer running Solaris or IRIX and a Mac OS X v10.3 computer, you'll find many of the same system daemons: init to start the system (process ID 1), the /etc/rc script for boot-time configuration and launching, at and cron for scheduling jobs, and inetd to manage access to starting daemons based on network events. While each of those systems developed variants over the years—anacron for cron, and xinetd for inetd, to name two—the fact remained the same: There were many ways to start jobs during and after bootup. Apple also brought methods into the mix with SystemStarter and mach_init.

The transition to launchd functions began with its introduction in Mac OS X v10.4.

Exploring launchd Functions

Think of launchd as a one-stop shop. If you need to perform some action with a job, use launchd to do any of the following:

▶ Launch a program initially or on a schedule.

▶ Ensure that your program gets restarted if it crashes.

▶ Load new jobs post-boot and unload jobs that are running. (Technically, a user space program called launchctl handles these actions, but it is a component of launchd.)

The Apple-created launchd system takes over for several other disparate components in Mac OS X, such as the following:

▶ init

▶ SystemStarter

▶ mach_init

▶ /etc/rc

▶ at

▶ cron

▶ watchdog

▶ xinetd

In Leopard, some of these subsystems, such as cron, still exist and function, but all have either been heavily deprecated or simply dropped. For example, watchdog is gone; to replicate its functions, you need to use launchd. at still exists, but is disabled by default. To use at, you need to enable it via launchctl using root-level privileges:

```
#launchctl load -w /System/Library/LaunchDaemons/com.apple.atrun.plist
```

Using launchd plists

How does launchd function, and how can an administrator interact with it? During boot-up, once the kernel is loaded and initializes itself, it launches launchd, which becomes PID 1 and manages the system from that point. Using launchd is as simple as installing a plist in the right place.

launchd relies entirely on properly formatted plists being in the right place. When launchd becomes PID 1 and takes over, it scans a series of directories. These directories follow the Apple schema for other file locations. Table 9-1 summarizes each location and its use for launchd:

Table 9-1 Directory Location of Plists and launchd Use

File Location	launchd Use
/Library/LaunchDaemons	Per-machine jobs provided by a sysadmin
/System/Library/LaunchDaemons	Per-machine jobs supplied by Apple
~/Library/LaunchAgents	Programs run in a user's session
/Network/Library/LaunchAgents	Per-user program installed by sysadmin; affects all systems on a network (bound to the directory service)
/Library/LaunchAgents	Per-user jobs installed by sysadmin; run for each user on a single machine
/System/Library/LaunchAgents	Per-user jobs provided by OS X

A plist is an XML-based file consisting of keys and values. Plists can be plain text or binary, but launchd uses only plain-text plists.

A launchd plist has only three required keys: Label, ProgramArguments, and KeepAlive. (KeepAlive is new to v10.5 and replaces the now-deprecated OnDemand.)

The Label key gives the launchd job a unique name. This name is entirely user-supplied, and can technically be any string. Popular convention, though, is the reverse-DNS naming scheme popularized by Java. A label is permanent, meaning that you can always refer to the job by this name (unlike a Process ID [PID], which, if the process restarts, will get a new PID).

ProgramArguments denotes the program to be run and, if applicable, any arguments that the program should be run with.

While launchd will load a plist without a KeepAlive key, its explicit use is recommended. The KeepAlive key in many respects replaces watchdog. If set to false, launchd will run the program only when asked to by some condition. If set to true, launchd will see to it that the program stays alive. If it crashes or exits, launchd will restart it. Here's a short example that will keep TextEdit running all the time:

```
<?xml version="1.0" encoding="UTF-8"?>
<!DOCTYPE plist PUBLIC "-//Apple//DTD PLIST 1.0//EN" "http://www.apple.com/DTDs/
PropertyList-1.0.dtd">
<plist version="1.0">
<dict>
    <key>Label</key>
    <string>com.radiotope.textedit</string>
    <key>KeepAlive</key>
    <true/>
    <key>ProgramArguments</key>
    <array>
    <string>/Applications/TextEdit.app/Contents/MacOS/TextEdit</string>
    </array>
</dict>
</plist>
```

Save this file in your home directory in the Library/LaunchAgents directory. Filename convention is to use the label plus ".plist."

Note that the plist requires a valid XML and DOCTYPE header. The remainder of the plist is wrapped in a <dict> tag, as each key is a part of this master dictionary. In this example, the value for label is the string com.radiotope.textedit.

KeepAlive is set to true, so once launchd runs TextEdit, even if it exits, launchd will restart it.

launchctl is the user-level interface to launchd. The load verb is used to load a job into launchd. Because the specification for this job is not disabled, and is set to be kept alive, launchd runs the job immediately:

```
$launchctl load ~/Library/LaunchAgents/com.radiotope.textedit.plist
```

Press Return to launch TextEdit. (If TextEdit appears behind Terminal.app, hide Terminal. app, or press the Command-Tab key to bring TextEdit to the foreground.)

Type something if you wish, but, more importantly, quit TextEdit. TextEdit should launch again immediately. Quitting TextEdit too quickly between restarts delays the next launch and logs a message in system.log as follows:

```
Apr 26 17:22:13 jack-kerouac com.apple.launchd[111] (com.radiotope.textedit):
Throttling respawn: Will start in 3 seconds
```

To verify that launchd still has a particular job loaded, you can use the list verb to display a context-sensitive list of all jobs. (For example, a user's list will appear differently than a separate user's list or root's list.) Filtering with grep will help you pick out a specific job:

```
$ launchctl list | grep textedit
32563   -       com.radiotope.textedit
```

When you want to quit TextEdit for good, switch back to the shell, and use launchctl to unload the plist:

```
$ launchctl unload -w ~/Library/LaunchAgents/com.radiotope.textedit.plist
```

The -w flag marks the job as disabled, so launchd will not start this job again at next login. You can also delete the plist.

As an administrator, it's important to understand the layers that launchd uses, as shown in this figure:

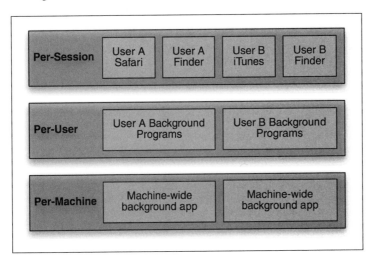

Per-session (agents) programs do the following:

▶ Interact with a user (have an interface)

▶ Come and go with login and logout

Per-user (background apps) applications do the following:

▶ As user agents, run as a user in the background

▶ Affect only one user

▶ Are designed for automation or personal processes

Per-machine (daemons) programs do the following:

▶ Arbitrate hardware systemwide (such as plugging in a new disk)

▶ Require codes to share hardware between user processes

Depending on the layer that you're targeting and the scope that you want to affect (one user on a machine, every user on a machine, or potentially every user on a network), you're told in which directory to create a plist.

When setting up a launchd plist to manage daemons or agents, it's important to follow certain rules that launchd expects of those programs. As specified in the launchd.plist man page, a daemon or agent launched by launchd must not do the following in the process directly launched by launchd:

▶ Call daemon(3)

▶ Do the moral equivalent of daemon(3) by calling fork(2) and have the parent process exit(3) or _exit(2)

A daemon or agent launched by launchd should *not* do the following as a part of its startup initialization:

▶ Set up the user ID or group ID

▶ Set up the working directory

▶ chroot(2)

- ▶ setsid(2)
- ▶ Close "stray" file descriptors
- ▶ Change stdio(3) to /dev/null
- ▶ Set up resource limits with setrusage(2)
- ▶ Set up priority with setpriority(2)
- ▶ Ignore the SIGTERM signal

Besides keeping a program running full-time, launchd can also start programs based on the following conditions:

- ▶ Activity on a network port
- ▶ Change in a file
- ▶ Change to a directory's contents
- ▶ File system mounting
- ▶ Set interval (for example, every 5 minutes)
- ▶ Specific date and time

For example, to have a program launch every time a volume is mounted, set the KeepAlive key to false, and the StartOnMount key to true:

```
<key>StartOnMount</key>
<true/>
```

To run a script or program every 5 minutes, use the StartInterval key:

```
<key>StartInterval</key>
<integer>300</integer>
```

The integer value is measured in seconds. To cause a job to start at a specific time, use the StartCalendarInterval key. This key uses a dictionary that uses the integer keys of minute, hour, day, weekday, and month to describe the time to run this job. Any missing values are considered wildcard values. For example, to run a job every day at 0300 hours (3 a.m.), specify the dictionary of keys like this:

```
<key>StartCalendarInterval</key>
        <dict>
```

```
                <key>Hour</key>
                <integer>3</integer>
                <key>Minute</key>
                <integer>00</integer>
        </dict>
```

The hour key looks for integers in a 24-hour range (0 to 23). The weekday key ranges from 0 to 6, with 0 being Sunday.

The Sockets key allows launchd to listen on a network socket on behalf of a program. The Sockets key expects a dictionary of Listeners—another key. To bind to a specific port, use the SockServiceName listener key. Its value is a string that represents the port to bind to, either as a service name or port number. The following example causes launchd to listen to port 8090, and start the program on activity on that port:

```
<key>Sockets</key>
        <dict>
                <key>Listeners</key>
                <dict>
                        <key>SockServiceName</key>
                        <string>8090</string>
                </dict>
        </dict>
```

Two keys, WatchPaths and QueueDirectories, trigger a program run on file system changes. WatchPaths watches individual files, while QueueDirectories watches directories and runs the specified program as long as the directory is not empty. Both keys expect an array of strings containing full paths to their target. In this example, if the file /Users/Shared/trigger.txt is created or modified, the program specified in the plist will be run:

```
<key>WatchPaths</key>
    <array>
            <string>/Users/Shared/trigger.txt</string>
    </array>
```

There are many more keys to fine-tune a program and how it runs. See the launchd.plist man page for more information. For more information on using man pages, see "Getting Help" earlier in this chapter.

Using launchd for Other System Efficiencies

launchd does more for a system and administrator than simply remove and consolidate legacy subsystems. It also makes the system more efficient in ways that the subsystems could not.

One way that launchd makes resource use of the system more efficient is by not running a program until it's actually needed. For example, when a plist specifies the KeepAlive key with a value of false, the program is not loaded until actually needed. This contingency prevents a program that may never be run from consuming any resources. The practice applies to plists using WatchPaths, QueueDirectories, and even Sockets. For plists that use Sockets to specify a network port on which to listen, launchd simply reserves the port, but does not run the program until activity occurs on the port.

Another way launchd optimizes systems is by booting them asynchronously. launchd can run any job, in any order; this speeds boot time dramatically. Long-time Mac OS X users may have noticed boot times getting faster. This speed-up is certainly due to the evolution of faster hardware, but launchd also plays a major role.

launchd also makes the job of administrators easier by consolidating job maintenance into a single interface. One interface makes it easier to understand which jobs are loaded and ready to run. Job maintenance becomes clearer because each job must be described in a plist, stored in a well-known location. Because each launchd plist can describe all attributes needed by a job, it's easier to change attributes across jobs.

Finally, launchd has been released as open source software under the Apache license. At http://launchd.macosforge.org you can find the source to the entire program. This is the most valuable way to become familiar with launchd.

Using Other Automation Technologies

On the Mac OS X timeline, launchd is a fairly new system, and the version that ships with Leopard is even more powerful than the introductory version that appeared in Tiger. Prior to the introduction of launchd, several subsystems existed to help boot the system, run jobs at startup, and periodically schedule jobs. Some of those subsystems, now considered deprecated, still exist. Others are a current part of the system and work in concert with launchd. Following are descriptions of subsystems that existed before launchd that you may need to convert into launchd jobs.

cron

A job scheduler, cron is deeply rooted in UNIX. launchd now has the capability to schedule a job as well as cron, and Apple has converted all system cron jobs to use launchd. But because many third-party utilities are still not launchd savvy, you can expect cron to hang around for a bit.

If you've worked with cron on another system, you can apply that knowledge to Mac OS X, and have cron behave as expected. If you don't have experience with cron, you're better off mastering launchd at this stage. However, you may run into cron jobs on older systems that you'd like to convert to a launchd plist. This section shows you how.

cron runs jobs based on a schedule set down by *crontab* files. Crontabs are plain-text files, in one of two types: the system crontab files and user crontab files. The two differ only slightly in format. The system crontab is stored in /etc/crontab, although this isn't present on v10.5 by default. User crontabs are stored in /usr/lib/cron/tabs. You should edit user crontabs using the cron command, with the -u switch to denote the user, and the -e switch to specify an edit.

In either type of crontab file to be converted to a launchd plist, there is one line per scheduled job. Each line contains a scheduling designation, and the program to execute. For example:

```
35 5 * * * /private/var/root/bin/backup.sh
```

The first five fields specify when to run the job. In order, they are:

▶   Minutes: The minutes after the hour, 0 to 59

▶   Hours: The hours of the day, 0 to 23

▶   Day: The day within a month, 1 to 31

▶   Month: The month of the year, 1 to 12

▶   Weekday: The day of the week, 0 to 6 (0 = Sunday)

The StartCalendarInterval array keys in launchd correspond directly to these fields from cron, and use the same integer ranges. A crontab requires that each field have a value. An asterisk (*) denotes a wildcard or "always" value, meaning that if the day field contains an asterisk, the job runs every day. In launchd, the *lack* of an entry makes it a wildcard. A launchd plist for the cron line above would look like this:

```
<?xml version="1.0" encoding="UTF-8"?>
<!DOCTYPE plist PUBLIC "-//Apple Computer//DTD PLIST 1.0//EN" "http://www.apple.com/
DTDs/PropertyList-1.0.dtd">
<plist version="1.0">
<dict>
        <key>Disabled</key>
        <false/>
        <key>Label</key>
        <string>org.example.backup</string>
        <key>ProgramArguments</key>
        <array>
                <string>/private/var/root/bin/backup.sh</string>
        </array>
        <key>KeepAlive</key>
        <false/>
        <key>StartCalendarInterval</key>
        <dict>
                <key>Hour</key>
                <integer>5</integer>
                <key>Minute</key>
                <integer>35</integer>
        </dict>
</plist>
```

Because this particular job runs as root, it needs to be stored in the /Library/ LaunchDaemons folder.

SystemStarter

SystemStarter is an Apple-created system to start daemons at boot time, taking dependencies into account. The advent of launchd caused the deprecation of SystemStarter. However, you may run into some legacy SystemStarter items that you want to convert to launchd.

SystemStarter scans the /Library/StartupItems directory for subfolders. (It also scans /System/Library/StartupItems; however, items in the System domain are not to be altered or used by administrators. This domain is under the Apple purview and may change with any given system update.) This folder contains two files that describe what to run and that program's dependencies: a plist and a shell script. The plist is always named StartupParameters.plist. The name of the shell script is based on the startup item and will have the same name as the enclosing folder. The following example is a StartupParameters.plist for the Apache web server under v10.3:

```
{
    Description     = "Apache web server";
    Provides        = ("Web Server");
    Requires        = ("DirectoryServices");
    Uses            = ("Disks", "NFS", "Network Time");
    OrderPreference = "None";
}
```

Description is a user-supplied description of the service. It does not influence the startup process.

Provides specifies the services that this startup item provides. In this example, the plist specifies that Apache provides a Web Server service.

Requires denotes dependencies for the service. Dependency tracking only works for other startup items. SystemStarter accomplishes this by scanning the Provides field of other startup items. Here, you can see that Apache requires DirectoryServices to be loaded before it can launch. If it cannot find this dependency, or the dependency fails to launch properly, Apache will not run.

Uses is similar to the Requires attribute; however, it does not stop the service from loading if the other services cannot be found. SystemStarter tries to load all the services in Uses prior to launching the item that this startup item specifies.

OrderPreference specifies the general time period in which a startup item will be executed. It is evaluated *after* the Requires and Uses attributes. Possible values for this attribute are First, Early, None (default), Late, and Last. None simply denotes no preference.

The shell script associated with this StartupItem is as follows:

```sh
#!/bin/sh

. /etc/rc.common

StartService ()
{
    if [ "${WEBSERVER:=-NO-}" = "-YES-" ]; then
    ConsoleMessage "Starting Apache web server"
    apachectl start
    fi
}

StopService ()
{
    ConsoleMessage "Stopping Apache web server"
    apachectl stop
}

RestartService ()
{
        if [ "${WEBSERVER:=-NO-}" = "-YES-" ]; then
    ConsoleMessage "Restarting Apache web server"
    apachectl restart
    else
    StopService
    fi
}

RunService "$1"
```

It is not necessary to describe this script line-by-line, because there is only one thing needed from it to create a `launchd` item: the actual daemon to execute, with its parameters, contained in the `StartService()` function. In this case, it's `apachectl start`. This command would be converted to `ProgramArguments` keys in a `launchd` plist. To see how Apple chose to approach this conversion, here's the `launchd` plist—/System/Library/LaunchDaemons/org. apache.httpd.plist—that exists in Leopard to control Apache:

```
<?xml version="1.0" encoding="UTF-8"?>
<!DOCTYPE plist PUBLIC "-//Apple Computer//DTD PLIST 1.0//EN" "http://www.apple.com/
DTDs/PropertyList-1.0.dtd">
<plist version="1.0">
<dict>
        <key>Disabled</key>
        <false/>
        <key>Label</key>
        <string>org.apache.httpd</string>
        <key>ProgramArguments</key>
        <array>
                <string>/usr/sbin/httpd</string>
                <string>-D</string>
                <string>FOREGROUND</string>
        </array>
        <key>OnDemand</key>
        <false/>
        <key>SHAuthorizationRight</key>
        <string>system.preferences</string>
</dict>
</plist>
```

If you've read "Using launchd" earlier in this chapter, this code should be entirely clear. What's worth noting is that even to launch a service like Apache, the `launchd` plist is straightforward and simple, with no oddball tricks. In the `ProgramArguments` array, Apple launches `httpd` directly. This direct approach is a better way to manage `launchd`, because `launchd` requires that the program to be run doesn't fork or background itself. In contrast, the `apachectl` script launches `httpd` and forks it off. Because this approach is unacceptable to `launchd`, the `plist` specifies the `httpd` daemon directly, with the `-D` and `FOREGROUND` parameters.

To cause a system daemon to run as root, store the launchd plist in /Library/LaunchDaemons.

A final note: Rather than SystemStarter's "fire-and-forget" method of launching, launchd can monitor any job and restart it if needed. To have launchd monitor and restart a job, set the OnDemand key to false—or, if you use the up-to-date KeepAlive key, set it to true.

periodic

Much of Mac OS X system maintenance is automated. Behind the scenes, log files are cleaned and rotated to stop them from filling up the system disk, databases are rebuilt, and more.

The periodic program scans folders for jobs to run periodically based on its configuration file, /etc/defaults/periodic.conf. Mac OS X comes with the presets of daily, weekly, and monthly. These simple directories are stored in /etc/periodic. Any scripts stored in daily are run daily at 3:15 a.m. The weekly scripts are run at 3:15 a.m. on Sunday, and the monthly scripts are run at 5:30 a.m. on the first day of every month. Not surprisingly, periodic is under the control of launchd. Three plists, located in the /System/Library/LauchDaemons directory, control the running of the periodic binary:

```
com.apple.periodic-daily.plist
com.apple.periodic-monthly.plist
com.apple.periodic-weekly.plist
```

You don't need to make any special arrangement to run a maintenance routine alongside the jobs supplied by the system. Each directory is a collection of loose scripts. Placing an executable in the appropriate directory will run it along with the others, which are run in alphabetic order. For example, following is the contents of the weekly directory on Mac OS X Server:

```
310.locate
320.whatis
500.weekly.applesaved
600.weekly.server
999.local
```

The numeric prefixes keep the jobs in order.

mach_init

Consider the `machd_init` process as a stepping stone from traditional UNIX `init` to today's `launchd` service. Processes to be run with `mach_init` are specified by plists placed in the /etc/mach_init.d or /etc/mach_init_per_login_session.d directories. The plist format is relatively close to those used in `launchd`. However, some key names differ, and `launchd` has many more options. The following is a sample plist stored in the Mac OS X Server v10.4 /etc/mach_init.d directory that launches `memberd`:

```xml
<?xml version="1.0" encoding="UTF-8"?>
<!DOCTYPE plist PUBLIC "-//Apple Computer//DTD PLIST 1.0//EN" "http://www.apple.com/
DTDs/PropertyList-1.0.dtd">
<plist version="1.0">
<dict>
        <key>ServiceName</key>
        <string>com.apple.memberd</string>
        <key>Command</key>
        <string>/usr/sbin/memberd -x</string>
        <key>OnDemand</key>
        <false/>
</dict>
</plist>
```

The `ServiceName` key would become a `launchd` `Label` key. The `Command` key becomes the `launchd` `ProgramArguments` key with one exception. `ProgramArguments` requires that each argument be separated. You can bring over the `OnDemand` key as-is, but it's best to convert it to the more modern `KeepAlive`. Here is this job as a `launchd` plist:

```xml
<?xml version="1.0" encoding="UTF-8"?>
<!DOCTYPE plist PUBLIC "-//Apple//DTD PLIST 1.0//EN" "http://www.apple.com/DTDs/
PropertyList-1.0.dtd">
<plist version="1.0">
<dict>
    <key>Label</key>
    <string>com.apple.memberd</string>
    <key>ProgramArguments</key>
    <array>
```

```
            <string>/usr/sbin/memberd</string>
            <string>-x</string>
    </array>
    <key>KeepAlive</key>
    <string>true</string>
    </dict>
</plist>
```

The conversion of this plist was a simple copy and paste with very small edits. You wouldn't need to convert this plist, as memberd is gone under v10.5, but it shows a good example of how to convert a mach_init item to launchd.

at

If you're coming from another platform and expect to use at, you can feel at home because the at system works on Mac OS X. It is disabled by default, but easy to enable. If you have no experience with at, use launchd. As stated in the section "Exploring launchd Functions" earlier in this chapter, launchd controls at. You can load the subsystem as follows:

```
#launchctl load -w /System/Library/LaunchDaemons/com.apple.atrun.plist
```

launchd calls the atrun subsystem every 30 seconds when the atrun plist is loaded. This means that the fine granularity that you would typically expect from at may not be as expected.

Because at is command-line driven, you can substitute the corresponding launchctl commands listed here. Rather than using the at command to schedule a job, you will need to create a launchd plist (see "Using launchd" and "Examples" in this chapter). You can use launchctl list to emulate atq . launchctl is context-sensitive based on the user running it. To get a list of machine-wide jobs, use sudo to invoke launchctl.

You can simulate atrm with launchctl unload -w (plist). launchd also allows stopping a currently running job using launchctl stop (label name).

Before making this conversion, reevaluate if the program being converted would be better off in an on-demand model.

rc

The /etc/rc boot-time script is completely gone as of Mac OS X v10.5. Prior to Leopard, the script in /etc/rc was run at boot time. In v10.4, launchd was made responsible for running rc.

If you need to run a script once at boot time, launchd can handle this for you. Create a basic plist, which should be saved in the /Library/LaunchDaemons directory. Set the KeepAlive key to false, and the RunAtLoad key to true. The latter key causes a job to run after launchd loads the plist.

init.d

Mac OS X has never used System V runlevels as some other flavors of UNIX do. Like StartupItems, these scripts have hooks for multiple functions, such as stopping or restarting a service. Much of this functionality is unnecessary with launchd. Because launchd maintains direct control over the jobs it launches, you don't need to write special code for the most common case, where the shutdown procedure is to look up a PID in a PID file and send it a SIGTERM.

init.d items are essentially equivalent to lines in /etc/rc that start a program at boot. Create a basic plist, save it in /Library/LaunchDaemons, and use the RunAtLoad key to start the job. As with /etc/rc, conversion time provides a time to evaluate if it is better to change to an on-demand model.

Examples

This section contains raw "cookie-cutter" examples of bash scripts and launchd plists that you can modify for your purposes.

Copy a file into each user's home directory (with home directories located in /Users). You will need to run this script with root privileges, because a standard user will not (or should not) have access to other users' top-level home:

```
#!/usr/bin/env bash


FILE_TO_COPY="/files/new_policy.txt"
for i in /Users/*; do
    cp ${FILE_TO_COPY} ${i}/
done
```

Perform an action on each user in Open Directory, except system users (assuming that standard users have a User Identifier [UID] greater than 499):

```
#!/usr/bin/env bash

for name in `dscl localhost -list /Search/Users`
do
    USER_ID=`dscl localhost -read /Search/Users/${name} UniqueID | awk '{print $2}'`
    if [ $USER_ID -gt 499 ]; then
            printf "${name}\n"
    fi
done
```

Change the `printf` line to perform the action in question.

Use `rsync` to back up critical system files; then move all backup data to a remote machine (preferably offsite):

```
#!/usr/bin/env bash
# Get config in /etc
rsync -a -q --delete /etc/ /backup/etc/

# Get /var/backups
rsync -a -q --delete /var/backups/ /backup/var/backups/

# Get Mail
rsync -a -q --delete /var/spool/imap/ /backup/var/spool/imap/
rsync -a -q --delete /var/imap/ /backup/var/imap/

# ship all backups to a remote computer
rsync -a -v --delete -e ssh /backup/ remote.example.com:/Volumes/Data/backup/remote/
```

Script the creation of a new user. Important variables are set at the beginning of the script.

```
#!/usr/bin/env bash
$USERNAME="backup_admin"
$HOMEDIR="/Users/backup_admin"
```

```
$PASSWORD="y7e3jsSRN"
$UID="505"

dscl localhost create /Local/Default/Users/${USERNAME}
dscl localhost create /Local/Default/Users/${USERNAME} PrimaryGroupID 0
dscl localhost create /Local/Default/Users/${USERNAME} UniqueID ${UID}
dscl localhost create /Local/Default/Users/${USERNAME} UserShell /bin/bash
dscl localhost create /Local/Default/Users/${USERNAME} NFSHomeDirectory ${HOMEDIR}
dscl localhost -passwd /Local/Default/Users/${USERNAME} ${PASSWORD}
sudo dscl localhost append /Local/Default/Groups/admin GroupMembership ${USERNAME}
mkdir -p ${HOMEDIR}
ditto -rsrc -V /System/Library/User Template/English.lproj/ ${HOMEDIR}
chown -Rf ${USERNAME}:admin ${HOMEDIR}
```

Back up a directory every time its contents change. This is a `bash` script and `launchd` combination. Because `launchd` does not perform these actions itself, you need a script to run the required actions. And because a script does not spontaneously run on its own, you need something to invoke it.

The script is a single line and uses `rsync` to copy a directory:

```
#!/usr/bin/env bash
rsync --delete -a /Users/Shared/source/ /Users/Shared/destination/
```

The folders listed in the `bash` script should be updated appropriately for your needs. The `launchd` plist to run this script takes advantage of the `QueueDirectories` key to watch the folder in question:

```
<?xml version="1.0" encoding="UTF-8"?>
<!DOCTYPE plist PUBLIC "-//Apple//DTD PLIST 1.0//EN" "http://www.apple.com/DTDs/
PropertyList-1.0.dtd">
<plist version="1.0">
<dict>
    <key>Label</key>
    <string>com.radiotope.backup_on_change</string>
    <key>ProgramArguments</key>
    <array>
```

```
            <string>/Users/marczak/bin/backup_on_change.sh</string>
        </array>
        <key>QueueDirectories</key>
        <array>
                <string>/Users/Shared/important</string>
        </array>
    </dict>
    </plist>
```

The program arguments must match the name and location of the script as saved on your system. Also, the QueueDirectories key must correspond with the source directory specified in the bash script.

Troubleshooting

Troubleshooting can be described as an art as much as a science, and this is often the case when trying to track down problems with scripts. Without explicit error messages, you may have hit a bug, or you may have a logic error that you introduced yourself.

All of the scripting languages and commands presented in this chapter have a specific syntax. If this syntax is violated, an explicit error message will be displayed. If a violation of syntax occurs in a running script, the line number of the offending statement is reported. These are the easy cases.

For times when a script runs but doesn't do what you expect, debugging-by-printing is a common technique to help understand the flow. Every scripting language has some method of quickly displaying output, from the bash printf to the AppleScript display dialog. Adding these methods in various places throughout your code offers an excellent way to analyze its flow.

For example, if you expect that a certain condition should be true, but the true branch isn't running, use a print statement to find out why:

```
printf "The value variable is ${value}\n"
if [ $value -gt 2000 ]; then
    # run some commands
fi
```

For scheduled jobs that run when you're not around, use the `logger` command to write information to /var/log/system.log for later inspection:

```
#!/usr/bin/env
logger Starting maintenance script
if [ -f /var/run/file ]; then
    logger state file exists, running commands
    # run some commands
fi
logger Maintenance complete
```

`logger` logs the lines into /var/log/system.log, where the logging system timestamps the entry. This can aid in seeing how long a script took to run.

In the "is it plugged in?" variety of errors, don't forget to check the basics:

▶ Does the first line of the script have a valid shebang (such as `#!/usr/bin/env bash`)? Without a valid shebang line to let the shell know which interpreter to use, an otherwise properly written script won't run.

▶ Is the script marked as executable? Use `ls` to verify and `chmod` to change the file permissions if necessary.

▶ Is the script in the current `$PATH`? If not, specify the absolute path to a script when called from `launchd`, `cron`, or other scripts.

▶ Is the script missing a dependency? If a command that the script relies on is missing, has moved, or has been changed, the main script won't run as expected.

When creating `launchd` plists, remember: plists are the only method of job specification. Without a properly formatted plist, `launchd` will not know how to run your job. Rather than hand-create a `launchd` `plist`, use the Apple Property List Editor.app—supplied with developer tools—or a third-party utility like Peter Borg's Lingon. Both will create proper XML for the `launchd` plist files.

Of course, it's tempting to hand-edit existing plists to make quick changes. Ensure that markup tags are properly matched, and all angle brackets are closed. After editing a plist, but before loading it into `launchd`, use `plutil` to check the validity of the file:

```
plutil -lint /Library/LaunchAgents/com.example.fileagent.plist
/Library/LaunchAgents/com.example.fileagent.plist: OK
```

If the `plutil` parser detects an error, it will report it:

```
XML parser error:
        Encountered unexpected character k on line 5
```

The error cites the line number where the XML parser encountered an error. On occasion, depending on the exact error, sometimes the error lies on the previous line than reported. Also, be aware that a parser can only check syntax. It cannot determine if you've misspelled a key or value.

The more you work with scripts and `launchd` plists, the more apparent errors will be to you without resorting to a lot of these techniques.

What You've Learned

This chapter introduces you to the many ways you can automate Mac OS X—that is, "How to make the computer do your work for you." You can apply system automation to most tasks to ease your job. The length of this chapter also underlines the importance of automation to administrators. Administrators are most effective when not bogged down with system minutiae. In this chapter, you learned the following:

▶   Many automation technologies are built into Mac OS X, out of the box.

▶   Apple-created technology such as AppleScript and Automator are available to automate many graphical user interface programs and system settings.

▶   Nearly all programming and scripting environments that you could want are also available as part of the system: bash, Perl, Python, PHP, Ruby, Tcl, and more.

▶   Each language available in Mac OS X has its strengths. For example:

  ▶   bash is perfect for batching other shell commands and scripts.

  ▶   Python can tap into Mac OS X native Cocoa APIs, and is already used extensively by Apple.

  ▶   Help is readily available via man pages, built into the system.

There are many Mac OS X–specific ways of changing user values and system settings:

▶ Use the defaults command to read and write user preferences.

▶ Use systemsetup and networksetup to alter nearly every setting in System Preferences.

▶ Use the Apple-created launchd system for job control. launchd replaces many earlier technologies. It's relatively easy to convert a former way of running a job into one that is compatible with launchd.

▶ launchd requires plists to know which jobs to run, and determines which layer a job affects by the directory in which the plist is placed.

Review Quiz

1. What are the automation technologies included in Mac OS X?
2. What is the default shell for newly created accounts in Mac OS X v10.5?
3. Which bash variables are inherited by subshells?
4. In which directories does the bash shell search when a command is typed at the prompt?
5. What is the command that runs the help system built into the shell?
6. What is the command that queries and manipulates user and system preferences?
7. What is the system in Mac OS X that boots the system and maintains job control?
8. What file format is used to specify to launchd what program to run and how to run it?

Answers

1. AppleScript, Automator, shell scripting, Perl, Python, PHP, Tcl, and Ruby.
2. The bash shell.
3. Any variables exported with the export keyword.
4. The directories in the $PATH variable, in the order they are listed.
5. The man command searches and looks up manual pages.
6. The defaults command can read and write preferences in property lists (plists).
7. launchd.
8. launchd requires a valid plist to describe a job.

10

Time   This lesson takes approximately 45 minutes to complete.

Goals   Learn to protect data against accidental and mechanical issues

Learn to create a data protection policy

Learn to choose an appropriate backup method

Learn how to automate backup solutions

Learn the locations of common data stores and their backup needs

Chapter 10
Ensuring Data Integrity

As a system administrator, it's not enough to automate alerts so that no log entry goes unnoticed, or to analyze current system utilization and shore up the network's defenses against unauthorized activity. You also need to attend carefully to the data that lives on each device. In Mac OS X, data integrity has been attended to as on other systems, but the OS also has unique aspects, such as metadata attached to files, that demand attention.

In Chapter 7 you learned how to protect the integrity of data through access controls that allow only authorized users to alter data. This chapter addresses the mechanics of data integrity: how to protect data from the accidental, mechanical, and human issues that arise in a technology-driven environment.

Determining Backup Strategies

Unfortunately, many technologists approach backup from the wrong angle: technology. All decisions about backup should start with, and be informed by, a backup policy. Most importantly, a backup policy should be created in conjunction with, *and signed off by,* senior management. Without high-level buy-in, backup will not serve the business properly. A backup policy does not need to be a lengthy document, but it does motivate all parties involved to think through all of the issues. Table 10.1 that follows shows a questionnaire listing the various issues that a policy should address.

The goal of backup is to prevent data loss. Once data is backed up, there are typically three reasons to restore it: A deleted or corrupt file needs to be restored, a crashed or deleted volume needs to be restored, or the business needs certain files restored from a point in time for legal reasons.

Backing up costs money. Casually deciding that everything on every system will get backed up every night will cause costs to soar as new storage for backups must be purchased, and the need for network bandwidth increases. At the same time, backing up too little on a system will cause problems when files that were excluded need to be restored.

Authors of a backup policy need to determine what data is important to the business and what the impact is if it is lost, damaged, or otherwise inaccessible. Each repository of data must be considered: traditional file systems, storage area network (SAN) storage, database servers, mobile devices, and grid storage. From there, it must be decided how *ephemeral* each piece of data is, that is, its life cycle. How often does the data change? Its life cycle will help determine the backup cycle.

As a technologist, you should also consult with your company's legal department. It may be a legal requirement that certain data is backed up and retained for a certain period of time.

It's valid to find that certain data should be excluded from a backup. Graphics workstations often contain large scratch files. Depending on company policy, users may have personal files on their work computers. Determining which data is to be backed up is called the *scope*.

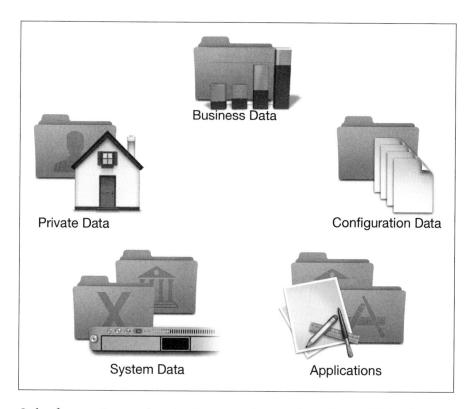

Business Data

Private Data

Configuration Data

System Data

Applications

Only after creating a policy should you evaluate and specify specific hardware and software for backup.

Regardless of the ultimate strategy chosen, the plan must include provisions for routinely testing backups. Backup destinations cannot be black holes into which data disappears. Backup logs need to be checked after each backup run. Tests need to be performed to validate existing backups. The worst time to find out that a backup was not successful is when trying to restore data for real.

The following table lists potential questions to ask when creating a backup policy.

Table 10.1   Questions to Determine a Backup Strategy

What gets backed up?	When does it get backed up?	How is the process handled?	Where?	Who backs up and restores?	In an emergency
Configuration files?	How frequently should data be captured?	How easily does data need to be restored?	Will the backup be stored?	Who can back up?	How is data restored from a server crash that destroys the data on disk?
Which configuration files?	How long does data need to be retained?	Can all files be backed up as flat files? Or does data need to be dumped by running a process?	Will it be stored online? Nearline? Offline or offsite, or both?	Who can restore?	How is data restored if the OS is destroyed?
Which data files?	How quickly does data need to be restored?	Are there regulatory requirements?		Does different data require different policies on who can back up or restore it?	Is replacement hardware available?
Is it necessary to back up log files? All user files?	When is a good time to run the backup? Does it interrupt service?	What type of media retention should be provided?			In case of a large, geographical region problem, how is data restored?
Which databases get backed up?		How long will backup media last (the media lifetime)?			(Note: Human wellness and communication during an emergency should be covered in a larger disaster recovery plan or business continuity plan.)
Can all files be backed up as flat files? Or does data need to be dumped by running a process?		How does running the backup or restoring it impact system performance?			
		What type of logical security (including encryption) is needed?			
		What physical security is needed?			

About Information Lifecycle Management

An important concept in the context of storage networking is Information Lifecycle Management (ILM). The idea is to ensure a match between data and an appropriate storage product. As information ages, it passes through a continuum in importance, from current work to archived projects that you never expect to work on again. A system's storage should reflect the changing nature of data. For example, current projects may be on storage that is both high-performance (so that you lose no time working) and high reliability (so that you don't miss a deadline due to equipment failure). Older projects, on the other hand, may not need the high performance because they are not under active development, but they may need to be accessed occasionally. As time goes on, you may not even need the projects to be available immediately; they need to be reliably stored, but it may be acceptable to have access times of up to a day to bring the material back online.

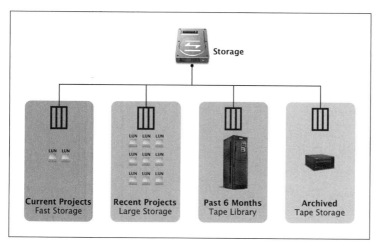

Managing information's lifecycle can be handled several ways. Often, a manual process moves completed projects into a designated target. You can also use an Xsan system, which can spread folders across different storage types, or *affinities.*

If you use an Xsan system, ADIC's StorNext Storage Manager can help you set up policies for a lifecycle management workflow. You can define service levels for different classes of data, and automate data placement and protection objectives. Xsan can act as a client to the StoreNext SAN volume and mount the volume. From a user's viewpoint, the volume looks and behaves like a standard Xsan volume.

Choosing Backup Methods

There are various accepted methods of performing backups. Nowadays, rarely does one size fit all. You can combine each of these methods, or apply different methods to different classes of data, to achieve the best overall solution. Perhaps some data is ideal for offsite into-the-cloud backup, while other data requires tape as a destination. It's important to categorize the data being stored by your company, and match appropriate backup policies to each type.

Using Traditional Backup to Tape

Storing files on disk and backing up to tape on a nightly basis is a traditional method of backing up data. Tape is a well-established, time-tested technology, and has the advantage of being more portable and durable than other technologies. While tape still gives the best cost-per-megabyte ratio, disk-based backup is approaching that ratio. However, tape is relatively slow compared to today's disk and network speeds.

As a mature technology, many backup applications are built with transferring data to tape in mind. Some currently available backup solutions that work with tape units are:

► Retrospect by EMC

► BRU by Tolis Group

► Time Navigator by A-Tempo

► NetVault by BakBone

As of this writing, BRU, Time Navigator, and NetVault also support the Xsan file system, which has special backup and restore needs. See the Apple Knowledge Base article "Xsan: Best Practices for Data Integrity" at http://docs.info.apple.com/article. html?artnum=303371.

Backing Up to Removable Media

According to your backup strategy, certain files or groups of files may take longer than acceptable to complete a backup to tape. In such cases, a good solution may be to back up to disk or other removable media. This backup can take the form of a centralized backup to a large Redundant Array of Independent Disks (RAID) bank, or the archiving of files to DVD or other local devices by individual departments.

When speed and minimal impact is essential, tape and disk backup may be combined. An initial copy is staged to a secondary server's disk, which is a fast process. A copy of the data then is picked up by a backup program and written to tape. Many backup applications perform the data staging phase as an integral part of the backup.

Backing Up "Into the Cloud"

More and more products are taking advantage of relatively fast bandwidth and inexpensive storage by backing up to remote locations over a wide-area network (WAN). The backup destination may reside at a commercial host's data center (such as Amazon's S3 service), or simply over a company virtual private network (VPN) to a remote office. The term "cloud" came into existence to refer to a service that exists over a network and grants a single interface to its offerings. Cloud services typically offer high scalability on the back end without a subscriber needing to understand the details of how the back end works. With respect to backup, you ship someone your data for storage, which is then available to you on demand. This cloud may be offered by a service provider or by a dedicated group within your company.

No matter who offers the service, the result is the same: Data is moved offsite and protected from any local geographical disaster. Examples of products in this category include the following:

▶ CrashPlan for Business: Code 42 Software

▶ Zettabits Storage System: Zettabyte Storage

Other companies have announced intentions to enter this market, but at the time of this writing, have no released products. This is a backup category to track closely.

Backing Up LAN-Free

LAN-Free Backup is a relatively new scheme, available only when a Fibre Channel SAN is in place. As the name suggests, in a LAN-Free backup, no data travels over the LAN. A backup server on the SAN has access to a directly attached storage unit or Fibre Channel tape unit in a switch. All data to be backed up is written to a volume or volumes on the SAN. From there, the backup can be picked up by the SAN-bound backup server.

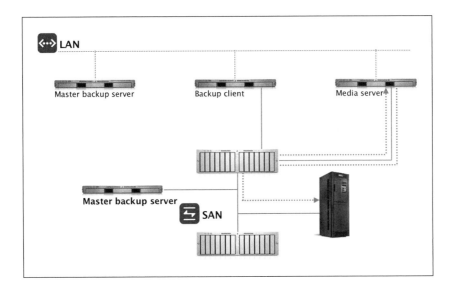

Comparing Backup Methods

All backup methods seek to match the appropriate data with appropriate storage. Not all data needs to be backed up using the same method. For all backup methods, you also need to consider restoring and restore speed. You must routinely perform restore testing.

All backup methods also must take into account the unique attributes of the Mac OS X HFS+ file system. Current versions of HFS+ can store access control lists (ACLs) for file system objects, along with metadata and general extended attributes, and forked files. (Forked files, a file type unique to the Mac OS, have a data fork and resource fork.) All of this metadata needs to be kept intact with its associated files. It's important that backup software for Mac OS X systems protects this information on backup and can also put it back properly on restore.

Without backing up and being able to restore metadata, consequences range from missing file icons to data not being usable. For more information, see "Other Backup Policy Considerations" in *Mac OS X Server Administration for Version 10.5 Leopard* at http:// manuals.info.apple.com/en_US/Server_Administration_v10.5.pdf.

An excellent test suite is Backup Bouncer by Nathanial Grey (http://www.n8gray.org/ blog/2007/04/27/introducing-backup-bouncer/). Backup Bouncer takes a source directory that is filled with files that have resource forks, extended attributes (EAs), and ACLs applied. You back this up with the software you're testing, and restore it elsewhere. Backup Bouncer then reports on how well the backup software performed in retaining various categories of file system attributes.

These file system attributes go beyond pure data; many are unique to the Macintosh platform and Mac OS X. It's important that a backup solution account for them. Some Mac OS X native solutions treat these attributes properly, but not all do. Non-native Mac OS X solutions, where Mac OS X is one of many client types able to be backed up, are typically even less capable of handling attributes properly. However, retaining these categories of attributes is critical for the file system, the proper functioning of services that rely on this metadata, and the OS itself.

Using Backup Tools

Mac OS X is flexible when it comes to backup. Many backup tools ship as part of the operating system. However, many times, the backup solution requires custom work to script and automate it—which may be perfectly appropriate. When the demands are too great for these built-in tools, third-party alternatives exist that can scale up and scale out, and are fairly ready out-of-the-box. Mac OS X Leopard also features the new Time Machine system for backup.

Some data is straightforward to back up: It lives as a plain-text file on a file system and can be copied elsewhere with any tool. Backing up other data—such as information stored in a database—falls into this category. While the database is running, its stores are open and volatile. In this case, it's best to take a database dump and back up the data dump. This strategy also gives you the flexibility to import the dump into a different version of the database software.

The most important strategy, regardless of the tool, is *automating* the backup process. Backup processes should happen automatically, without any human intervention. Humans are, well, human. It will be the day that an administrator needs to leave the office early for a personal reason that the administrator will forget to start or schedule that backup process—the one that's later needed for a critical restore. An automated process is also better at monitoring and reporting on each backup job than a person.

Using Command-Line Utilities

Mac OS X is rich with applications that can copy data and schedule tasks. Several utilities ship with Mac OS X for copying and scheduling jobs. In most cases, Apple has even updated traditional UNIX utilities to account for the attributes unique to the HFS+ file system, such as ACLs and extended attributes (EAs).

rsync

An open source command-line utility that provides fast incremental file transfer, rsync can compare and transfer files in one direction, copying only differences between two files or directories. Due to the copy-only-differences algorithm, rsync can be very efficient, even when synchronizing two large directories over relatively slow links. Many switches alter rsync's behavior, but usage is easy. Like most transfer programs, rsync needs to be supplied with a source and destination. For example, to sync the main /etc directory with a backup copy, use the following rsync command:

```
# rsync -av --delete /etc/ /backups/etc/
```

The switches in this example are as follows:

▶ -a works in archive mode

▶ -v indicates verbose operation

▶ --delete to delete file on target if the same file does not exist on source

The source is the contents of the /etc directory, while the destination is /backups/etc/. Running the rsync command copies files from /etc to /backups/etc. If it is run again immediately, it is likely that no files actually get copied. This is the power of rsync: In this case, it realizes that there is no need to perform any work. In addition, rsync has been patched to also be able to sync metadata such as arbitrary EAs, ACLs, Portable Operating System Interface (POSIX) permissions, and resource forks. This capability is turned off by default; the -E (capitalization is important) switch enables it. In Mac OS X with HFS+ file systems, you should always include the -E switch unless you know that the data being backed up has no EAs. The one downside to this resynching of metadata is that, when used with the -E switch, rsync will *always* sync resource forks whether or not they've been modified. However, that data typically is minimal, and using rsync will still save great amounts of time.

To generate a preview of what rsync would do without actually doing it, use the --dryrun flag. rsync will determine the changes needed and act as if it's copying data, but won't actually do so. This can quickly give you an idea of which files will be copied and how many bytes will be transferred overall.

rsync can also copy data over a network connection using Secure Shell (SSH). This is beneficial in that it can move data from one machine to another, potentially offsite, and encrypt the data while doing so. The -e switch (lowercase!) enables this behavior:

```
# rsync -avEe ssh /etc/ user@host:/backups/etc/
```

In this example, the source remains the same as the previous example, but the destination is now prefixed with information for the remote host. The login information is separated from the remote path by a colon. If this is a new host, ssh will prompt to accept the remote fingerprint and enter a password. To automate a nightly rsync-over-SSH process, generate keys so that SSH can identify this user without requiring a password. See "Generating a Key Pair" in Chapter 7 for details.

rsync is available on all UNIX platforms and can rsync from one platform to another. Just be aware that when transferring from Mac OS X to a non–Mac OS X server, metadata may get lost. It's safest to transfer Mac OS X data to destinations that understand HFS+. Transferring plain-text files with no real metadata is acceptable. A good strategy, and one that's recommended, is to combine general UNIX using Mac OS X as an rsync destination.

To restore files backed up using rsync, simply copy them back from the destination. This can be done using means other than rsync; however, if the destination is offsite, rsync may be the quickest way to restore the data needed. The same command that copied files offsite can reverse its source and destination parameters to copy back. To restore files from the command shown above:

```
# rsync -avEe ssh user@host:/backups/etc/ /etc/
```

See the rsync man page for more options. For instructions on using man pages, see "Getting Help" in Chapter 9.

ditto

ditto is a Mac OS X–specific tool that was written to copy files while supporting HFS+ metadata. ditto will copy ACLs, resource forks, and arbitrary metadata. Its general form is ditto [source] [destination]. For example, to copy the directory my_files to my_files_ backup, you can use the following command:

```
$ ditto my_files my_files_backup
```

This simple command creates a directory for my_files_backup if it doesn't already exist, and copies all files and subdirectories from my_files into it. It also copies the metadata for each file. There is no output on success. To gain more insight while the command is running, use the -v and -V flags, to list each directory and file copied, respectively.

ditto also can create archive formats from directories. The default is a cpio archive. To specify this functionality, use the -c switch:

```
$ ditto -V -v -c my_files my_files.cpgz
```

You can extract cpio archives using the ditto -x switch, along with the Mac OS X Archive Utility.app, located in /System/Library/CoreServices. You can also query and manipulate these archives with pax. (See its man page for more details; see "Getting Help" in Chapter 9 for instructions on using man pages.) To extract the files archived with the previous example, you can invoke ditto with the following parameters:

```
$ ditto -V -v -x tmp.cpgz tmp
```

The -x switch to ditto extracts the archive specified in the source position, and creates the destination, if necessary.

Due to its ability to create archives and send its data to stdout, ditto can be combined with ssh to send data remotely. Unlike rsync, ditto always copies all files—but this is often desired. For example, to copy the entire folder my_folder to a remote server over SSH, you can combine ditto with other tools, as follows:

```
$ ditto -c my_folder -|ssh user@host ditto -x - ./my_folder
```

The hyphen (-) as a source or destination denotes stdin or stdout. The pipe symbol (|) connects the output of the first command (ditto) to the input of the second (ssh), which extracts the data on the remote side. Combining ditto with other tools is a very handy trick when you need to move Mac data laced with attributes to a remote machine.

To restore data copied with ditto, simply copy it back from the destination. You can accomplish this restoration with means other than ditto, such as the Finder. The backup and restore commands will be the same, with the source and destination reversed. If backing up to an archive, change the -c (create archive) in the command to -x to extract the archive, or use /System/Library/CoreServices/Archive Utility.app. Double-clicking the .cpgz file in the Finder will launch the Archive utility; or use a .cpgz file with the open command: open backup.cpgz. See the ditto man page for other options; for instructions on using man pages, see "Getting Help" in Chapter 9.

asr

An efficient way to clone entire volumes, for backup or distribution, is asr, or Apple Software Restore. The command-line-driven asr copies entire *volumes*, either file-by-file, or disk block–by–disk block, to other volumes (including disk image–based volumes). The clone of a bootable volume will also be bootable. However, this is not the tool to use to copy individual files.

Like other copy tools, parameters to asr include a source and destination, which can be specified as a disk image, /dev entry, or volume mountpoint. To allow for a block copy, the volume must be able to be unmounted, or mounted read-only. Since the boot volume cannot be unmounted, it cannot be a source for a block copy.

As an example, to block-copy the mounted volume HD_Master to the destination volume Backup, you could use the following asr command:

```
# asr restore --source /Volumes/HD_Master --target /Volumes/Backup --erase
```

The use of the term "restore" in asr can be misleading. In essence, all copies are restores. In the case of asr, it is restoring one volume to another, whether or not it's the initial copy. Available in some form or another since Mac OS 8, asr began as a way to rapidly restore entire systems. To restore cloned data, simply swap the source and target parameters. For more information on asr, see the wonderfully detailed man page; for instructions on using man pages, see "Getting Help" in Chapter 9. For system cloning with asr, see *Apple Training Series: Mac OS X Deployment v10.5* (Peachpit).

Other Command-Line Utilities

An exhaustive list of every data transfer and manipulation command available is beyond the scope of this book. Following is a short list of other commands that you should investigate further on your own:

► serveradmin—Mac OS X Server Admin command-line equivalent. Can be used to dump settings to a file, and for restoration of these settings. (See "Automating Data Backup" below for examples of serveradmin in use.)

▶ scp—Secure copy. Use SSH to securely copy data to or from a remote machine.

▶ hdiutil—Manipulate disk images: create, attach, verify, burn, and so on.

▶ tar—tar archiving utility. Create and extract tar archives.

▶ pax—Multiple format archive utility. Read and write file archives and copy directory hierarchies.

▶ zip—Compress (archive) and extract zip files.

▶ kdb5_util—Kerberos database maintainance utility. Used to dump the Kerberos database.

Time Machine

Time Machine, or "backups for the rest of us," is very different from traditional file-to-tape backups, and a very powerful backup system that can store multiple versions of files. Unquestionably, Time Machine is an impressive way to back up. Its simple interface masks a complex system underneath, only some of which is appropriate to go into in depth here. Time Machine is nontraditional and rather unconventional at times. It makes backup effortless for the end user and smaller environments, but needs to be evaluated by system administrators for any scenario involving more than five users or a certain threshold of data. Administrators need to account for how Time Machine differs from other backup methods when planning for system backup.

Time Machine works well in home settings, where typically fewer computers than in office environments back up to any given destination. Time Machine can back up to locally attached or network storage. Much of Time Machine's power comes from its use of Leopard's fsevents API. fsevents allows Time Machine to be informed of changes on disk rather than having to scan an entire volume for changes against another list.

As an administrator, you should consider several things before deciding whether to use Time Machine as a backup mechanism. These include limitations on what administrators can control, Mac OS X Server, behavior and event handling, rotation of backup media, and backup of FileVault-protected homes.

Unlike most systems that administrators work with, Time Machine requires little to no configuration or maintenance. However, the downside is that system administrators have little that they can control. On its own, Time Machine will back up once an hour to the destination configured in the Time Machine Preference pane. The destination can include network-mounted storage on an Xserve or other appropriate Apple Filing Protocol (AFP) device.

Time Machine may not be a good strategy for Mac OS X Server. On Mac OS X Server, Time Machine backs up only servers running in standard or workgroup mode.

Time Machine does not allow for rotation of backup media. In other words, you can choose only one destination in the Time Machine Preference pane:

▶ If this destination is a locally attached disk, it cannot be removed and taken offsite, or easily substituted for another.

▶ If the destination is a server, however, the server's backup share can then be backed up.

▶ If the destination specified is a network share, a disk image per client is created on the share point and used repeatedly. This configuration allows many clients to back up to the same share point, but may increase network traffic and slow user connections.

Last but not least is one serious drawback for mobile users: Time Machine backs up FileVault-protected home systems only when the associated user is not logged in. A warning appears if Time Machine, when enabled, detects any FileVault home system that is logged in.

It may be undesirable to have a backup system that works only when users are logged off. Some companies may require encrypted home directories. Plus, Mac OS X is designed to be able to run long periods of time without logging out or rebooting.

Time Machine Details

Several launchd-controlled daemons and property lists for preferences determine Time Machine's behavior. The global preference file is /Library/Preferences/com.apple.TimeMachine.plist. This stores preferences such as the Time Machine currently enabled state and exclusions. The primary daemon is /System/Library/CoreServices/backupd, which is controlled through launchd via the /System/Library/LaunchDaemons/com.apple.backupd.plist file.

backupd is the main daemon that handles the actual work; Time Machine also reacts to several events. One event is time—once an hour, Time Machine gathers the list of changed files and sends them to the backup disk. The daemon that makes this happen is /System/Library/LaunchDaemons/com.apple.backupd-helper.plist launchd LaunchDaemon, by calling /System/Library/CoreServices/backupd.bundle/Contents/Resources/backupd-helper. You can change the interval in the plist file:

```
# defaults write /System/Library/LaunchDaemons/com.apple.backupd-auto StartInterval
-int (integer in seconds)
```

The default time is 3600 seconds, or one hour.

Time Machine also reacts to disk mount events, in order to ask the user whether a given drive should be used as storage for backup. These disk mount events are handled by /System/Library/LaunchDaemons/com.apple.backupd-attach.plist, which looks for mount events and runs backupd-helper with an -attach switch. You can turn off this behavior by adding a key to /Library/Preferences/com.apple.TimeMachine.plist:

```
# defaults write com.apple.TimeMachine DoNotOfferNewDisksForBackup -bool YES
```

If desired, you can push out this setting with managed preferences.

Comparing Backup Tools

You can use multiple backup methods, in sequence, to move and store data. Shell utilities, commercial applications, and Time Machine each have strengths and weaknesses for the different classes of data that need to be backed up, as the following table shows.

Table 10-2   Comparing Backup Options

	Shell Tools	Commercial Apps	Time Machine
Makes a bootable backup	`asr`, `ditto`, `rsync`	Some[1]	No
Copies metadata	`asr`, `ditto`, `rsync`	Some[1]	Yes
Cost	Included with Leopard	Typically $500 to $6,000 or more, depending on application	Included with Leopard
Restores by file	`ditto`, `rsync`	Yes[1]	Yes (not for FileVault users)
Backs up to tape	No[2]	Yes[1]	No
Backs up over the network	`ditto` and `rsync` when combined with `ssh`	Yes[1]	Yes
Backs up database	Need to dump database tables first, and then back up the dump	Some[1]	Not appropriate for all types of server-based data

[1] Check with the application vendor for specific information.

[2] Use Tolis Tape Tools to write to tape.

Automating Data Backup

Backup should always be automated. (See Chapter 8, "Automating Systems," for information on automation in general.) You can use scripts to automatically schedule a script to run at a certain time, perform specific backup tasks, and remove data after use (called data wiping). Automating backups provides consistent operation and the ability for administrators to build smaller blocks into a larger whole that can tackle more complex jobs.

Here's a short sample script that you can build on.

```
#!/usr/bin/env bash

logger -p local0.notice -i -t Nightly Starting nightly routine

# Backup Open Directory
LOCATION=/var/backups/odbackup-`date "+%Y%m%d"`
echo "dirserv:backupArchiveParams:archivePassword = s3kret" > sacommands.txt
echo "dirserv:backupArchiveParams:archivePath = $LOCATION" >> sacommands.txt
echo "dirserv:command = backupArchive" >> sacommands.txt
chmod 600 sacommands.txt
/usr/sbin/serveradmin command < sacommands.txt

# Dump Server Admin Settings in use
/usr/sbin/serveradmin settings afp > /var/backups/afp.sabackup
/usr/sbin/serveradmin settings dhcp > /var/backups/dhcp.sabackup
/usr/sbin/serveradmin settings dirserv > /var/backups/dirserv.sabackup
/usr/sbin/serveradmin settings dns > /var/backups/dns.sabackup
/usr/sbin/serveradmin settings mail > /var/backups/mail.sabackup
/usr/sbin/serveradmin settings network > /var/backups/network.sabackup
/usr/sbin/serveradmin settings smb > /var/backups/smb.sabackup
/usr/sbin/serveradmin settings swupdate > /var/backups/swupdate.sabackup

# Dump MySQL Data
/usr/bin/mysqldump -u root --password=s3kret --all-databases > /backup/sqldump.sql

# Backup changes in /etc
rsync -a -q --delete /etc/ /backup/etc/

# Sync /var/backups to main backup directory
rsync -a -q --delete /var/backups/ /backup/var/backups/

# Sync Mail
rsync -a -q --delete /var/spool/imap/ /backup/var/spool/imap/
rsync -a -q --delete /var/imap/ /backup/var/imap/

# Clean up old backups
```

```
find /var/backups/ -mtime +14 -delete

logger -p local0.notice -i -t Nightly Syncing data offsite
rsync -a -v --delete -e ssh /backup/ backup.example.com:/Volumes/Data/backup/

logger -p local0.notice -i -t Nightly Finished
```

You can schedule a script like this with launchd. Since a backup script needs to run with
root privileges to have permission to read sensitive files, you should store a launchd plist in
/Library/LaunchDaemons. An example launchd plist, named nightly.sh and stored in /usr/
local/sbin, schedules the sample script:

```
<?xml version="1.0" encoding="UTF-8"?>
<!DOCTYPE plist PUBLIC "-//Apple//DTD PLIST 1.0//EN" "http://www.apple.com/DTDs/
PropertyList-1.0.dtd">
<plist version="1.0">
<dict>
    <key>Label</key>
    <string>com.example.nightly </string>
    <key>LowPriorityIO</key>
    <true/>
    <key>Nice</key>
    <integer>1</integer>
    <key>ProgramArguments</key>
    <array>
            <string>/usr/local/sbin/nightly.sh string>
    </array>
    <key>StartCalendarInterval</key>
    <dict>
            <key>Hour</key>
            <integer>4</integer>
            <key>Minute</key>
            <integer>35</integer>
    </dict>
</dict>
</plist>
```

This example plist schedules the script to run at 4:35 a.m. every day. It is also tasked with a nice value of 1, and the `launchd LowPriorityIO`, which ensures less impact on the server.

The example script backs up key data files and dumps the OD database and MySQL database files, to ensure a clean backup.

You can also use scripts for specific backup tasks—for example, a script can back up detailed client information to a disk image in response to a user problem. You can see a functioning tool in "The Collector," a sample troubleshooting tool that creates a disk image, and then stores relevant client information on it (logs, hardware information, and so on). This is available from the Peachpit website at http://www.peachpit.com/acsa.adv-sys-admin.

It's also important to automate data wiping. To stop people from retrieving data that you believe is deleted, erasure must be performed in a way that makes it very difficult to recover it. Apple includes two utilities to clean a volume. The first is part of the `diskutility` tool: the `SecureErase FreeSpace` command. This is designed to work on an entire volume. The command is straightforward and passes in a level and target volume:

```
# diskutil SecureErase FreeSpace 1 /
Started erase on disk disk0s2 MacintoshHD
Creating temporary file
[ \ 0%................................................. ]
```

The command essentially writes large temporary files—consuming all free space on the disk—and securely erases them by overwriting them with multiple passes of other data. You can specify the level to which data can be overwritten with one of the following options:

▶   Single-pass random erase

▶   US DoD seven-pass secure erase

▶   Gutmann 35-pass secure erase

The higher the level, the longer the operation takes. If only a specific file needs to be targeted, the `srm` (secure remove) command can be substituted for `rm`. Like `rm`, `srm` simply takes a pattern to target. For example, to securely erase all files in a directory that begin with "2006," you can use the following command:

```
$ srm 2006*
```

When no option is specified, srm uses the Gutmann 35-pass secure erase, equivalent to option 3 of the diskutil SecureErase command. An option of -m performs a medium erase of US DoD seven pass, and the -s switch performs a simple one-pass erase. You can use srm in conjunction with other commands, such as find, to erase data with more specific attributes. To use srm in the preceding sample script, for example, you would use the find command rather than find's simple -delete switch. You could rewrite that line as:

```
find /var/backups/ -mtime +14 -exec srm {} \;
```

About Common Data Stores

To help you determine what data to back up and how, the following sections list locations for Mac OS X configuration files and data stores for Apple services that ship with Leopard.

In general, Mac OS X places initial configuration files in several locations. These files are also often updated with configuration changes made with graphical user interface tools. These files need to be backed up, to restore a system that reflects changes made since initial installation.

One of the most important and active directories is /etc, which contains configuration files for the mail system, SSH, and SSH server keys, Samba, emond, and more. Particular care should be taken to back up and version (create a new version of) the files in this small but critical directory.

▶   Service states: /System/Library/LaunchDaemons/*

▶   General configuration files: /etc/

▶   System keychain: /Library/Keychains/System.keychain

iCal Service

iCal uses extended attributes (EAs) extensively to mark and describe its data. A backup solution that does not retain EAs cannot properly restore iCal data. You can change the location of data through Server Admin. Following is the default location:

Configuration files: /etc/caldavd/caldavd.plist

Data: /Library/CalendarServer/Documents/

This is the organization of the data store within the default location:

▶ ./principles/<users | groups>—Contains folders for each user or group that has been granted calendar access and that has logged in to the service at least once

▶ ./principles/<resources | locations>—Contains folders for each resource or location that has been granted calendar access and that has had its calendar accessed at least once

▶ ./principles/sudoers—Contains folders for each calendar serviceP administrator

▶ ./principals/__uids__—Contains folders for every user, group, resource, or location, using its directory-record unique identifier as the name

▶ ./principles/<users | groups>/<username>—An HTTP resource that represents the calendar user or group settings in the directory service

▶ ./principles/<users | groups>/<username>/calendar-proxy-read and ./principles/<users | groups>/<username>/calendar-proxy-write—Identifies the principals used to provide calendar delegate rights to other users

▶ ./calendars/<users | groups>—Contains folders for each user or group that has created at least one event, "to do," or calendar

▶ ./calendars/<resources | locations>—Contains folders for each resource or location that has accepted at least one event, "to do," or calendar

▶ ./calendars/<users | groups | resources | locations>/<name>/calendar—Contains iCalendar (.ics) files of each event in the principle's calendar

▶ ./calendars/<users | groups | resources | locations>/<name>/inbox—Contains iTIP file invitations to other users' pending events

▶ ./calendars/<users | groups | resources | locations>/<name>/outbox—Contains iTip file invitations waiting to be distributed to invitees

▶ ./calendars/<users | groups | resources | locations>/<name>/dropbox—Contains files attached to events, either from a user's self-created event or from participant events

iChat Server

iChat Server relies on both plain-text configuration files and a database, running under MySQL. For a proper backup, data in MySQL needs to be dumped with the `mysqldump` utility.

▶ Configuration files: /etc/jabberd/*

▶ Data: `mysqldump jabberd2 > jabberd2.backup.sql`

Security and FileVault KeyChains

▶ /Library/Keychains/System.keychain

QuickTime Streaming Server
Configuration files:

▶ /Library/QuickTimeStreamingServer/Config/

▶ /Library/QuickTimeStreamingServer/Playlists/

▶ /Library/Application Support/Apple/QTSS Publisher/

Data (default locations):

▶ /Library/QuickTimeStreamingServer/Movies/*

▶ ~user/Sites/Streaming/*

Firewall Service
While the /etc/directory should be backed up in its entirety, it is listed here separately as a reminder to version this directory before changes are made.

▶ /etc/ipfilter

NAT Service

▶ Configuration files: /etc/nat/

Mail
The mail service comprises several subsystems, each with its own configuration files and data stores. To restore the mail system to the same configuration that it was at any given point, you must account for each subservice.

Postfix SMTP:

▶ Configuration files: /etc/postfix/

▶ Data: (default locations) /var/spool/postfix/

Cyrus IMAP and POP:

- ▶ Configuration files: /etc/imapd.conf /etc/cyrus.conf
- ▶ Data: (mail database default location) /var/imap
- ▶ Mail data store: /var/spool/imap
- ▶ Mail database location config directory: /var/imap
- ▶ Mail data store location partition-default: /var/spool/imap
- ▶ Additional data store partitions: (no default value)
- ▶ partition-xxx: /var/spool/mail_xxx

(There can be multiple additional data store partitions as configured in Server Admin.)

AMAVIS:

- ▶ Configuration files: /etc/amavisd.conf
- ▶ Data: (default locations) /var/amavis/

ClamAV:

- ▶ Configuration files: /etc/clamav.conf
- ▶ /etc/freshclam.conf
- ▶ Data: (default locations) /var/clamav/
- ▶ /var/virusmails/

Mailman:

- ▶ Configuration files: /var/mailman/
- ▶ Data: (default locations) /var/mailman/

Spamassassin:

- ▶ Configuration files: /etc/mail/spamassassin/local.cf
- ▶ Data: (default locations) /etc/mail/spamassassin/

MySQL

MySQL may contain configuration information in /etc/ (it's not required), and in the database tables.

- ▶ Possible configuration file for MySQL: /etc/my.cnf
- ▶ Data: (default locations) /var/mysql/

To dump all tables in information (which may require authenticating):

```
mysqldump --all-databases > all.sql
```

PHP

PHP has no default configuration file, but the administrator can create one (such as copying /etc/php.ini.default to /etc/php.ini and modifying it), and should back it up if present: /etc/php.ini

- ▶ Data: (default locations) as designated by administrator

Web Service

- ▶ Configuration files: /etc/httpd/* (for Apache 1.3)
- ▶ /etc/apache2/* (for Apache 2.2)
- ▶ /etc/webperfcache/*
- ▶ /Library/Keychains/System.keychain
- ▶ Data: (default locations) /Library/WebServer/Documents/
- ▶ /Library/Logs/WebServer/*
- ▶ /Library/Logs/Migration/webconfigmigrator.log (Apache config migration log)

Wiki and Blog Server

The Wiki and Blog services are sensitive to the metadata associated with their files. Ensure that any backup solution takes this into account.

- ▶ Configuration files: /etc/wikid/*
- ▶ /Library/Application Support/Apple/WikiServer
- ▶ (wiki themes and template files)

▶ Data: By default, wiki and blog content is stored in the /Library/Collaboration/ folder. This folder can be changed in the Web Services pane in Server Admin.

The following list shows the default wiki file and folder hierarchy. This includes where all wiki files are stored and the folder structure for the wiki content. In the list, *groupname* is the name of the group, *pagename* is the name of the wiki page, and *page* is the name of the webpage.

▶ ./Groups/*groupname*/—Contains all files for one group's services

▶ ./Groups/*groupname*/wiki/*pagename*.page/—Contains the component files of a wiki page

▶ ./Groups/*groupname*/wiki/*pagename*.page/*page*.html—Contains the main text of the wiki (html content)

▶ ./Groups/*groupname*/wiki/*pagename*.page/*page*.plist—Contains the metadata for the wiki page

▶ ./Groups/*groupname*/wiki/*pagename*.page/revisions.db—Contains the version history database for that wiki page

▶ ./Groups/*groupname*/*pagename*.page/images/—Contains the images for that wiki page

▶ ./Groups/*groupname*/*pagename*.page/attachments/—Contains all attachments for that wiki page

Blog data is maintained for both users and groups.

User blogs are in /Library/Collaboration/Users/*username*/weblogs. It contains bundles with a .page extension that represent each blog entry. These bundles in turn house a plist with page metadata, and a separate HTML file containing the actual content.

Group blogs are in /Library/Collaboration/*groupname*/weblogs. Like user blogs, this directory houses bundles that represent each blog posting.

The filenames for blog pages are generated automatically. The bundle contains references to this (and potentially) other referenced filenames. None of these filenames should be altered manually.

Each <*groupname*> directory contains an index.db file that provides an ID to help link various collaboration components together. It will be re-created if deleted.

Each <*groupname*> directory contains a discussions subdirectory. This is where comments left by readers for a particular page are stored. The discussion directory for a given group contains a discussion.db file (sqlite) and a welcome.plist file. It also contains plist files for each page.

- ▶   Log files (default location): /Library/Logs/wikid/*

Restoring Backed-Up Data

In general, the method that you use to restore backed-up data will depend on the method that was used to back up the data in the first place. This is particularly true for commercial applications that tend to use proprietary storage formats.

Data backed up to storage that exposes backed-up files directly is one exception to this rule. ditto, asr, and rsync back up to standard volumes accessible by Mac OS X. If only a portion of files are needed from the backup, the volume backed up to can be mounted and the required files simply copied.

The most important rule about restoring data is to test the process. Restore tests need to occur on a regular basis; this is the only way to ensure that the data being backed up can be restored without problems. When working with production data, an important test is to restore critical data to a test server. Services that benefit from restoring to a test server are Mail, Blog, and Wiki.

In the case of Time Machine, it's important to test restoring and building a system from scratch. A system backed up by Time Machine can be entirely restored by booting from the Mac OS X v10.5 installation media, installing Mac OS X, and following the prompts to restore Time Machine data.

Server settings backed up with the serveradmin settings command can be restored by using file redirection with the files created during the backup, as in this example:

```
sudo serveradmin settings all < mysettings.txt
```

Troubleshooting

Overall, backup schemes have many points of entry and many moving parts. You're *always* relying on something else besides the backup tool itself. Is the source and destination disks' integrity verified? Is there sufficient capacity on the destination disk or tape? Is the backup software picking up on unique Macintosh file system attributes? Is the network available when attempting a network transfer?

Troubleshooting needs to follow a methodology, much like that covered in Chapter 12, "Troubleshooting." However, here are some common errors.

First and foremost: Is the backup policy being followed? This is less of a technical issue, certainly, but can lead to implementation problems. Is the right tool being used for the right data? Are users allowed to back up or restore data? If a service level agreement (SLA)—an agreement between IT and end users regarding how quickly a service is to be performed—is specified in policy, is the transfer time adequate? Does more bandwidth need to be put in place to satisfy an SLA?

Once in the technical realm, again, you need to follow a methodology. Be attentive to error messages logged by a backup program, either directly on the console or in a log. Even if a program has a log, always check the system log for issues.

Permissions and metadata can also be the source of issues. Since all processes run in a security context, the backup process needs sufficient privileges to access the files that it's backing up. Watch logs and read backup reports for listings that mention "unable to open file" or "permission denied."

If a backup method does not initially back up or later restore file system attributes, such as resource forks, you may run into problems, depending on the type of file. A typical sure sign of missing attributes will appear in the Finder.applications file, which may display an icon with the international "No" symbol, signifying that they cannot be run on this platform.

Data files that are missing their resource forks or other attributes may display a blank or generic UNIX icon.

If files mistakenly were copied as a backup to a non-HFS+ volume, any files with resource forks will have them split off as dot-underscore files. So, a file named roses.psd that has a resource fork will be copied as two files: roses.psd and ._roses.psd. You can rejoin these two halves with the `FixupResourceForks` utility, which acts only on an entire directory, not on individual files. Copy all files from the non-HFS+ volume to a directory on an HFS+ volume. Supply the directory name to `FixupResourceForks`. To rejoin each file contained within the top level with its missing piece, use this command:

```
$ FixupResourceForks FixupFiles
```

If the only backup destination is a non-HFS+ volume, consider creating a disk image within the non-HFS+ space and copy files to that container. Copying files to this disk image will allow you to accurately maintain all HFS+ attributes.

What You've Learned

Data integrity protects data from inadvertent or malicious alterations, including deletion. It's important to take proactive steps to protect the integrity of data by controlling access, and protecting against mechanical failure and human error. Disk drives fail, memory chips have error rates, and people make mistakes. When planning backup, it's important to understand what to back up, with what frequency, and also what *not* to back up.

This chapter presented the following points:

▶ Before anything else, create a backup policy. When created with senior management, a backup policy is aligned with the business it is protecting. All actual backup purchases and decisions should flow from the policy.

▶ Include a plan for backup testing and verification. Incomplete or inaccurate backups are of little value.

▶ Match the classification of data to the storage that holds it.

▶ Choose the appropriate location of the backup storage, for the needs of the class of the data. There are several destinations for backup storage: disk, tape, or offsite "in the cloud."

▶ It's absolutely critical to test restores of backups.

▶ It's imperative that you take into consideration the unique attributes of the Mac OS X HFS+ file system—ACLs, resource forks, and arbitrary metadata—when backing up and restoring files.

▶ Don't rely on a single backup method as an all-or-nothing proposition. Use various methods as required for given situations.

▶ As needed, use the Mac OS X command-line utilities that focus on transferring files and that are built into the distribution. Commands such as `rsync`, `cp`, and `mv` have been updated to handle extended attributes. Commands such as `ditto` and `asr` are unique to Mac OS X and can retain most, if not all, file system object attributes.

▶ Consider the unique, powerful Time Machine backup solution for smaller environments, but evaluate it for any scenario involving more than five users or a certain threshold of data. The Time Machine functionality is handled by the backupd daemon. There are three launchd plists that handle the behavior of Time Machine. There is also a main preference file.

▶ Automate backup. The more people that get involved in the process, the more room there is for human error.

▶ Manage the automation process entirely with tools built into Mac OS X: scripting utilities such as rsync and asr can be combined with launchd for scheduling. Automated backup of key files can be useful for troubleshooting.

▶ Use the built-in Mac OS X utilities to securely wipe storage space, which make it difficult for an attacker to retrieve deleted data.

Review Quiz

1. What is the first step in backing up data?

2. What unique properties need to be considered when backing up and restoring Macintosh data?

3. What is the medium used in a LAN-free backup?

4. Which Mac OS X built-in command-line utility is available to perform a block-based clone of an entire volume?

5. What is unique about backing up data from databases?

Answers

1. The creation of a backup policy, specifying scope of backup and with senior management sign-off.

2. Metadata in the form of extended attributes, file system access control lists, resource forks, and general file system metadata.

3. LAN-free backups travel over a SAN.

4. asr, the Apple Software Restore utility.

5. Databases should either be shut down before backup, or dumped to separate files that get backed up.

Part 4 Optimizing and Troubleshooting

11

Time

Goals

This lesson takes approximately 60 minutes to complete.

Learn to establish metrics against which you can measure performance

Learn the components of high availability services

Learn to create software-based redundant disk and network services

Learn to configure IP failover server pairs

Chapter 11
Ensuring Reliability

In previous chapters, you've learned about ensuring the integrity of data against human error or maliciousness. This chapter looks at the other side of that equation: maintaining the integrity and reliability of systems against mechanical failure, with a focus on Apple-branded technology systems. This process requires planning, understanding of business needs, and technical skills.

The administrator's goal is to provide "high availability"—that is, service availability—which is a composite of each subsystem on which a service relies. High availability includes the reliability of the software itself and the operating system, down to the hardware that it's running on. Company policy should determine the necessary availability of service, as discussed in Chapter 10, "Ensuring Data Integrity."

Establishing Reliability Metrics

With so many systems that are interdependent, the adage "If you can't measure it, you can't manage it," is possibly more important than ever. Unfortunately, many administrators manage by gut feelings, rather than measured metrics. Often, when you actually measure, you'll find that reality is counter to your beliefs.

It is up to administrators and senior management to establish reliability metrics and thresholds in policy. When a threshold is crossed for a given period of time, a course of action must be taken to bring metrics back to acceptable levels.

One oft-cited metric is *uptime*. Uptime measures the time that a computer system or service has been "up and running." It is typically seen as a measure of reliability. When used carefully, and within a framework of metrics, uptime can be a valuable measurement. However, like statistics, metrics can be bent to almost any meaning. A system could have a long continuous uptime, for example, but as a result of poor maintenance, the database on that system could be giving out bad data.

Most company senior management personnel do not understand the effect that demanded uptime will have on costs, and ask for "five-nines"—or "99.999%" uptime. Each "nine" increases the vigilance that an IT department must give to systems. It also increases a system's cost, as money must be spent on higher quality components or redundant systems, and possibly both. Analyzing this metric shows that, the higher the metric is, the more difficult it may be to meet.

For example, the true length of a year on Earth is 365.2422 days, or about 365.25 days. The following table gives rounded values for each level of "nines" and how much uptime per year that specifies, and perhaps more to the point, how much downtime per year that allows.

Table 11-1   Level of "Nine" and Corresponding Uptime and Downtime per Year

	Uptime per year	Downtime per year
99.000%	361.598 days	88 hours
99.900%	364.885 days	9 hours
99.990%	365.214 days	53 minutes
99.999%	365.256 days	5 minutes

IT departments must also respond to other metrics, such as providing return on investment (ROI) and service level agreements (SLAs). These topics are beyond the scope of this chapter. However, all members in an IT department should familiarize themselves with these and other metrics.

Maintaining High Availability

One factor that impacts high availability of software and hardware is the age of this software and hardware. Software ages only with respect to other software components. For example, when an OS is upgraded, many software components suddenly become outdated ("legacy"). Hardware aging often results in physical failures.

To create highly available systems, a system administrator must account for each system, and their dependencies and possible failure, as shown in the following list of vulnerable systems:

▶   Power

▶   Hardware

▶   Power supply

▶   Memory

▶   Logic board

▶   Disks

▶   Communication cards (SCSI, Fibre Channel, and so on)

▶   Network

▶   Service (software)

(This chapter does not discuss memory, logic boards, or communication cards.)

Each of these systems can protect against failure in a number of ways, with the most common being *redundancy*. Redundant systems provide a spare that can take over in the event of failure, avoiding a single component that could take a service offline in the event of failure.

Remember Murphy's Law: "Whatever can go wrong, will go wrong"; these components form a chain of dependencies that is only as strong as its weakest link.

Planning Power Redundancy

The Intel-based Xserve has the option to provide power-supply redundancy. While this is a welcome improvement, not all systems have this capability. Additionally, if power supplies aren't receiving power, it doesn't really matter how redundant they are. To combat this, systems can include *Uninterruptible Power Supplies* (UPSs). Essentially, a UPS is a large battery acting as a hot spare (online and ready to take over) to facility power. In larger setups, generators start when facility power fails. This way, power is restored from some source before UPS batteries are drained.

Properly implementing a UPS requires some analysis. The following steps you through an overview of the planning process:

Step 1: Identify devices that require UPS backup

While not all devices require battery backup, more devices than just servers need UPS batteries for high availability. Be sure to include all devices in the chain of dependencies, including network switches, modems, external online storage such as Redundant Array of Independent Disks (RAID) units, and Fibre Channel switches.

Step 2: Calculate power consumption

For instructions on determining the total power consumption of electrical devices and how to size a UPS, see "Determining Heat Dissipation and Load, Power, and Cooling" in Chapter 1. A system, however, is a dynamic thing. Don't forget to periodically revisit the load placed on the UPS devices supporting upgraded equipment that may draw more power than the previous piece, or in racks that are being added to.

Step 3: Determine the required run time

Estimate or measure the time you need a UPS to support all of its equipment after power fails. This includes the time to send notifications and start generators, or the time to gracefully shut down your servers and other devices.

Step 4: Identify the required battery capacity

Unless someone in the group has prior experience in determining the right battery capacity, you will need outside help. Most vendors will be happy to aid in the process. Alternatively, most vendor websites have run-time calculators to help size a UPS for your needs. For example, APC's UPS selector can be found at http://apc.com/tools/ups_selector/. An alternate vendor, Liebert, tends toward larger installations, and will have a representative assist when necessary (http://www.liebert.com).

Step 5: Research and select UPS vendors and models

While you may already have a good idea of a preferred brand of UPS, manufacturers change products and capabilities all the time. Ensure that a particular brand supports Macintosh environments. (This shouldn't make a difference, but nevertheless, some manufacturers *still* throw up their hands upon hearing "Macintosh.") Also, check with any value-added resellers (VARs) that your company works with; they may have bundles and real-world experience with various models and interaction with Mac OS X.

Step 6: Verify electrical ratings and wiring in your facility

Larger UPS devices typically call for 30-amp circuits, and place their own load on an electrical system as they charge batteries and run tests. Have a licensed electrician evaluate the electrical plant where any UPS will be installed. Let UPS systems save you from problems rather than create them.

Step 7: Determine the UPS communication method

You must also determine how UPS communicates over the system, whether through Mac OS X or other systems such as Linux and Windows. Most UPS models contain the ability to signal status over an IP-based network or serial ports. The appropriate software is required to interpret these signals and shut down as appropriate.

Mac OS X has built-in support for communicating with a UPS over a USB cable. If Mac OS X detects a supported UPS, you can use the Energy Saver Preference pane to determine shutdown aspects of the OS.

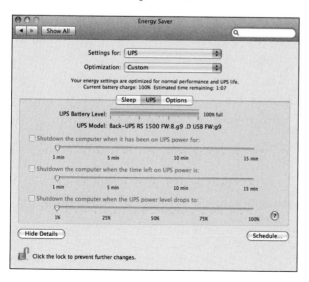

Mac OS X–compatible software is available from some UPS manufacturers. Additionally, open source software has sprung up to enable network-based shutdown of systems. For example, apcupsd, the APC UPS monitoring daemon, supports Mac OS X systems as well as Linux and Windows, allowing a common interface across multiple platforms (http://www.apcupsd.org/).

Step 8: Test the UPS

Testing the solution is always critical—as Chapter 10, "Ensuring Data Integrity," covers— and a UPS setup is no exception. Have a test plan that simulates power outages. Most UPS devices can also perform self-tests and report on battery statistics. Be sure to include power systems in a test plan.

Implementing OS Power-Supply Controls

When a server is presented with the condition of running on battery power from a UPS, you need to decide what actions to take, before and after power is lost and restored. These decisions include when to shut down the system and switch to battery power, and when and how to reboot the system.

You can perform the bulk of the setup in the UPS tab in the Energy Saver Preference pane. Alternatively, you can issue equivalent commands at the command line or in scripts via the pmset utility. For example, to set the UPS battery percentage level where Mac OS X will begin a shutdown, use this command:

```
# pmset -u haltlevel 15
```

This command instructs Mac OS X to halt the system when the attached UPS reaches 15 percent of battery capacity. See the pmset man page for more options; for instructions on using man pages, see "Getting Help" in Chapter 9.

When a UPS-signaled condition causes Mac OS X to shut down, it calls a special shut-down file. The /usr/libexec/upsshutdown script handles shutdown for low-power situations. This example added an extra parameter to the shutdown command: the -u switch, which instructs shutdown to leave the system in a faux-dirty state (unclean shutdown—typically on sudden loss of power when files are not properly closed), so that the system will restart automatically when power returns, because the system has no reason to restart automatically on a clean shutdown. You need to configure automatic reboot for the system to be left in a dirty state.

To adjust the configuration of automatic reboot, you can use the Energy Saver Preference pane, or the `systemsetup` command-line utility. To see if the system is set to restart after a power failure:

```
$ systemsetup -getrestartpowerfailure
```

To set the system to restart after a power failure, you can also use `systemsetup`. For example, to enable restart after power failure supply, use on to the `-setrestartpowerfailure` switch:

```
# systemsetup -setrestartpowerfailure on
```

You also need to deal with external devices that may not have these controls. It may be appropriate to delay the startup of a server until external devices have the chance to start up. This is especially important when using large external RAID arrays. To determine the delay of how long the system waits to restart after a power failure, use `systemsetup`:

```
$ systemsetup -getWaitForStartupAfterPowerFailure
```

You can also set this delay using `systemsetup`. Supply a value, measured in seconds, to the `-setWaitForStartupAfterPowerFailure` switch:

```
# sudo systemsetup -setWaitForStartupAfterPowerFailure 360
```

This example delays a server startup for 6 minutes after power is restored following a dirty shutdown.

Automatic restarting of a server on OS freeze is available only to server-supported hardware (Xserve and Mac Pro). This restart is taken care of by a daemon that "tickles" a hardware timer (the "doomsday clock"). The hardware timer counts down from 5 minutes, and, unless reset, will forcibly reboot the system. The `watchdogtimerd` daemon, controlled by the `launchd` /System/Library/LaunchDaemons/com.apple.watchdogtimerd.plist file, resets the timer every 4 minutes. If the timer doesn't hear from `watchdogtimerd`, it assumes that the OS is unresponsive and forcibly restarts the system.

Creating Disk Redundancy

Disk drives, based on several moving parts, ultimately will fail. Sometimes defects in the manufacturing process cause failures. This section describes one way to protect systems from any single disk failing, by using RAID, or a redundant array of inexpensive disks.

Mac OS X has built-in software RAID options, including the capability to build mirrored RAID sets. The Disk Utility.app can handle most RAID tasks; the command-line-based `diskutil` is more powerful in many ways, including scriptability.

To create a mirrored RAID set, first you need to know the disk device IDs. You can use `diskutil` to provide this information with its `list` verb:

```
$ /usr/sbin/diskutil list
/dev/disk0
   #:                        TYPE NAME              SIZE        IDENTIFIER
   0:        GUID_partition_scheme               *149.1 Gi    disk0
   1:                         EFI                 200.0 Mi     disk0s1
   2:            Apple_HFS Macintosh HD           148.7 Gi     disk0s2
/dev/disk1
   #:                        TYPE NAME              SIZE        IDENTIFIER
   0:     Apple_partition_scheme                 *100.0 Mi    disk1
   1:         Apple_partition_map                 31.5 Ki      disk1s1
   2:             Apple_HFS Data                  100.0 Mi     disk1s2
/dev/disk2
   #:                        TYPE NAME              SIZE        IDENTIFIER
   0:     Apple_partition_scheme                 *100.0 Mi    disk2
   1:         Apple_partition_map                 31.5 Ki      disk2s1
   2:         Apple_HFS Disk Image               100.0 Mi     disk2s2
```

If both disks are new, or have no data on them, the `diskutil createraid` verb can be used to create a mirrored RAID set. Taking disks from the previous example list, you would issue the following command to mirror disk1s2 and disk2s2:

```
# diskutil createraid mirror Data HFS+ disk1s2 disk2s2
```

This command creates a mirror RAID set named Data from the two disks disk1s2 and disk2s2.

When creating new RAID sets or adding disks, if possible, it is better to specify the entire disk instead of a partition on that disk. This allows the software to reformat the entire disk using the most current partition layouts. When using whole disks, the type of partitioning used is selected based on the platform type (APMFormat for the PowerPC [PPC] platform, GPTFormat for Intel). GPT and APM partition formats cannot be mixed in the same RAID set.

AppleRAID has the capability to create a mirrored RAID from an existing disk with another disk the same or greater size (although space beyond the size of the original disk will be wasted). The `diskutil enableraid` command can RAID-enable an existing disk, which allows adding a new disk. For example, if the example disk disk1s2 is a single disk that you want to turn into a mirror, you could issue the following command:

```
# diskutil enableRAID mirror disk1s2
Changing filesystem size on disk 'disk1s2'...
Attempting to change filesystem size from 104857600 to 104824832 bytes
Waiting for new RAID to come online "CA9B6A1C-58B9-48C5-9437-CC4911DCB3E5"
Found new RAID set
[ \ 0%................................................... ] Changing filesystem size
on disk 'disk9'...
The disk has been converted into a RAID
```

In the example given, disk9 refers to a new RAID device. This device will contain any devices that make up the RAID set, including the original disk disk1s2. (Disks that were originally partitioned on Mac OS X v10.2 or earlier or were partitioned to be Mac OS 9–compatible may not be resizable.) Once this disk has been degraded, it can be repaired (or given its initial partner disk) using the `diskutil repairMirror` command. For example, to add the blank disk2s2 to the newly degraded RAID disk9 created in the previous example, you could issue the following command:

```
# diskutil repairMirror disk9 disk2s2
Note:  Syncing data between mirror partitions can take a very long time.
Note:  The mirror should now be repairing itself  You can check it's status using
'diskutil listRAID.
```

Notice the notes—syncing the mirrors really does take a long time. The larger the disks, the longer the process takes. To display the status of RAID devices, issue the command diskutil listRAID :

```
$ diskutil listRAID
RAID SETS
---------

===============================================================================
Name:              Data
Unique ID:         CA9B6A1C-58B9-48C5-9437-CC4911DCB3E5
```

```
Type:                 Mirror
Status:               Online
Size:                 104824832 B
Device Node:          disk9
Apple RAID Version:   2
---------------------------------------------------------------------------
#   Device Node     UUID                                    Status
---------------------------------------------------------------------------
0   disk1s2         1A20A082-5342-4624-A259-F91CB69CB00A     Online
1   disk2s2         0AF106BF-5FD0-403B-86D8-035150E6F872     Online
===========================================================================
```

If a RAID set is degraded or rebuilding, its status is listed as such.

One downside to AppleRAID is that a failed disk does not notify administrators of its failure. However, you, as administrator, can easily script a warning using the diskutil listraid, grep, and launchd commands (and some inspiration from Chapter 9, "Automating Systems"). See the diskutil man page for further RAID options.

In addition, some third-party RAID utilities, such as SoftRAID (http://www.softraid.com), offer monitoring and other capabilities. The Apple Xserve and Mac Pro utilities offer hardware RAID options that extend RAID capabilities to RAID 5 configurations.

Creating Network Redundancy

From two or more similar network interfaces, you can create an aggregate that acts as one. (Typically, aggregate networks are created to increase bandwidth.) The new, bonded interface can suffer network outages on all physical interfaces but one and keep running. The network switch that these interfaces connect to must support the 802.3ad Link Aggregation Control Protocol and be configured accordingly. The process of switch configuration differs from manufacturer to manufacturer, and is outside the scope of this book. Once you have configured a switch properly, you can configure Mac OS X.

Follow these steps to create the aggregate network and then configure the interface:

1   Choose System Preferences from the Apple menu. In System Preferences, click the Network Preferences tab to display the pane.

2   Click the Preference button at the bottom of the pane, and choose Manage Virtual
Interfaces.

3   Click the Add (+) button and choose New Link Aggregate. Enter a name of your
choice for the new Link Aggregate interface. Select the options for the interfaces that
should belong to this bonded group, using the checkboxes.

4   When you have finished, click the Create button.

The system now recognizes this interface as new, and as such it must be configured. To
configure the interface, use the Network Preference pane or the `networksetup` command,
which you can also use to create and destroy hardware bonds.

To use the `networksetup` command to create a bonded interface as you would from the
Network Preference pane, issue the following command:

```
# networksetup -createBond bond0 en0 en1
```

This command creates a new, aggregate interface named `bond0`, by combining the `en0` and
`en1` interfaces. See the `networksetup man` page for more options.

Once you configure this new bonded interface, it has a single IP address and MAC
address. For all intents and purposes, there is still a single route into the server. If one
cable is physically damaged or unplugged, network traffic continues to pass on the
remaining interface without interruption.

Monitoring High Availability

As systems expand, automated solutions are nearly the only way to keep up. Mac OS X offers several automated systems that provide high system availability.

The Mac OS X diskspacemonitor can monitor free space on volumes and automatically take action when defined thresholds are reached. The speed of a disk drops the closer it gets to capacity. More importantly, when a disk fills completely, writes fail and files are not properly closed, leading to possible corruption.

The Mac OS X IP failover capability allows a warm standby server to monitor a primary, and take over in the event of hardware failure on the primary. Like disk RAID, this strategy allows continued availability even in the face of complete hardware failure. In the case of IP failover, however, the failure can entail an entire server.

Using diskspacemonitor

diskspacemonitor is a relatively simple but important script on Mac OS X Server that automates disk-space checking and response when thresholds are crossed. An administrator can fully configure it.

To determine whether diskspacemonitor is enabled, use the status command:

```
# diskspacemonitor status
Not enabled.
```

To enable diskspacemonitor, use the on command:

```
# diskspacemonitor on
```

No output is returned from this command. Turning diskspacemonitor on enables the launchd task at /System/Library/LaunchDaemons/com.apple.diskspacemonitor.plist. Once enabled, diskspacemonitor is configured in the /etc/diskspacemonitor/diskspacemonitor.conf preference file. It is three short lines:

```
monitor_interval=10
alert_threshold=75
recovery_threshold=85
```

monitor_interval is the interval in minutes between diskspacemonitor checks.

`alert_threshold` is the percentage full at which `diskspacemonitor` will run the alert scripts in /etc/diskspacemonitor/action.

`recovery_threshold` is the percentage full at which `diskspacemonitor` will run the recovery scripts in /etc/diskspacemonitor/action.

The action directory contains two predefined scripts:

▶   /etc/diskspacemonitor/action/alert, to alert the administrator that a warning threshold is exceeded

▶   /etc/diskspacemonitor/action/recover, to recover disk space by compressing, rolling, and deleting log files.

Administrators may add their own scripts:

▶   /etc/diskspacemonitor/action/alert.local

▶   /etc/diskspacemonitor/action/recover.local

The administrator-supplied scripts run at the appropriate threshold, and then the standard scripts are invoked.

Thanks to the configuration files provided, simply turning on `diskspacemonitor` causes a Mac OS X Server system to alert an administrator of impending low disk conditions, and automatically roll old log files on actual low disk conditions.

Using IP Failover

IP failover allows a backup server to notice when a primary server goes offline and to come online in its place. Apple has made the initial setup and configuration of IP failover simple, but the reality is more complex. An administrator must be diligent in selecting appropriate services for failover and testing the implications, as well as configuring servers appropriately.

For example, failover for a server providing static- or database-driven web services is fairly straightforward, as web setups can be replicated to the backup server with a database server running on another machine. In this case, failing from the primary to the secondary requires no *state*. In a more complex web environment, common storage must be mapped to keep session information and Secure Sockets Layer (SSL) transactions intact. Apple has enabled a way to easily fail over Apple Filing Protocol (AFP), but doing the same for Windows services (Samba) is far from built-in.

Additionally, if you plan to fail over a given service, it must be configured properly on both the primary and secondary server: IP failover goes into effect upon an entire server going offline, and not simply when service levels drop (like a load balancer).

About the Failover Scheme

A failover scheme has two parts. On the master, the `IPFailover` startup item (/System/Library/StartupItems/IPFailover) launches `heartbeatd` during startup. Upon launch, `heartbeatd` checks its argument list, and moves to the background. `heartbeatd` sends out a message every second via port 1694. This is the signal to the backup server in the failover pair that the primary is still alive and well (or can at least get a heartbeat signal out). These messages are directed at the address specified in the FAILOVER_BCAST_IPS entry in the /etc/hostconfig file.

On the backup server, the `IPFailover` startup item starts `failoverd`, which listens for the heartbeat message on port 1694. If it stops receiving the heartbeat message, it begins the failover process.

On detecting a failure, `failoverd` takes over the master host's public IP addresses, to maintain service availability to incoming clients. `failoverd` also invokes `NotifyFailover` to notify the administrator by email, and `ProcessFailover` to acquire the monitored IP. (See the following illustration.)

The `ProcessFailover` script also executes scripts located in the /Library/IPFailover/<IP_Address> folder, where `IP_Address` is the address of the primary server. You must create this folder; it does not exist by default. This folder can contain four scripts: PreAcq, PostAcq, PreRel, and PostRel. These scripts perform actions you determine at each stage of a failure. The names define the context of when the scripts will run (before IP acquisition, after acquisition, before IP release, or after IP release). The capability of customizing actions for their specific configuration is where the real power and flexibility of IP failover comes into play.

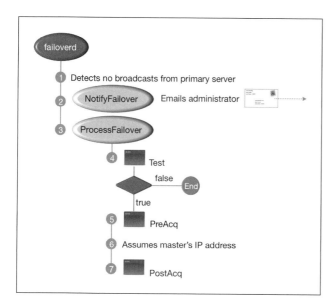

Configuring Failovers

A failover setup has a few basic requirements: nearly identical hardware and software for the master and backup servers, multiple common network interfaces (Ethernet or FireWire), and the ability to connect to common networks and common storage.

Initial failover configuration requires several steps:

1   Configure the primary Ethernet interface of each server to connect to the primary network. Each server should have its own IP address and be connected to the same subnet.

2   Configure Domain Name System (DNS) for the interfaces. A DNS administrator should also:

▶   Map the IP address of the master server to a virtual DNS name (for example, store.example.com) that users use to connect to your server. This allows you to change the IP address of the master server transparently to users.

▶   Map the IP addresses of the master and backup servers to DNS names (for example, master.example.com and secondary.example.com) that you can use to refer to the two computers when setting up IP failover.

3   Directly connect the master and backup computers together using a second Ethernet interface or IP over FireWire. This is an important step because the two computers communicate failover events over this connection. In addition, the administrator should do the following:

▶   Configure the TCP/IP settings of the secondary Ethernet interface or IP over FireWire interface on both computers.

▶   Assign each computer a private network IP address, separate from the primary interface. For example, use 10.1.0.2 and 10.1.0.3, while the primary interfaces are configured with 192.168.200.2 and 192.168.200.3.

▶   Make sure the secondary connections are on the same subnet.

4   Configure the master server following these four steps:

▶   Add or edit the FAILOVER_BCAST_IPS entry in /etc/hostconfig to specify the addresses to send heartbeat messages to.

▶   It's most efficient to send the heartbeat messages to specific addresses, rather than a broadcast address. For example, if the primary IP address of the master server is 17.1.0.50 and the secondary IP address is 10.1.0.2, add the following line to the /etc/hostconfig file: `FAILOVER_BCAST_IPS="10.1.0.3 17.1.0.51"` This line instructs the master server to send the heartbeat messages to the primary and secondary IP addresses of the backup server.

NOTE ▶ To edit the /etc/hostconfig file, you must be root. Use the `sudo` command when opening this file using your preferred command-line editor.

▶   Add or edit the `FAILOVER_EMAIL_RECIPIENT` entry to specify the mail address to send notifications to. If you don't add this entry, mail notifications go to root, which typically routes to no one.

▶   Restart the server.

5   Configure the backup failover server following these four steps:

> ▶   Add or edit the FAILOVER_PEER_IP_PAIRS entry in the /etc/hostconfig file to specify the IP address of the primary network interface on the master server. For example, if the IP address of the primary network interface on the master server is 17.1.0.50, add the following entry: `FAILOVER_PEER_IP_PAIRS="en0:17.1.0.50"`

> ▶   Add or edit the FAILOVER_PEER_IP entry in /etc/hostconfig to specify the IP address of the secondary network interface on the master server. For example, if the IP address of the FireWire port on the master server is 10.1.0.2, add the following entry: `FAILOVER_PEER_IP="10.1.0.2"`

> ▶   Disconnect the direct connection between backup server and master server. If you're using IP over FireWire for the secondary interface, disconnect the FireWire cable connecting the two computers.

> ▶   Restart the backup server. When the backup server has started up, reconnect it to the primary server.

Configuring Failover Services

To have a backup server take over the services of a failed master requires additional instructions. The instructions in "Configuring Failovers" simply bring a backup server on-line in place of a failed master; there's nothing that makes it take over for services configured on the master.

Many services have failover or high-availability capabilities built in, and wouldn't need to rely on the Apple IP Failover scheme. For instance, Open Directory has a Master and Replica configuration that provide a high availability configuration. MySQL has facilities for replication and may be better served by its native failover capabilities than by trying to use the Apple IP Failover.

Typically, good candidates for Mac OS X Server in an IP failover pair are services that do not fail over on their own. The specific service will determine how it should be configured. Generally, the master and backup in the pair will need some common storage to maintain state. The following example uses AFP. For services other than AFP, you need to become familiar with the service, determine if server-based failover is appropriate, and plan a method for the backup server to take over for a failed master.

In the case of network disconnect, AFP can allow initially authenticated clients to reconnect to the server using a reconnect token rather then reauthenticating with user credentials. The reconnect token contains information that allows the server to verify session and user data on the server.

When the client initially logs in (using user credentials), the server sends the client a reconnect token. This token is encrypted with the server reconnect key located in /etc/AFP.conf and is only readable by the server.

Following a disconnect of an established session, the client attempts a reconnect by sending the reconnect key to the server. The server decrypts the reconnect token using the server reconnect key. Then the server verifies that it is a valid, authenticated session token, by verifying data in the reconnect token with data on the server (for example, user data obtained from the user record). When the information is verified, the server completes the reconnect.

In the case of failover, the server reconnect key used to initially encrypt the reconnect token handed to the client must be used by the backup server to handle all reconnects.

By default, the server reconnect key is stored in /etc/AFP.conf. This file must be placed on a shared storage that both servers can access.

The path to the key is specified by the reconnectKeyLocation attribute value, found in the preference file /Library/Preferences/com.AppleFileServer.plist.

Changing the value of reconnectKeyLocation in the server preferences file ensures that both servers use the same reconnect server key.

Troubleshooting

Following are suggestions on troubleshooting issues that may arise with AppleRAID and IPfailover.

When creating a RAID set using AppleRAID, using the command-line tool often gives more specific error messages than the graphical Disk Utility.app. Additionally, notice the primary warning for new RAID sets: Do not use disks previously formatted with a Mac OS 9 wrapper without reformatting.

Remember to check RAID sets often with the `diskutil listRAID` command to determine if any sets are having problems.

If an existing RAID set continually degrades by itself, check each disk in the set for bad blocks. You can perform this check with the command-line `diskutil` and third-party applications.

If a disk is having a physical problem, system.log typically will display kernel-level messages to that effect.

Troubleshooting IP failover is a matter of knowing the service. As you learned in this chapter, `IPFailover` depends on two daemons: `heartbeatd` and `failoverd`. Both are launched by a `StartupItem`, and depend on the correct entry existing in /etc/hostconfig.

Furthermore, the heartbeat packets are delivered on port 1694: Make sure that this is not blocked. If you find that a backup unexpectedly is trying to take over for a master, make sure that the physical network connecting the backup and master is sound.

Finally, like other services, the logs always contain clues. Check system.log. Also check the specific `IPFailover` log— /Library/Logs/failoverd.log—all failover activity is recorded there.

What You've Learned

You should understand these points about providing highly available services:

▶   Before getting too deep into the technology behind providing high availability, determine exactly which services require this level of reliability.

▶   Uptime is a measure of the time that a computer or service has been up and running. It is a metric that must be used carefully.

▶   Reliability is often measured in "nines." Each added nine dramatically reduces the window in which a service can be unavailable.

▶   High availability is a chain of all components on which a service relies. This includes power, hardware, network components, and the service itself.

▶   Power redundancy is handled by redundant power supplies and battery-backed UPS devices.

▶ Mac OS X has built-in capability to monitor and react to a UPS connected via a USB cable.

▶ The `pmset` and `systemsetup` commands can query and manipulate system settings that determine thresholds at which to react to UPS battery events and power failure conditions.

▶ Disk Utility.app and the `diskutil` command-line tools are capable of creating RAID sets based on AppleRAID in software.

▶ `diskspacemonitor` is a useful script that not only monitors disk-free conditions, but can also take actions (read: run scripts) based on free space thresholds.

▶ Server-based IP failover is built into Mac OS X Server. While the basic configuration is relatively simple, understanding and implementing failover for particular services may present challenges.

▶ `heartbeatd` and `failoverd` are the two daemons responsible for sending and listening to the primary server's heartbeat. If the backup server running `failoverd` does not receive a heartbeat, it starts the failover process.

▶ `failoverd` uses the NotifyFailover and ProcessFailover scripts to notify admins, and acquire the targeted IP, respectively.

▶ Four scripts, PreAcq, PostAcq, PreRel, and PostRel are available to perform custom actions at each stage of the failover process.

Review Quiz

1. What is the difference in downtime per year between a 99.99% available service and a "five-nines" 99.999% available service?

2. Which command-line tool is used to alter on-battery behavior of a Mac OS X system?

3. Which command-line tool is used to create mirrored disk sets?

4. What are two advantages of creating a bonded network interface?

5. What are the two processes responsible for monitoring an IP failover pair?

6. What are the four scripts run by `ProcessFailover` to run actions on failover state change?

Answers

1. The 99.99% available per year service can be down for 53 minutes per year. A "five-nines" 99.999% available service can only be down for 5 minutes per year. That's a difference of 48 minutes per year.

2. The `pmset` (Power Management Settings) command.

3. `diskutil`

4. A bonded network interface creates redundancy and improves throughput.

5. `heartbeatd` and `failoverd` send and receive the heartbeat signal, respectively.

6. The four scripts are PreAcq, PostAcq, PreRel, and PostRel.

12

Time   This lesson takes approximately 60 minutes to complete.

Goals   Learn to follow a troubleshooting methodology
Learn where to find help
Learn command-line tools to assist in the troubleshooting process

Chapter 12
Troubleshooting

Troubleshooting is as much art as it is science. Each chapter in this book has included troubleshooting advice specific to the chapter's subject, and focused purely on the technical resolution. This chapter takes a more general look at troubleshooting and teaches you how to develop a good troubleshooting methodology that you can apply to *any* situation.

Following a Methodology

When a new problem surfaces—one that you haven't seen or resolved before—it's important to follow a troubleshooting *methodology*. By doing so, you can systematically narrow down the problem to find the cause of the problem and, hopefully, a resolution.

Troubleshooting has two goals: fix the problem properly, and fix it quickly. To fix a problem properly, you must do the following:

▶ Follow systematic troubleshooting procedures.

▶ Use up-to-date references and tools.

▶ Create no new problems.

Several actions are keys in troubleshooting: documenting your work, following your methodology, and backing up.

If you are in a shared support environment, or if you rely on outside contractors, documenting a fix for a particular problem is a very effective way to ensure that you or your team does not have to start from scratch every time a problem appears.

Bearing in mind the old adage "haste makes waste," be sure to stick with your methodology, rather than thrash or rush and perform sloppy work. It's too easy to introduce *new* problems while trying to fix the current issue.

Always create a backup before modifying files and settings. If you're going to perform work that may alter user data, or affect a system in a way that you're not entirely sure about, create a backup of any files that may be affected. Additionally, it may be wise to clone the entire computer before performing a systemwide alteration.

Here are some tips that you should keep in mind throughout the troubleshooting process.

Take Notes

The expected short tasks often end up taking much longer than expected. What starts out as a simple troubleshooting job can sometimes unravel into a major task.

Start taking notes from the very beginning of the troubleshooting process, even if it seems like a simple problem. Document each setting that is changed, added, or removed. After you complete the fix, review your notes to see where you might have been more effective.

Use Your Resources

Consulting with available resources is a great way to find information about the product and problem that you're troubleshooting. Even if you're not sure what you're looking for, browsing through references such as the AppleCare Knowledge Base or technical mailing lists, or searching the web can be helpful when you don't know what to try next. You might come across an article related to the issue you're trying to resolve. Don't hesitate to ask questions of coworkers or other reputable technical authorities, because they can provide valuable clues.

Consider the Human Factor

When you've been working long and hard on a problem that has you stumped, it can help just to take a break. Frustration can affect your ability to think logically. Sometimes you may be too close to a problem to see it—a short break might lead you to consider new solutions or approaches.

Also consider your user or customer. Some users are anxious, on deadline, or feeling stress or pressure for other reasons. Do not give half-answers or make comments ("Uh-oh, this doesn't look good") that might be alarming during the troubleshooting process. Don't hesitate to suggest that your user take a break while you're working.

Follow an Order of Elimination

Approaching a problem methodically is efficient and cost-effective. Most problems can be categorized and eliminated with careful troubleshooting.

Check for problems in the following order:

1. User-related problems

   Check for user-related problems while gathering information, duplicating the problem, and trying quick fixes. These include incorrectly set preferences, inadvertent errors, incompatibilities, and incorrect assumptions.

2. Software-related problems

   Software can cause symptoms that look like hardware problems. Always check for software problems before assuming the problem is hardware-related. Report bugs if you find them (this is an instance where your notes will be helpful).

3. Operating system–related problems

   Attempt to identify operating system–related problems from general symptoms that affect all applications, or from specific symptoms, such as problems that prevent the startup process from completing.

4. Hardware-related problems

   When you are convinced that the problem is not caused by user error or software, you should troubleshoot it as a hardware issue. Hardware problems are beyond the scope of this book; the AppleCare Knowledge Base at http://www.apple.com/support is a valuable resource.

Taking General Steps

Often, solving a problem requires you to rethink exactly what the problem is. Sometimes what appears to be a bug isn't a bug at all. Remain objective, and be careful not to convince yourself of incorrect truths. Using a consistent methodology will keep you on the right track.

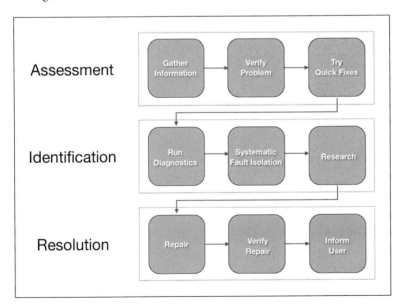

The illustrated troubleshooting sequence shows the main steps of one troubleshooting methodology. It is used inside Apple to resolve issues and is an expansion on the scientific method.

The first row includes steps that help assess a problem; the second row shows steps where the cause is identified and troubleshooting steps take place so that complete understanding is gained; and the third row involves fixing the problem and wrapping up the issue.

A formalized process that goes with this methodology is shown in this flowchart:

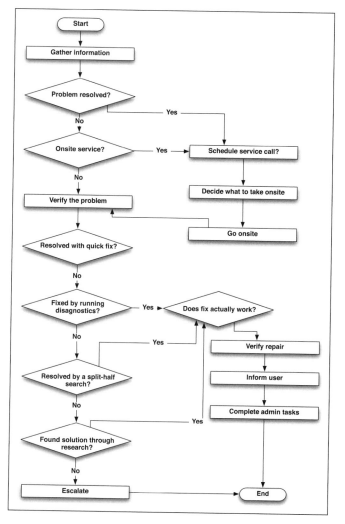

The process shown here is used by the AppleCare support group to ensure that it handles all issues properly and tracks them accurately. The flowchart describes a series of loops that are performed until the system is returned to normal operation. Imagine you're a desktop support technician called to work on a malfunctioning computer. According to the flowchart, the first step is to gather information. You immediately encounter a decision point: Was it a simple problem, and did gathering information alone resolve the problem? If it doesn't, you then verify the problem, that is, you see if you can reproduce it, and you try a quick fix. (You can skip the onsite service decision, since you already have the computer in front of you.)

Let's say you think you have identified the problem, so you skip to repair or replace. (In a software context, this choice can be stated as "troubleshoot or reinstall.") After completing the repair (often a quick fix is a repair), you ask yourself if the problem is resolved. No? Then you loop back to trying quick fixes. You may try a number of quick fixes before either resolving the problem or deciding that no more quick fixes apply and you need to go on to running diagnostics. You may realize that you have exhausted your knowledge and need to research. You may decide that it is time to escalate the problem to a senior technician. Or, you may determine the problem is fixed and enter the documentation and notification stage.

Assessing the Problem

Asking the proper questions is perhaps the most powerful troubleshooting tool in your arsenal. Getting a clear picture of what is not working is crucial if you want to find the solution. Try to get as complete and specific a picture as possible about what problems are occurring, when they occur, and what error messages are displayed. Search the Knowledge Base if you think this might be a common problem.

Tips for Gathering Information

Following are tips on how to ask the right questions to get the answers you need, starting from a broad view:

1. Start with open-ended questions such as "What is the issue?" or "What is happening onscreen?" Open-ended questions generally start with words like how, why, when, who, what, and where. They can't be answered by "yes" or "no." You usually gather more information this way, even if some of it is not exactly pertinent to the problem at hand.

2. Without interruption, let users explain in their own words what they have experienced. The explanation may help you avoid assumptions about the source of the problem, because you may hear that more things are broken than you expected.

3. As you begin to understand the basics of the problem, start asking closed questions that require more limited, specific answers. Examples of closed questions are "What version of the operating system are you using?" and "Is there an icon on your desktop?" Users either can tell you the version or that they don't know (in which case, you would guide them to the information). Closed questions often can be answered by "yes," "no," or a value such as "10.4."

4. Verify your understanding of what the user has told you. Restate what you have been told and get the user's agreement that you understand the problem. An example of restatement would be, "Okay, so what's happening is that when you do X, Y occurs. Is that correct?"

5. If the user agrees with your understanding, continue to gather information. If the user does not agree with your understanding, clarify what you misstated and again verify your understanding. Do not continue with the troubleshooting until the user agrees that you understand the problem.

Using "The Four Cs"

Another useful methodology is "The Four Cs." This systematic strategy applies to networks, both Ethernet and Fibre Channel–based, and examines the following:

► Connections (networks and cables)

► Components (hardware failures)

► Configurations (software settings)

► Combinations of problems in the first three groups

Examining Connections

There was a time when you could purchase a personal computer and not connect it to anything else, except perhaps a printer. Those times are long gone. Networks have a place in connecting home machines to other machines and the Internet up through racks of machines running in a cluster configuration that coordinates activities via Ethernet.

Understanding these components and how they fit with others is critical in the trouble-shooting process. If networking is not your strength, consider consulting with someone who has the expertise necessary to initially set up or troubleshoot for you.

Examining Components

Troubleshooting down to the component level—server, network card, or disk drive—is an essential skill. Often, individual components have methods of notification that can alert administrators before they fail.

Examining Configurations

After verifying that system connections and components are in perfect working order, a simple error or misconfiguration can result in various levels of performance and reliability of the system. Networks rely on intricate combinations of active background processes, static configuration files, and dynamic transactions. The more familiar you become with these aspects of a network's structure, the more quickly you will be able to troubleshoot problems related to the configuration of the system.

Examining Combinations of Problems

Never underestimate the ability of several components to fail at the same time. Also, there are times when several components just do not work together despite what "should" be happening. Challenge your assumptions and look for bad interactions between compo-nents or multiple failures. If at all possible, bring components from a troubled system into a known-good test environment. Swap components in series and in multiples.

Using Troubleshooting Tools and Resources

This section covers using tools generically for overall troubleshooting use. See the "Troubleshooting" sections in the individual chapters for information on how to use sys-tem tools in the chapter-specific situations.

Seeing What the User Sees

On a 1-to-1 scale, nothing is better than being able to actually see the same screen as the user while troubleshooting. It may be difficult for people outside of the technology field to describe a problem in the same manner you would. It's also possible that you're troubleshooting an application that you're not entirely familiar with. Mac OS X gives you several options for viewing a screen remotely.

Using Apple Remote Desktop to Troubleshoot

While Apple Remote Desktop (ARD) covers a broad range of tools, the ability to remotely view the screen of another Mac OS X computer is one of the top reasons for its use. Since the client portion of ARD is part of the out-of-the-box system since Mac OS X v10.4, it is a very good choice in Macintosh environments.

ARD leverages the open source Virtual Network Computing (VNC) product. This means two things. First, generic VNC clients, such as Chicken of the VNC, can be used to connect to an ARD-configured Mac. Second, the ARD Admin console can connect to Windows or Linux machines running a VNC client.

See http://www.apple.com/remotedesktop for more details.

Using Screen Sharing to Troubleshoot

New to Leopard is an additional way to view a remote screen: the built-in screen sharing, essentially a stripped-down version of ARD. Screen Sharing has been integrated with iChat, allowing two network-connected users to view one screen. Participants may request to view the remote screen, or allow their screens to be shared.

Screen sharing is also integrated into the Finder, which offers a screen sharing button while browsing network computers. Finally, you can use a vnc:// URL in the "Connect to Server..." menu item in the Finder to allow connections to arbitrary machines running the ARD client. For more on screen sharing, see "Installing Remotely Using a Graphical Interface" in Chapter 2, "Installing and Configuring Systems."

See http://www.apple.com/macosx/features/ichat.html for more information.

Determining the State of the System

When working on larger problems—issues that affect an entire system, or multiple users on a machine—it's always beneficial to be able to gather the system state. Getting the big picture is crucial in these situations. Here are tools to help you do that.

Using System Profiler

Built into Mac OS X as a graphical user interface and shell-based utility, System Profiler can report on almost any aspect of the system: hardware characteristics, installed applications, system software versions, and more. For more on System Profiler, see "Creating Reports" in Chapter 8, "Monitoring Systems."

Using Logs

Never underestimate the amount of information you can gather from log files. You should *always* consult log files when troubleshooting a problem (and often even before then). Some programs may have their own logging facilities, which should be documented. Contact the application developer when no logging ability seems to exist.

Most importantly, many subsystems can turn on enhanced logging with greater debugging information. When the standard depth of logging isn't delivering enough information for solving a problem, look for a way to increase the verbosity of logs. Many of the subsystems accessed via Server Admin.app have a Logging tab that allows administrators to increase or decrease the amount of logging a given service provides. Unfortunately, outside of the Logging feature, methods to achieve deeper logging are fragmented. Many times, applications handle this in different ways. For some specific programs, see this chapter's "Trying Examples" section.

For details on reading log files and their typical locations, see "Reading Log Files" in Chapter 8, "Monitoring Systems."

Performing Verbose Boot

Sometimes, an issue will arise that takes place before the operating system is ready to accept logins. Mac OS X can drop the graphical login and present a text-based verbose boot to aid in the troubleshooting process. This is also a good way to get familiar with the system in general.

To perform a verbose boot, after you hear the boot chime, hold down the Command and V keys. During that boot and shutdown sequence, the familiar graphical screens (gray screen with the Apple logo on boot, and solid blue on shutdown) will be replaced by scrolling text that describes startup and shutdown events.

To make a system boot permanently in verbose mode, use the `nvram` command. `nvram` allows manipulating nonvolatile RAM, where certain boot parameters are stored. To set the verbose flag, issue this command with root-level access:

```
# nvram boot-args="-v"
```

To reverse this setting, set the `nvram boot-args` value to an empty string:

```
# nvram boot-args=""
```

Sometimes, messages may scroll by too quickly to read fully. There is a period of time when messages cannot be written to /var/log/system.log; however, immediately after boot, the message buffer still contains boot-time messages. You can use the dmesg (diagnostic message) command to print kernel messages. Simply type dmesg with root-level privileges at a prompt:

```
# dmesg
```

Because the kernel is the interface between hardware and the operating system, using dmesg can often help you find issues related to peripherals causing problems.

Using Command-Line Tools

While the graphical user interface makes many tasks much easier, speed and power for troubleshooting lie under the covers on the command line. Because this book has presented command-line tools throughout, this section summarizes command-line tools, options, and recommended use.

ps

The ps utility displays all currently running processes visible to a given user. When ps is run with root-level privileges, it gives a high-level snapshot view of the number and type of programs running on a system. For more on ps, see "top, CPU%, and Load Averages" in Chapter 10, "Monitoring Systems."

strings

The strings tool searches a file and prints out the human-readable portions. This is primarily useful with binary files and can be very useful in trying to glean what an executable does or how it does it. strings simply takes a filename as its argument:

```
$ strings filename
```

A match is a "string" if four or more alphanumeric characters appear contiguously.

fs_usage

According to its man page, fs_usage "presents an ongoing display of system call usage information pertaining to filesystem activity." fs_usage is useful for determining which files an application touches while it is running.

For more on fs_usage, see "Other System Monitoring Utilities" in Chapter 8, "Monitoring Systems."

Dtrace and Its Utilities

The Dtrace subsystem is a powerful troubleshooting tool new to Leopard. Exposed in the graphical user interface as Instruments.app and in the shell as dtrace, it allows an administrator to instrument just about any aspect of the system. Dtrace does, however, ship with some utilities that use the dtrace framework to accomplish their specific goal.

For example, the opensnoop script uses dtrace to single out file-system open calls. When opensnoop is run with root-level privileges and no arguments, all open files are printed to stdout. This result is very similar to fs_usage, but typically has less impact on a system.

Another example of a utility based on dtrace is syscallbyproc.d. Running this utility with root-level access with no arguments will sample the system until you stop it with a break (Control-C). Once stopped, syscallbyproc.d prints a count of all processes that made system calls and their frequency during the sample time, sorted by frequency. Using this utility is another way to determine which process is having the largest impact on the system.

For more on dtrace, see "Instruments and Dtrace" in Chapter 8, "Monitoring Systems," the dtrace man page, and the developer documentation on DTraceToolKit.

otool

Primarily a developer tool, the otool command displays specified parts of object files or libraries. It is only installed with the Xcode tools. It can also be useful to administrators trying to troubleshoot issues involving frameworks and libraries.

otool has many options. The -L switch displays the names and version numbers of the shared libraries that the object file uses. This can be a great asset when tracking down library version conflicts.

lsof

lsof lists currently open files. Because the Berkeley Software Distribution (BSD) layer treats all objects as files, lsof is a very powerful troubleshooting utility. If you run it with no arguments and root-level access, lsof will display all open files. Its -p switch will limit output to open files of the given process ID. Used with the -i switch, lsof can list open network sockets.

For more on lsof, see "Other System Monitoring Utilities" in Chapter 8, "Monitoring Systems."

netstat

When it comes to network statistics, netstat is very handy. It can report on details as varied as ports being listened to by an interface, network interface card (NIC) error statistics, how much data has been sent and received by an interface, and more. As such, netstat is good at providing details as well as a long-distance view.

For more on netstat, see "Other System Monitoring Utilities" in Chapter 8, "Monitoring Systems."

tcpdump

A network packet-capture utility, tcpdump displays or views the contents of all packets on a network interface, or just those that match a Boolean expression. It is based on the open source packet-capture library, libpcap. tcpdump is an ideal troubleshooting tool for anything network-related, from a simple confirmation that data is reaching a particular interface, up through decoding protocol peculiarities. To control the interface being monitored, tcpdump requires root-level or admin-level access.

For more on tcpdump, see "Other System Monitoring Utilities" in Chapter 8, "Monitoring Systems."

vm_stat

The vm_stat utility reports on machine virtual memory statistics. It can display aggregate data since boot, or show update values at a given interval. It is most useful in determining if a system is short on real RAM and swapping to disk too often.

For more on vm_stat, see "Determining Hardware Utilization" in Chapter 4, "Assessing Systems."

iostat

iostat displays an impressive amount of data about kernel I/O statistics on terminal, device, and CPU operations. The first statistics that are printed are averaged over the system uptime. To obtain information about the current activity, you can specify a wait time that causes iostat to display delta information at the specified interval.

For more on iostat, see "Determining Disk Utilization" in Chapter 4, "Assessing Systems."

Finding Help

The first thing to remember when troubleshooting a problem is that you're not alone. Typically, you're not even the first to experience a particular issue. The Macintosh community is tightly-knit, and solutions to problems disseminate quickly. This section talks about how to find help when you need to solve a problem.

Using man Pages

This book has presented many solutions that involve work in a shell, due to their power and speed. The command line is an environment that may be new to many administrators. When trying to remember a command or its syntax, *use the man pages built into the system*. There's very little need to struggle—just look it up. The man command allows lookups of commands directly, or for keywords in the pages.

For more on the man command, see "Getting Help" in Chapter 9, "Automating Systems."

Using Documentation

Often, people miss the official documentation produced by Apple for Mac OS X Server. PDF files containing several hundreds of pages can be found online at http://www.apple.com/server/resources.

This documentation is well written and often contains information that tends to confuse people who haven't read it. Remember: Mac OS X tends to do some unique things under the hood. While the Apple documentation may not answer every single question you have, it will give you a solid foundation on which to move forward.

Searching the Web

As stated earlier, the Macintosh community is fairly vocal. There are websites that present Mac technical topics, archives, forums, and more. This also includes the support section of the Apple website.

Found at http://www.apple.com/support, the Apple support section contains guides to downloads, manuals, Knowledge Base articles, and more. The main page is a portal into all of the support and help resources that Apple offers. While there are subsections that cover each product, Knowledge Base articles are categorized by keyword. Knowing the keyword for your product can help streamline results. All keywords begin with the letter *k*. The keyword for Mac OS X is *kmosx*. To target a specific version of Mac OS X, use the point release number. For example, articles covering Mac OS X v10.5 use the *kmosx5* keyword. Apple maintains a search help page at http://www.apple.com/it/support/help/search/.

The Apple presence on the web outside of the Apple website is strong. The Mac Fix It site specifically deals with early notification of problems users have after applying certain patches. Found at http://www.macfixit.com, the site features a free front section with current news and a paid inside section. The fee covers staffing costs: The site is actually staffed and run as a real business, to answer questions posed by users.

Another popular resource for system administrators is AFP548. Named after the protocol and port number used in the Apple Filing Protocol, http://afp548.com contains articles and a forum section where articles are written, questions are asked, and answers are given. Often, people in this forum are on the cutting edge of Macintosh technology, and find answers before most others.

Finally, don't forget searching the web with a tool like Google. You never know what blog or archive may contain the answers you seek. If you are receiving a specific error message, search for it explicitly. This is where good knowledge of logs come into play. Rather than search for "PPP won't connect," search for "L2TP error sending CDN (Can't assign requested address)"—a message obtained directly from a log file.

Keep in mind when searching the web that not all information you find may be helpful. In fact some resources may suggest doing things that may exacerbate the issues that you're currently experiencing. It's important that you analyze a number of sources and opinions before forming your own.

Being Forewarned Is Forearmed

Many resources exist that continually keep you informed about new technology, techniques, and issues in the Macintosh community. Reading and participating on a regular basis increases your knowledge and preparedness dramatically.

Mailing lists are one such resource. Apple runs many lists, found at http://lists.apple.com/. Each list is typically active, and is populated by exceptionally knowledgeable and helpful individuals. Do remember, though, that these are not typically Apple employees, but simply volunteers who strive to help the community.

Another important mailing list for Apple system administrators is the Mac Enterprise list. The Mac Enterprise charter is to disseminate information on best practices for Mac OS X and Apple products in an enterprise setting. While most action happens on the mailing list, there are also webcasts and articles found on the main website, http://www.macenterprise.org/.

MacTech is a monthly magazine focusing on in-depth how-to articles, reviews, and coverage of new techniques relating to IT and Mac development. Following a publication like *MacTech* keeps you abreast of ways to automate and enhance the systems you support before you may need to tackle a problem yourself. Subscriptions and archives can be found at http://www.mactech.com.

Lastly, go now and sign up for a free developer account at http://developer.apple.com. The Apple developer site contains documentation, source code, and more to help inform and troubleshoot Macintosh issues. Most importantly, you need a developer account to file bug reports. The Apple bug-tracking system is named "radar," and can be accessed at http://radar.apple.com. You'll need to sign in with your developer account. Filing bug reports is an important way to help Apple prioritize issues. Your voice helps make change happen.

Consulting Experts

Due to any number of circumstances, you may need outside help. If you're implementing a technology for the first time, or even if the project scope is too large for the existing team, don't discount hiring a consultant or freelancer. Apple maintains a list of independent (not employed by Apple) consultants through the Apple Consultants Network. The portal page to the network is at http://consultants.apple.com/, and contains case studies and a search section that helps you find qualified consultants in your area.

Trying Examples

Following are some examples of how to use tools presented in this chapter.

Finding Running Processes

Use ps to gain information on all currently running processes, including the associated account:

```
# ps aux
```

Paired with grep, filter down to processes in question. For example, find all processes named ssh:

```
# ps aux | grep ssh
```

Using Strings

Using strings as a troubleshooting tool is more art than science.

To examine an executable binary, simply include the filename as a parameter to strings. There's often a lot of output, and using a pager like less can help stem the flood of information. To examine the ManagedClient binary and pass it through less, use the following command:

```
$ strings /System/Library/CoreServices/ManagedClient.app/Contents/MacOS/ManagedClient
| less
```

Used with grep, this command is an interesting way to find absolute file paths embedded in binaries. By looking for the forward slash (/) symbol as the first character, you'll often find the preference files that the binary uses:

```
$ strings /System/Library/CoreServices/ManagedClient.app/Contents/MacOS/ManagedClient
| grep "^/" | less
```

Finding Listening Network Ports

Network services listen to specific ports for connecting clients (called binding to a port). Only one program at a time can bind to a given port number. If a program tries to bind to an already reserved port, an error will be generated, typically written to a log, and the operation will fail. The netstat command can be used to determine what ports are currently bound:

```
# netstat -an
Active Internet connections (including servers)
Proto Recv-Q Send-Q  Local Address          Foreign Address         (state)
tcp4      0      0  192.168.92.38.51125    192.168.181.151.22     ESTABLISHED
tcp4      0      0  192.168.92.38.51106    192.168.171.92.8194    ESTABLISHED
tcp4      0      0  *.88                   *.*                    LISTEN
tcp6      0      0  *.88                   *.*                    LISTEN
tcp4      0      0  *.22                   *.*                    LISTEN
tcp6      0      0  *.22                   *.*                    LISTEN
Active LOCAL (UNIX) domain sockets
Address   Type   Recv-Q Send-Q   Inode     Conn     Refs  Nextref Addr
 5713f68 stream     0      0        0  54b03b8      0        0
 54b03b8 stream     0      0        0  5713f68      0        0
 789bcc0 stream     0      0        0  5199a18      0        0
...remainder of output removed for space considerations
```

In this case, since you're only interested in connections that are listening on certain ports, you can filter with grep:

```
# netstat -an | grep LISTEN
```

Another option to find bound ports is the lsof command. The -i switch lists open network activity. Again, use grep to filter on listening ports:

```
# lsof -i | grep LISTEN
launchd         1        root   13u  IPv6 0x4a59be8   0t0  TCP localhost:ipp (LISTEN)
launchd         1        root   14u  IPv4 0x4e02e64   0t0  TCP localhost:ipp (LISTEN)
launchd         1        root   58u  IPv6 0x4a59984   0t0  TCP *:ssh (LISTEN)
launchd         1        root   60u  IPv4 0x4e02a68   0t0  TCP *:ssh (LISTEN)
krb5kdc         87       root   12u  IPv6 0x4a59258   0t0  TCP *:kerberos (LISTEN)
krb5kdc         87       root   13u  IPv4 0x4d2266c   0t0  TCP *:kerberos (LISTEN)
AppleVNCS       270      mike   4u   IPv6 0x4a58ff4   0t0  TCP *:vnc-server (LISTEN)
Microsoft 12724          mike   43u  IPv4 0x814266c   0t0  TCP *:3998 (LISTEN)
```

lsof is a little more powerful than netstat when determining open ports because it will also list the program that is bound to a given port.

Using Debug Logs

There are several canonical ways that programs understand to produce more detailed output and logging information. This section gives only a high-level overview, because each method depends on the program in question.

Setting the Verbose Command-Line Switch

Many programs simply use a -v switch to indicate that you want verbose output. For example, if ssh is not connecting or not accepting keys, use the -v switch:

```
$ ssh -v brian@www.example.com
OpenSSH_4.7p1, OpenSSL 0.9.7l 28 Sep 2006
debug1: Reading configuration data /etc/ssh_config
debug1: Applying options for *
debug1: Connecting to www.example.com [192.168.59.78] port 22.
debug1: Connection established.
```

```
debug1: identity file /Users/brian/.ssh/identity type 0
debug1: identity file /Users/brian/.ssh/id_rsa type -1
debug1: identity file /Users/brian/.ssh/id_dsa type -1
debug1: Remote protocol version 2.0, remote software version OpenSSH_4.2p1
FreeBSD-20050903
debug1: match: OpenSSH_4.2p1 FreeBSD-20050903 pat OpenSSH*
debug1: Enabling compatibility mode for protocol 2.0
debug1: Local version string SSH-2.0-OpenSSH_4.7
debug1: SSH2_MSG_KEXINIT sent
debug1: SSH2_MSG_KEXINIT received
debug1: kex: server->client aes128-cbc hmac-md5 none
debug1: kex: client->server aes128-cbc hmac-md5 none
debug1: SSH2_MSG_KEX_DH_GEX_REQUEST(1024<1024<8192) sent
debug1: expecting SSH2_MSG_KEX_DH_GEX_GROUP
debug1: SSH2_MSG_KEX_DH_GEX_INIT sent
debug1: expecting SSH2_MSG_KEX_DH_GEX_REPLY
debug1: Host 'www.example.com' is known and matches the DSA host key.
debug1: Found key in /Users/brian/.ssh/known_hosts:10
debug1: ssh_dss_verify: signature correct
debug1: SSH2_MSG_NEWKEYS sent
debug1: expecting SSH2_MSG_NEWKEYS
debug1: SSH2_MSG_NEWKEYS received
debug1: SSH2_MSG_SERVICE_REQUEST sent
debug1: SSH2_MSG_SERVICE_ACCEPT received
debug1: Authentications that can continue: publickey,password,keyboard-interactive
debug1: Next authentication method: publickey
debug1: Trying private key: /Users/brian/.ssh/id_rsa
debug1: Trying private key: /Users/brian/.ssh/id_dsa
debug1: Next authentication method: keyboard-interactive
```

You can extract further detail if you specify the verbose switch (-v) more than once:

```
$ ssh -vvv www.example.com
```

Using Configuration File Settings

Many programs look to a configuration file to obtain their runtime settings. For example, Samba, the SMB server used in Mac OS X Server, uses /etc/smb.conf to store and read its runtime settings. In its [global] section, one line determines how verbose logging will be:

```
log level = 2
```

The log level can range from 1 to 10, with 10 being the most information possible. Change the value and restart the smbd daemon for the change to take effect immediately.

See the documentation for other programs as needed to determine proper settings.

Presence of Debug File

Some programs look for a file on disk to determine if they should perform extra logging. A perfect example of this is the Apple DirectoryService subsystem. Since DirectoryService is active before it's possible to log in, it provides a way for an administrator to specify debug logging as soon as it starts. If the file /Library/Preferences/DirectoryService/ .DSLogAtStart is present, DirectoryService will log debugging information to /Library/ Logs/DirectoryService/DirectoryService.debug.log. Simply create an empty file using the touch command:

```
# touch /Library/Preferences/DirectoryService/.DSLogAtStart
```

This tactic makes it possible to troubleshoot issues with Directory Service–based accounts authenticating at the login window. Using ssh, an administrator can access a machine as a user is logging in at the console. The DirectoryService debug log can give clues as to why failures are occurring.

Using Environment Variables

Some applications will check for the presence of a particular environment variable to determine the logging level required. (For more on environment variables, see "Using Bash" in Chapter 9, "Automating Systems.") As an example, most Cocoa applications respect the MallocStackLogging variable. It can be set per running instance. For example, to generate a stack log for iTunes, you could run it with the variable set:

```
$ MallocStackLogging=1 /Applications/iTunes.app/Contents/MacOS/iTunes
```

While this leans slightly more toward the developer side, often, any information available will help narrow down an issue's root.

What You've Learned

Troubleshooting is part art and part science. When you're trying to solve problems, it's important to employ a consistent troubleshooting methodology as well as patience. Important points to take away from this chapter are as follows:

▶ The two goals in troubleshooting are to fix the problem properly and to fix it quickly.

▶ Always create a backup before modifying files and settings.

▶ Documenting your work is a critical step in the troubleshooting process.

▶ To get information on the problem, start by asking broad questions and only then start to get more specific.

▶ Always clarify with the user your understanding of the issue.

▶ "The Four Cs" methodology consists of examining connections, components, configuration, and combinations.

▶ Several screen-sharing technologies make it easier to see what the user is seeing.

▶ Reading log files is a critical step in finding problems.

▶ Many command-line tools can help you determine the state of a system and instrument-specific parts of a running system.

▶ You're not alone—there are many resources available to help when a problem arises. These include built-in documentation and web searches, as well as human help in the form of colleagues and consultants.

▶ A free developer account allows you to file bugs in the Apple bug-tracking system at http://radar.apple.com.

Review Quiz

1. Why is it important to follow a methodology when troubleshooting?

2. What are The Four Cs?

3. What is the command used to cause a Macintosh to boot in verbose mode with no keypress at boot time?

4. What is the Apple bug-tracking system called, and how do you access it?

Answers

1. It helps you remain consistent, and follow a systematic plan.

2. Connections, components, configurations, and combinations.

3. The `nvram` command manipulates the nonvolatile RAM available at boot. Issuing `nvram boot-args="-v"` sets a verbose boot.

4. The Apple bug-tracking system is called "radar." It is accessible at http://radar.apple.com, and sign-in requires a valid developer ID.

Appendix

Documenting Systems

Documentation is a process, an ongoing cycle of steps, to keep written values in sync with reality. Whether you're documenting the initial configuration, as described in the same-named topic in Chapter 1, or keeping track of system changes, documentation is an important—and often indispensable—part of the system administrator's job. This chapter offers additional ideas and tools for administrators to use in gathering data and documenting their systems.

Gathering Data

Mac OS X has several ways of gathering data from remote systems, some built-in and some available for purchase. Off-the-shelf software includes software from Apple and third parties.

The built-in command-line system_profiler utility, along with Apple Remote Desktop, is covered in Chapter 8, "Monitoring Systems." In addition to those tools, this chapter lists some other options for gathering data.

Capturing Graphical Information

Sometimes, a value that needs to be documented exists only in the graphical user interface. Mac OS X has two built-in screen-capture utilities that are perfect for documenting these values: Grab and screencapture. With what you want to capture visible onscreen, press Command-Shift-4 and drag the area to be captured; Mac OS X then creates a Portable Network Graphic (PNG) file on the current user's desktop. You can also make screen captures of a remote machine while it's being viewed, using a one-button-click function in Apple Remote Desktop.

Finally, you can use the shell-based screencapture utility, either in scripts or for remote capture. Simply run the utility with the name of the file in which the current screenshot will be saved:

```
screencapture prodx_serial.png
```

If you're performing screencapture over SSH, due to security domains under Mac OS X, you must run this utility in the same mach bootstrap instance as the current loginwindow context. Pass in the PID of the current loginwindow instance to the launchctl bsexec parameter:

```
sudo launchctl bsexec PID screencapture screen.png
```

or, to perform this dynamically:

```
sudo launchctl bsexec $(ps ax | grep [l]oginwindow | awk '{print $1}') screencapture
screen.png
```

For viewing or storing in a central location, copy the file from that machine using scp.

Collecting Other Mac OS X Information

Mac OS X Server can run in one of four configurations: standard, workgroup, advanced, and Xsan metadata controller. (The fourth option is available only if, at install time, a Fibre Channel card is installed in the machine.) To determine a server's current mode of configuration, use the built-in `serveradmin` tool with admin-level credentials.

While `serveradmin` can return a large amount of information, part of the information needed resides in the `info:serviceConfig:IsStandardConfig` key:

```
serveradmin settings info:serviceConfig:IsStandardConfig
```

If this command returns yes, the server is running in either standard or workgroup mode. To determine which mode, use a follow-up query to `serveradmin`:

```
serveradmin settings info:serviceConfig:IsWorkgroupServer
```

A result of yes means that the specified server is running in workgroup mode. A result of `_empty_dictionary` combined with a yes from `IsStandardConfig` means that this is a standard server. If both keys are lacking, the server is running in advanced mode.

For methods of saving service configurations, see "Exporting Settings and Data" in Chapter 3, "Upgrading and Migrating Systems."

Reporting with Third-Party and Custom Software

There are several third-party packages for reporting on Mac OS X systems available, but perhaps none as common as Apple's own Apple Remote Desktop (ARD). ARD has powerful reporting capabilities, especially when combined with the ARD Task Server setup.

Using Apple Remote Desktop for Reporting

Developed by Apple, ARD ties in nicely with Mac OS X systems. Since v10.4, each Mac OS X install loads the ARD Agent by default, but does not enable or configure it. However, it's easy to set up and enable ARD Agent with the `kickstart` script, located at /System/Library/CoreServices/RemoteManagement/ARDAgent.app/Contents/Resources/.

`kickstart` is used to configure and control ARD Agent. The utility has a slightly obtuse syntax, preferring hyphens preceding most parameters—even values of parent parameters.

The following example configures and enables ARD Agent on a Mac; you can perform these same tasks over SSH on a remote Mac:

```
# ./kickstart -activate -configure -users marczak -access -on -privs -all
-allowAccessFor -specifiedusers -clientopts -setmenuextra -menuextra no -verbose
-restart -agent
Starting...
Activated Remote Management.
Stopped ARD Agent.
Stopped VNC Privilege Proxy
Stopped VNC Server.
Stopped RFB Register MDNS
marczak: Set user remote access.
/usr/bin/dscl -f '/var/db/dslocal/nodes/Default' localonly -create "/Local/Target/
Users/marczak" naprivs '-2147483648'
Set the client options.
Setting allow all users to NO.
Setting all users privileges to 1073742079.
Done.
```

-activate enables the agent; -configure is a parent parameter and requires further options. This example passes in a user name (-user marczak), enabling access (-access -on) and granting all privileges (-privs -all).

A new-to-v10.5 option is -allowAccessFor -specifiedUsers. This option corresponds with the new graphical user interface option in the Sharing preference pane.

You must specify the users to which access will be granted in the -configure option.

-clientopts is another parent parameter with several suboptions. In the previous example, the menulet is disabled using -setmenuextra -menuextra no. The -verbose command simply causes kickstart to print details about what it's currently doing. Finally, when you have finished, specify options, use -restart -agent option to restart the agent, which is required for any new options to take effect.

Once ARD Agent is running on all machines, you can run reports for documentation purposes. For example, you can report how much RAM is installed on each station, or what version of the operating system is running. With Apple Remote Desktop, you can find out quickly. With a separate copy of Apple Remote Desktop running as a task server, you can set machines to automatically generate new report data and upload the data periodically to the task server. This automatic reporting lets you, as an administrator, fetch the most recent data about a machine even if it's not currently powered on.

To run reports, select the machines to report on, and click the Reports button in the toolbar. (If this button is dimmed, make sure that the user account under which you're running has admin privileges on the local machine.)

Prebuilt reports range from the traditional System Overview and User History reports to the unique File Search and Network Test reports. Many reports allow you to fine-tune them to filter down to just the information required. You can create a recurring schedule for report runs using the Schedule button in the report dialog box.

Customizing Reports

Don't discount the write-it-yourself approach. Mac OS X is loaded with tools that allow you to completely customize a reporting solution. In fact, you'd be using many of the tools presented in this book: system_profiler, scripting, launchctl, and more. A full client-server solution is waiting to happen, thanks to the combination of Mac OS X Server as a central repository, and a pre-loaded install of the open source MySQL database. You can make the reporting as simple, full-featured, or custom as you want. See Chapter 8, "Monitoring Systems," for an introduction to the basics and ideas on setting up your reports.

Trying Other Reporting Applications

Before you reinvent the wheel, know that you're not the first one in the world trying to solve a particular issue of reporting. Look for a prebuilt solution. Good off-the-shelf and open source projects exist for system monitoring, system configuration, deployment, trouble-tracking, and other similar tasks.

Sites like http://freshmeat.net and http://macforge.net can help you track down these open source projects. If you find one that's interesting, and it's not built specifically for Mac OS X, check MacPorts (http://www.macports.org/) to see if there's a port available. Sites with forums and mailing lists such as MacEnterprise (http://www.macenterprise.org) and http://www.afp548.com typically discuss these products and their uses in various Mac environments. You're not alone, and there are many people willing to help. Combining a little open source and the desire to write your own solution is the true win: finding an open source project that you contribute to and improve.

Creating Documentation

Documentation comes in many forms. No single answer addresses all situations. The size of a company and the industry it's in may dictate regulations that require documenting certain activities. Check with your legal department about any requirements for compliance.

Following are some general guidelines that should keep you on the right path, including various electronic strategies.

Use a Template or Checklist

Create a boilerplate documentation sheet for equipment in your environment. A boilerplate ensures that all values are included when documenting new equipment. Often, equipment manufacturers will supply templates that can serve as a good base. (For an Apple-specific example, see http://images.apple.com/server/macosx/docs/Worksheet_v10.5.pdf.)

In general, you should capture the following information:

▶ Hardware configuration (CPU, RAM, hardware serial number, physical disk information, and so on).

▶ OS information (version, serial number, and so on) and other software information (manufacturer, title, version, and so on).

▶ Site-specific information such as asset-tag data, group configuration, administrator passwords and setup routines (for example, a section may be "How to create a new user").

Keep It Electronic

Online documentation has begun to replace the traditional method of documentation: writing documentation in a word processor, printing it out, and putting it on a shelf. Printed documentation has some disadvantages compared to its online counterpart. Paper gets lost, fades, is not backed up, can't easily be restricted in access, and isn't eco-friendly.

Now the tools and capability exist to create online documentation that can be updated in a collaborative fashion and that is free of printed documentation's limitations. Regardless of its final form, documentation probably will start out in electronic form, such as Pages, Word, or a plain-text file.

If you're creating electronic documentation, be sure to store your source files electronically. Protect them with controls built into Mac OS X, such as file system access control lists (ACLs), and encrypted disk images. Storing these files electronically also lets you back them up as part of your routine system backups.

If company policy requires a printed hard copy, store the printout in a binder to protect it and keep it together. And store this binder in a safe location: the Network Operations Center in larger organizations, possibly a locked cabinet or closet in a smaller organization.

Use Wikis

Furthering the "keep it electronic" mantra, a time-tested, collaborative tool that works perfectly for system documentation is a wiki. A *wiki* is a collection of web pages that can be modified or added to by anyone accessing the pages, using a simplified markup language. Nicely, Mac OS X Server features a built-in, very impressive wiki product. Wikis allow teams of people to create and update documentation. This keeps the documentation up-to-date, accessible, and searchable. Company policy and procedure is also ideal content for a wiki.

Control Access and Provide Audit Trails

Staying on the "keep-it-electronic" path allows proper access controls to be put in place. Wikis allow for per-user and per-group access control. If your documentation is simply a word-processing file, it can also be protected with file system access controls (permissions and access control lists).

Also, keeping documentation in an electronic format allows for an audit trail—a list of which user accounts have accessed or modified documentation files. This is important for companies that require it for regulation purposes. Ensure that these controls are in place and an access log is being kept.

Automate

Automate the process of keeping documentation up-to-date using scripts that collect system data and bring it into a database, or interpret the results and "humanize" it on the fly (taking the raw data and outputting something that people can easily read). In a larger organization, this may take the form of reporting "agents"—programs that run on each machine and report in to a central location. For consultants servicing new and existing clients, automating the documentation *generation* process can save time and create consistent sets of data. Use a custom-built or FileMaker tool that gives a checklist or simple sheet to enter data to create a nicely formatted report for your client.

Stay Organized

Nothing is worse than needing a piece of information and not being able to locate it easily. There are many approaches to staying organized.

If your documentation is online or in a Wiki, as suggested in the previous "Wiki" topic, search functions can help you find information.

If you've chosen to use one master document for all systems, break the information down into logical groupings. Sample section ideas are overview, system specifics, vendor contact information, and master passwords.

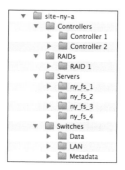

If you're following a one-document-per-system approach, you can use a simple file system structure to serve as a template. For example, a top level could represent a site, subfolders could represent servers, Redundant Array of Independent Disks (RAID) units, clients, and more at the site.

No matter the approach used—Wikis, word processing, or file system layout—organize yourself so you can find the information you've collected!

Summary

Proper documentation is what lets you take a vacation. It also lets you hand off responsibilities to less experienced administrators, confident that they will be able to refer to an authoritative source for procedures. This in turn lets you work on the bigger, better, more interesting projects. If you're a consultant, handing off proper documentation of a project or network setup to company principals is critical, and allows you to work with other clients, safe in the knowledge that company A has the information it needs while you're working with company B.

In this chapter, you have learned that:

▶ You can use `screen_capture` to capture a screen shot for documentation purposes.

▶ If you want to run `screen_capture` as root, but a different ID is logged in at the console, then you must use the `launchctl bsexec` parameter to be able to run in the same machine.

▶ More than just screen sharing, Apple Remote Desktop is a valuable tool in gathering reporting data from all Mac OS X machines. Pairing Apple Remote Desktop as a task server increases this value.

▶ You can configure the Apple Remote Desktop client (ARDclient) and start it remotely via SSH using the `kickstart` command. You can find the command at /System/Library/CoreServices/RemoteManagement/ARDAgent.app/Contents/Resources/kickstart.

Remember that the documents that make up your master documentation are fluid, changing entities. As hardware, software, procedures, and policies change in the physical world, documentation must be kept in sync. Parts of that can be achieved automatically, but should always be checked for accuracy. Advanced system administrators document!

Index

Symbols

#! shebang, using in Python, 235

$ (dollar sign) prompt, using with Terminal.app, 223

% (percent sign), appearance in sudoers file, 146

* (asterisk), using with crontabs, 248

._ (dot-underscore) files, occurrence of, 290

/ (forward slash), using in less, 193

: (colon), using with paths, 225

; (semicolon), using with selectors, 188

@ (at) symbol, using with log entries, 188

~/.bash_profile home directory, contents of, 226

< (less-than symbol), using with scripts, 224

> (greater-than symbol), using in scripts, 224

0 and 1 load averages, explanations of, 196

-0 switch, using with MacPorts, 29

' (single quotes), using with ManagedClient.app file, 40

A

A choice, using in dsimport, 58

A IPv4 address record, description of, 94

AAAA record, description of, 94

absolute path, specifying for scripts, 225

account authentication. *See also* authentication
  with PAM, 147–149
  setting password policies, 146–147
  with SSH and digital key pairs, 149–152
  with sudo tool, 145–146

account authorization, editing system rights, 166–168. *See also* authorization

account management group, using in PAM, 147

accounts in Mac OS X, types of, 141

ACEs (access control entries)
  checking, 168
  considering in order, 171
  defining in BIND, 97

ACL permissions
  description of, 168
  setting, 170–171
  viewing, 171

ACLs (access control lists). *See also* SACLs (system access control lists)
  defining in BIND, 97
  troubleshooting, 180

action scripts, resource for, 212

Activity Monitor.app
  Disk Activity tab in, 200
  Disk Usage tab in, 200
  Network tab in, 202

Adaptive Firewall
  availability of, 118
  configuration files for, 126

address groups, defining for firewall, 119

admin users, permissions granted to, 141

advanced configuration, advisory about, 22

AFP (Apple Filing Protocol), blocking, 123–124

AFP throughput, displaying value of, 69–70

AFP users, gathering information on, 70

AFP548, getting help from, 331

agents, managing with launchd plists, 243

AirPort base station
  configuring RADIUS from, 129–130
  disabling, 143

Alert log level, defined, 187

allow-transfer directive, using in BIND, 96, 98, 102

AMAVIS, data store for, 286

apachectl start command, using in SystemStarter, 251

apcupsd monitoring daemon, availability of, 299

Apple Filing Protocol (AFP), blocking, 123–124

*.apple firewall files, description of, 126

Apple services website, 120

Apple Software Restore (asr) backup utility, features of, 275

Apple support section, accessing online, 330

AppleRAID
  downside to, 304
  features of, 303
  troubleshooting, 312–313

AppleScript language, using, 236–238

AppleScript reference, downloading, 238

Application Level Firewall, configuration of, 127–128

applications. *See also* programs
  starting with launchd daemon, 244
  triggering on file system changes, 245

archive formats, creating from directories, 274

ARD (Apple Remote Desktop)
  creating reports with, 214–216
  troubleshooting, 325
  using for reporting, 343–345

ASL (Apple System Logger)
  logging messages in, 187
  in syslogd daemon, 186
  using logger with, 189

asl.db, interacting with, 189, 192